*f*P

TOO LATE
TO SAY GOODBYE

A True Story of
Murder and Betrayal

Ann Rule

Free Press
New York · London · Toronto · Sydney

FREE PRESS
A Division of Simon & Schuster, Inc.
1230 Avenue of the Americas
New York, NY 10020

The names of some individuals in this book have been changed.
Such names are indicated by an asterisk (*) the first time each appears in the book.

Photo Credits
Photos: 1, 2, 3, 4, 5, 24, 25, 26, 27, 28, 29, 30, 31, 32, 33, 35, 36, 51, 52, 59
(Barber Family)
Photos: 6, 7, 8 (Shelly Mansfield)
Photos: 9, 10, 11, 13, 14, 15, 18, 19, 20, 58 (Hearn Family)
Photos: 17, 21, 22, 23, 43 (Richmond County Crime Scene Photos)
Photos: 34, 37, 38, 39, 40, 42 (Gwinnett County Police Department
Crime Scene Photos)
Photo 41 (Marcus Head)
Photos: 47 (Chris Thelen), 48, 49, 50 (Annette Drowlette, Augusta Chronicle)
Photos: 53, 55, 56, 57 (Vino Wong, Atlanta Journal Constitution)
Photos: 16, 44, 45, 46, 54, 60, 61 (Ann Rule)

First Free Press hardcover edition April 2007
FREE PRESS and colophon are trademarks of Simon & Schuster, Inc.

For information about special discounts for bulk purchases,
please contact Simon & Schuster Special Sales at 1-800-456-6798
or business@simonandschuster.com

Manufactured in the United States of America

1   3   5   7   9   10   8   6   4   2

Library of Congress Cataloging-in-Publication Data
Rule, Ann.
Too late to say goodbye : a true story of murder
and betrayal / by Ann Rule.—1st Free Press hardcover ed.
p. cm.
1. Corbin, Jennifer, d. 2004.   2. Hearn, Dorothy.
3. Murder—Georgia—Case studies.   4. Murder victims—Georgia—Biography.
5. Murder—Investigation—Georgia.   I. Title.
HV6533.G4R86 2007
364.152'3092—dc22   2007009168
ISBN 13: 978-0-7432-3852-6
ISBN 10: 0-7432-3852-4

To All Women Who Are Living in Fear of Recrimination
And Stalking, in a Kind of Captivity, At the Hands of
Men They Once Loved and Trusted
In the Hope
That They Will Find a Safe Way Out
And
To Domestic Violence Groups
Who Are Doing Their
Best to Help

ACKNOWLEDGMENTS

IN ANY NONFICTION BOOK, the input of experts and those who have actually experienced the events therein is essential. This is never more true than in a book about actual criminal cases. The crimes itself, the victim(s), the suspects, the survivors, friends, and the investigators, prosecutors, and judges cannot be fully explored without the contributions of those who were *there*. When I traveled to Georgia in 2006, I knew only the most basic facts of this true story, and, as always, I worried that I would never discover enough to write the case in the depth I hoped for. Looking back now, I cannot thank the people I met enough for their willingness to show me the multifaceted aspects of two extraordinary investigations into a tragic and convoluted progression of events.

I have always found the residents of Georgia to be gracious and welcoming and my research in Gwinnett County and Richmond County certainly enhanced that impression. Public officials and private individuals in both counties were very open as they allowed me to research vital information, and consented to interviews. They shared their feelings and opinions with me, kept me from getting lost on unfamiliar freeways and country roads, filled me in on Georgia law, and explained the intricacies of advanced forensic science techniques.

Dozens of people who knew and loved Dolly Hearn, Jenn Corbin, and Bart Corbin shared their memories with me, even though they were saddened and shocked by events they could never have foretold.

I'd like to note the following people who were significant in helping me find the truth in *Too Late to Say Goodbye*:

Max, Narda, and Rajel Barber; Heather and Doug Tierney; Barbara and Dr. Carlton Hearn Sr. and Gil Hearn; Catherine Siewick, and Jane Hearn.

Detective Marcus Head, Sergeant E. T. Edkin of the Gwinnett County Police Department.

Gwinnett County District Attorney Danny Porter and his staff—particularly Chuck Ross, Jack Burnette, Russ Halcome, Mike Pearson, and Jeff Lamphier.

Judge Michael C. Clark and Greg Lundy.

Richmond County District Attorney Danny Craig and his staff: Jason Troiano and Parks White.

Scott Peebles and DeWayne Piper of the Richmond County Sheriff's Office.

Danny Brown, M.D., of the Georgia Bureau of Investigation.

And, in no particular order, a number of individuals who went out of their way to help me with various aspects of my research: Major Cathie Higgins, Jennifer Rupured, Stacey Ducker, Katherine Sherrington Meyer, Shelly Mansfield, Sheila Hanna, Prioleau Murray, Beverly Knowlton Fournier, Teresa Yawn, Dot Nelems, Darlene Hurst, Julie Hurst, Grace Yrizarry, Randy Ransom, Jennifer Grossman, Renee Walker, Pamela Earley, Loriann Hargis, Dienne Ogletree, Dara Prentice, Bob Reynolds, Sharon Shaw, Nancy J. Fontaine, Beverly Hawkins, Rosemary Heatherly, Ramona Lindsay Cathey, Karen Pirkle, Ilene Nicols, Valynda Vaughn, Pam Prouty, Bill Bufford, Kim Covington, Angie Echols, Maria Bips, Angela Hart, Millie Cartznes, Debbie Whitley, Amanda Jones, Tim Garrett, and Jo Busch, and the hundreds of "ARFs" (Ann Rule Fans) who post on my website's guestbook at www.annrules.com.

To my fellow journalists: Andria Simmons, *The Gwinnett Daily Post,* Lateef Mungin, and Anna Varela, *The Atlanta Journal Constitution,* and Steve Huff at truecrimeblog@blogspot.com.

To Drs. Amy Harper, Steven Smith, Kjersten Gmeiner, and Edward Benson of Group Health and their staffs, for their understanding and expertise.

And, finally, in this book that took two-and-a-half years to bring to fruition, I thank the Free Press/Simon & Schuster team that always stands behind me—or pulls me forward: Fred Hills, my editor for eighteen years, whose tenacity helped me weave any loose ends or frustrating details into a book that came in on time, Carolyn Reidy, president of Simon & Schuster, always an inspiration, my encouraging publisher Martha Levin, her assistant, Maria Bruk Auperin, who kept the puzzle pieces where they belonged and never lost her cool, Hilda Koparanian in charge of production, Erich Hobbing the artist responsible for what

I think is an outstanding book design and who also is responsible for the photo section, and Carol de Onís and Tom Pitoniak who oversaw the copy editing, detecting all the troublesome spots my own eye missed. I know I've said it before, but it's still true: no author writes a book alone.

To my perennial "first reader," and gentle critic: Gerry Hay.

And, as always, to the best literary agents an author could hope for, in gratitude for the many, many years we have been together: Joan and Joe Foley.

Cast of Characters

JENNIFER MONIQUE BARBER CORBIN 1971–2004
DR. BARTON THOMAS CORBIN, HER HUSBAND

Dalton and Dillon Corbin, her sons
Max and Narda Barber, her parents
Rajel Barber and Heather Barber Tierney, her sisters
Doug Tierney, her brother-in-law

Eugene and Connie Corbin, Barton's parents
Bradley Corbin, Barton's twin brother
Bobby Corbin, Barton's younger brother
Edwina Tims, Bradley's wife
Suzanne Corbin, Bobby's wife

* * *

DOROTHY CARLISLE "DOLLY" HEARN 1962–1990

Dr. Carlton Hearn Sr. and Barbara Hearn, her parents
Carlton Hearn Jr. and Gil Hearn, her brothers

AUGUSTA INVESTIGATION, 1990
RICHMOND COUNTY SHERIFF'S OFFICE

Captain Gene Johnson
Lieutenant John Gray
Sergeant Ron Peebles
Sergeant Billy Hambrick
Coroner Leroy Sims
Dr. Sharon Daspit, Medical Examiner
Dr. Farivar Yaghmai, Neuropathologist
Bruce Powers, Chief of Security, Medical College of
Georgia

AUGUSTA INVESTIGATION, 2004
RICHMOND COUNTY SHERIFF'S OFFICE

Detective Sergeant Scott Peebles
Crime Scene Investigator DeWayne Piper
Detective Don Bryant

RICHMOND COUNTY
DISTRICT ATTORNEY'S OFFICE

Richmond County District Attorney Danny Craig
Deputy District Attorneys: Parks White and Jason
Troiano

Dr. Danny Brown, Georgia Bureau of Investigation Medical Examiner

GWINNETT COUNTY INVESTIGATION, 2004
GWINNETT COUNTY POLICE DEPARTMENT

Detective Marcus P. Head
Lieutenant Troy C. Hutson
Sergeant Vic Pesaresi
Sergeant E.T. Edkin
Officer Travis Wright
Officer Michelle Johns
Corporals: Eddie Restrepo, Curtis Clemmons, Fred S. Mathewson, Austin M. Godfrey
Investigators: Michael Marchese, Dave P. Henry, S. Milsap, Chris Penn, Jason Carter, (Norcross Police Department) David Cheek, Gary Linder, C.T. Fish, James R. West, R.C. Nelson, L.B. Davis, G.R. Thompson, Mark A. Lester
Crime Scene Technicians: Amber Roessler, J. Abousselman.

GWINNETT COUNTY
DISTRICT ATTORNEY'S OFFICE

District Attorney Danny Porter
Senior Assistant District Attorneys: Tom Davis and Chuck Ross
Chief of District Attorneys Investigators: Jack Burnette
Investigators for the District Attorney: Bob Slezak, Jeff Lamphier, Mike Pearson, Russ Halcome, Kevin Vincent, Manny Perez

Chief Anthony Everage, Troy Police Department, Alabama

J.D. Shelton, Investigator, Alabama Attorney General's Office

GWINNETT COUNTY
MEDICAL EXAMINER'S OFFICE

Carol A. Terry, Medical Examiner
Ray Rawlins, Forensic Investigator
Zubedah Mutawassim, Forensic Technician

SUPERIOR COURT JUDGES

In Richmond County: Judge Carl C. Brown
In Gwinnett County: Judge Michael C. Clark, Judge Melodie Snell Connor, Judge Debra Turner.

DEFENSE ATTORNEYS

David Wolfe, Bruce Harvey, and Steve Roberts

Preface

April 24, 2007

WITH EVERY BOOK I write—and this is number 27—
I realize more just how many lives are affected when one
cruel and conscienceless person decides to take another
human being's life. Murder is not only a matter of a single
death; there are many "little deaths" as homicide repli-
cates its evil in countless lives left behind, changing them
forever. Even if there are no more homicides committed by
a particular killer, I know now that violent death never
stops reverberating among those who suffer such terrible loss. The pain resonates like an echo in a series of
tunnels—parents lose beloved children, spouses are torn
from one another, and children too young to fully grasp
the finality of death are destined to mature to a bleak point
where they will have to understand what forever means.
Families will never again have a complete Christmas or

Thanksgiving or reunion; there will always be empty chairs. Friends will grow older and no longer resemble their yearbook pictures—but certain youthful images of lost loved ones will remain engraved on their memories. And even police officers, detectives, prosecutors, defense attorneys, and judges will do what has to be done before moving on to future murders, but all with their lives subtly altered.

Never was this more true than in two complex and drawn-out investigations in the state of Georgia, probes that occurred, technically, in different centuries. Of course, that doesn't mean they happened many years apart, but simply that the millennium intervened. Even so, one of these tragedies was almost relegated to the past, where it might well have remained were it not for a second shocking event that brought old questions back into the light of day.

And, with the second death, even more sorrow. Could all of this be traced back to one person, a most unlikely suspect, one who may have gone through life totally without conscience, empathy, or remorse?

Perhaps.

*   *   *

OF THE 159 COUNTIES in the state of Georgia, Gwinnett County—northwest of Atlanta—stands out for its amazing exponential growth. In the last two decades, sleepy country towns surrounded by acres of raw land have attracted developers who then created whole neighborhoods with picturesque names drawn from history, nature, or their own imaginations. Houses, apartments, and condos soon burst from the red Georgia clay like the kudzu vine, a slithering, green noxious weed that threatens to creep relentlessly over everything in the state.

For the first few years of development, Gwinnett residents either boasted or complained that theirs was the fastest growing county in America. In the twenty-five years leading up to 2006, the population exploded from 200,000 to almost 800,000. In 1981, the Gwinnett County District Attorney's Office had six attorneys on staff and a handful of investigators, a number quite adequate to carry out the DA's business. The current Gwinnett County District Attorney, Danny Porter, was once one of those Assistant DAs. By 2006, after four terms as the District Attorney, Porter had a staff of ninety—including thirty-four lawyers and twenty-three investigators.

By 1990, the historic red-brick courthouse in Lawrenceville was bursting at the seams. The new $72 million Gwinnett County Justice and Administration Center on Langley Road opened in 1991. The modern structure with twenty-two courtrooms featured polished steel banisters, etched-glass walls and dividers, polished parquet floors, and skylights where the drum of a hard rain was almost louder than thunder. It was an expansive complex, yet it too soon began to strain against its walls.

In the District Attorney's office, a law library had to be sacrificed to make more office space; small cubicles were made even smaller and arranged in what became a challenging maze for the uninitiated.

The visitors' parking lot was the site of a very large monument dedicated "To America's Sons and Daughters Who Served Honorably in the Armed Forces." The sixty-one acres around the justice center were landscaped with chinaberry trees, pin oaks, crepe myrtles, lilies and begonias, azaleas and holly. Both the front and rear entrances were welcoming, but just inside those doors were the guards and metal detectors that have become ubiquitous in courthouses and law enforcement structures across America.

For some who came to this building in Lawrenceville, Georgia, there would be justice and triumph, and for others, heartbreak.

TOO LATE
TO SAY GOODBYE

PART ONE

Jennifer Barber Corbin

"JENN"

CHAPTER ONE

DECEMBER 4, 2004

THE SHRIEK OF SIRENS piercing the chill December morning on Bogan Gates Drive was almost as alien as the thackety-thackety of helicopters overhead would be. This quiet street in Buford is a relatively new part of an upscale neighborhood, home to young and middle-aged professionals and their families. The houses here have mostly red-brick façades with glossy black shutters, not unlike homes in Atlanta's more affluent districts, but on a smaller scale. In 2004, the average price of a home in Bogan Gates was between $200,000 and $300,000—the homes would cost twice that in Denver or Seattle or Philadelphia. Buford is an ideal suburb for those who commute the thirty-five miles to Atlanta: large enough with over 14,000 residents to merit local shopping centers, but small enough to dissolve the tension that comes with driving the I-285 beltway that encircles Atlanta with bumper-to-bumper traffic. And Bogan Gates Drive itself is an oasis of serenity with its manicured lawns and colorful gardens. Children play under the watchful eyes of all the adults there. If some stranger should insinuate himself into this enclave, he would not go unnoticed.

A negative note, at least for some, is that close neighbors tend to know each other's secrets. There isn't the anonymity that exists in apartment buildings in large cities. Neither is there the loneliness that city dwellers sometimes feel. Even so, some families on the street have secrets that none of their neighbors could possibly imagine.

That doesn't stamp Bogan Gates as different; every community has its mysteries and even its surprising secrets. When reporters for television news and local papers sweep into such places, they are certain to obtain instant interviews with shocked residents who invariably say: "Something like that just doesn't happen here—not in our neighborhood!"

But, of course, it does.

On this day in early December, Bogan Gates Drive just happened to be the site of one of the most horrific crimes in Georgia.

The town of Buford, its name as Southern as a name can be, sits close to Lake Lanier. This popular vacation spot's waters meander for mile after mile, cutting channels deep and wide into the shoreline, leaving inlets that resemble the bite marks of a giant alligator. Buford is surrounded by other small townships: Flowery Branch, Sugar Hill, Suwanee, Duluth, Oakville, Alpharetta. It is very close to the border between Gwinnett and Forsyth counties. Forsyth County once had a reputation as one of the most racially prejudiced areas in America. A sign beside the road there could read "Boiled Peanuts," or it might say, "Nigger, Get Out of Forsyth County, Before Sunset." But no longer. Oprah Winfrey once broadcast her show from Forsyth County, pulling aside the blinds to reveal raw prejudice. Today, those with set ideas about racial disparities have learned not to voice them aloud.

Buford, in Gwinnett County, is far more in tune with the twenty-first century, a bedroom community tied to a thriving metropolis. Young families who live there can enjoy relatively small-town warmth, or drive to Atlanta for more cosmopolitan pleasures.

The family who lived at 4515 Bogan Gates Drive fit comfortably into Buford's demographics. Dr. Barton T. Corbin, forty, had recently moved his dental practice to Hamilton Mill—less than ten miles away. His wife, Jennifer "Jenn" Corbin, taught at a preschool in the Sugar Hill Methodist Church. Although Dr. Corbin's efforts to build a new practice often kept him away from home, and Jenn was the parent who spent more time with their children, they both seemed to dote on their sons, Dalton, seven, and Dillon, five. They went to the boys' ballgames and participated in school events at Harmony Elementary School, where Dalton was in second grade and Dillon in kindergarten.

Married almost nine years, the Corbins appeared to have all those things that most young couples long for: healthy children, a lovely home, admired professions, close family ties, and myriad friends.

Jenn Corbin, thirty-three, was tall and pretty, a big-boned blond who usually had a smile on her face, no matter what worries might lie behind it. Bart was also tall, taller than Jenn by two or three inches, but beyond that he was her opposite. His hair was almost black, his eyes even darker, his pale skin surprisingly dotted with freckles. He was a "gym rat" whose muscular physique showed the results of his predawn workouts. When Bart was dealing with a problem, however, or worrying over his finances, he lost weight rapidly and became angular and bony. Then his cheekbones protruded and his profile turned sharp as an ax, almost Lincolnesque.

Many of his female patients found Bart strikingly handsome; some others were a little put off by his intensity. But most of Bart Corbin's patients seemed to like him. He often traded dental care with his personal friends for some service he needed, using an old-fashioned barter system.

To an outsider, the Corbins' marriage appeared solid—her sunniness balancing his sometimes dark moods. In truth, tiny threadlike fissures had crept silently through the perceived foundation of their marriage, weakening its structure from the inside out until a single blow could send it crumbling.

Most people who knew the Corbins weren't aware that Jenn had fled their home shortly after Thanksgiving of 2004, and that a divorce might be forthcoming. Those who did know were shaken that "Bart" and "Jenn" might be splitting up. To the world, they were a team, their very names strung together like one word when their friends talked about them. *Bart-n-Jenn.*

Jenn Corbin was responsible for that. She had struggled to maintain the façade that kept the foundering state of her marriage virtually invisible to the outside world. For at least eight years she continued to hope that she and Bart could somehow work out their problems and build a happy relationship. If they did accomplish that, there was no reason for anyone to know. If their union was irretrievably broken, people would know soon enough.

And know they would because, by the fall of 2004, Jenn had given up. Her parents, Narda and Max Barber, and her sisters, Heather and Rajel, knew that, although even they were reluctant to accept it. Jenn had tried to understand her husband and to make allowances for behavior she didn't understand. She had forgiven Bart for betrayals most other women would not put up with. It was he who had laid down the ground rules in their marriage, and she had accepted them. She hadn't gotten married with the idea that if it didn't work out, they could always get divorced. She and her sisters were born to parents who had married only once—and who had just happily celebrated their fortieth anniversary.

Jenn Corbin was one of those people whom almost everybody liked, probably because she liked everybody. She thought of others before she took care of herself and she protected her small sons like a lioness would, doing everything she could to be sure they were serene and happy. She was the same way with the youngsters she taught in preschool at the church. She had a warm lap and sheltering arms when their tears came.

Jenn was a Barber before she became a Corbin, raised in a loving and a very close family. When she and Bart married, her family had opened up the circle and welcomed him in. Except for his occasional flashes of temper, Bart was a lot of fun and he happily participated in holiday celebrations, outings on the Corbins' and Barbers' adjoining houseboats, or on picnics and trips. They all shared the kind of extended family loyalty that isn't seen very often.

Although Bart's mother, Connie, and his brothers— Brad, Bart's twin, and Bobby didn't spend much time with the Barbers, their connection was amiable enough, if a bit distant. Bart's father, Gene Corbin, had remarried and wasn't often in touch.

The Corbins' marital difficulties didn't stem from in-law problems. Rather, Bart's new dental clinic was struggling, and a renewal of old issues had left their marriage on the precarious edge of oblivion. But with Christmas only three weeks away, Jenn was looking forward to finishing the decorations on a tall tree that sat in the Corbins' formal dining room. Her little boys shouldn't have to miss out on Santa Claus because of an adult situation that wasn't their fault. She was halfway through with the tree, and she had stacked boxes nearby that held her treasured sentimental ornaments, new ones she had purchased during the year, and, most precious, Dalton's and Dillon's handmade art work they were so proud of. Jenn already had wrapped and hidden lots of presents for the boys.

* * *

IT WAS 7:30 on this Saturday morning, December 4, 2004, when Steve and Kelly Comeau, who lived across the street from the Corbins' house, were startled to hear someone knocking at their front door. They were still in bed; Steve had been out late helping a friend hang pictures, and on the way home he had stopped to help a stranded driver change a flat tire. When he answered the door, he looked down to see Dalton Corbin, age seven. Dalton's face was red and his cheeks were streaked with tears. He wore pajamas and appeared to be very upset.

"My mom isn't breathing," Dalton said. "My daddy shot my Mommy—I need you to call 911."

Skeptical, Steve Comeau nevertheless called 911,

while Kelly followed Dalton across the street to check on Jenn Corbin. She didn't even think about danger to herself, because she doubted that Dalton could really have seen what he said he had. Jenn was most likely just sleeping heavily.

The Corbins' overhead garage door was open. Kelly hurried beneath it, found that the door to the kitchen was unlocked, and headed down the hall toward the master bedroom, calling out Jenn's name. There was no answer.

There was light in the bedroom, although Kelly couldn't remember later if it was daylight or from a lamp. She could see Jenn lying diagonally across the bed. It was an odd position, and Kelly felt a little shiver of alarm. She told herself that Jenn was only sleeping, and she reached out to touch Jenn's right shoulder. Kelly moved her fingers slightly, pressing harder, but there was no reassuring thrum of blood coursing there. And Jenn's flesh was cold.

Jenn wasn't breathing. Kelly saw a trickle of blood coming from her nose, and a few bright red stains on the bedclothes beneath Jenn's head. She caught a glimpse of what looked like a pistol butt poking out from a coverlet next to her still body. Feeling as if she were in the midst of a nightmare, Kelly backed away from the bed, careful not to touch anything.

"She was way gone," Kelly would later recall to DA's Investigator Kevin Vincent. "Her body was frozen—ice cold. She was way, way gone. I didn't check for a pulse. I knew she was gone a long time before."

Kelly Comeau felt a ringing in her ears, and her whole body prickled with the shock that washed over her as she tried to deny to herself what she saw. Jenn Corbin was only thirty-three years old. She was healthy and vibrant and there was no reason at all for her to have a handgun in her bed. A thought swept through Kelly's mind: not at Christmastime!

It seemed to her that she had been in Jenn's bedroom—the room Jenn had decorated so beautifully—for a very long time, but it had actually been only moments. Kelly wanted to pull Jenn's green nightgown up over the breast that was partially exposed, but she knew she shouldn't touch anything.

There was nothing else she could do for Jenn. Her two little boys were Jennifer Corbin's biggest concern—always—and she would never have wanted them to see her this way. But Dalton and Dillon had indeed seen their mother dead, and Kelly's heart constricted at the thought. Would they ever forget it? No child should ever have to live with such memories.

*   *   *

KELLY TRIED TO USE the cordless phone Dalton Corbin took from the dining room table and handed to her. Its battery was dead and it didn't work. By now Dillon had come out of his room, too. With the boys trailing her, Kelly ran to her house and called 911 herself.

All she could repeat to the radio operator was that there was a dead woman in the house across the street—her friend, Jennifer Corbin. The dispatcher at the Gwinnett County Police Department's Communications Center told the Comeaus that patrol officers had already been dispatched and would be there momentarily. Officers Travis Wright and Michelle Johns were the first to arrive. An engine with EMTs and the paramedics' rig from Gwinnett County Fire Company #14 followed close behind them.

Kelly Comeau told Michelle Johns and Travis Wright

where the master bedroom was. They could hear a dog barking frantically inside. The patrol officers walked cautiously through the Corbins' open garage door with their weapons drawn, calling into the house before they entered. No one answered.

Zippo, the Corbins' dog, ran out, and Johns asked Kelly to lock him up in the backyard. The patrol officers were fully aware that this situation was one of the most dangerous any police officer can encounter. Although the 911 operator had done her best to calm down Kelly Comeau so she could determine what had happened and who might be in the house—possibly waiting there with a loaded gun—she wasn't able to elicit many facts. There was no description of a suspect; no one knew his—or her—sex, race, size, or what clothes the shooter had worn.

Neither of the Comeaus knew who might be in the house across the street. Jenn's SUV was parked outside, but Bart's pickup truck and his yellow Mustang convertible were gone.

Only now did Kelly realize that she might have been in danger herself when she entered the Corbins' house. She had been so concerned for Jenn and then so shaken by finding her body, she hadn't even thought of it. But if Jenn's killer was still inside, the first officers responding could be targets, too.

What had happened was too much to take in without facing each detail, each little shock, every ragged facet of tragedy one by one.

There was a strong likelihood that Jenn's killer had disappeared into the night, hours before. Even so, Wright and Johns, their hearts beating erratically, continued their exploration of the two-story brick house. No police officer is ever blasé about walking into a strange building where he might be caught in the sights of a gun. The patrol officers extended both arms and pointed their handguns toward the shadows. They made a quick sweep of the rooms and the hallway to reassure themselves that no one was hiding there.

There was no sound at all beyond their own breathing.

When they were satisfied that the house was empty, they waved to the EMS team to follow them into the house. The patrolmen and medics entered the master bedroom, and found it just as Kelly Comeau had reported. The woman who lay across the king-sized bed had what appeared to be a single gunshot wound near her right ear. The butt of a handgun rested three or four inches from the palm of her right hand, although her fingertips were less than an inch away from it.

Oddly, the barrel of the revolver was hidden beneath the rose-patterned comforter. There was a pale blue and white flannel coverlet with a snowman pattern at the foot of the bed, and a cordless phone next to it.

The medics checked the woman for any sign of life, and found none at all.

Patrol Sergeant E. T. Edkin joined his officers, and he saw immediately that there was nothing more anyone could do for the blond woman. Edkin was a veteran officer, a weight lifter with massive biceps. He had worked in the Homicide Unit for years, and had been a frequent partner to Detective Marcus Head, who was now on his way from home after being called out by the 911 operator. In December 2004, Edkin had temporarily left Homicide after being promoted to sergeant. It was standard policy. He would go back to working murder cases soon, but as a supervisor of detectives there.

"It wasn't my case," he said later. "I called the dispatchers at the Com Center and asked that crime scene investigators and someone from the Medical Examiner's Office be notified."

At first look, it appeared that the dead woman had killed herself. Still, with his years of experience working homicides, Edkin could not help but question whether this was in fact a suicide. He didn't comment on it, but went about setting up a perimeter around the Corbin's house and yard to bar anyone unauthorized from entering.

Edkin had Michelle Johns stay in a spot where she could watch the home's windows so that no one could exit or enter. Kelly Comeau approached her and asked if someone could get clothes for Dalton and Dillon—who were shivering in their pajamas. Johns was able to do that and still maintain her watch on the windows, and she went upstairs where she grabbed underwear, pants, shirts, shoes, socks, and jackets for Dalton and Dillon from what was obviously a children's bedroom. She glanced into another bedroom on the second floor and saw clothes belonging to an adult male hanging neatly in the closet.

Then she handed the children's clothes to Kelly so the little boys could change out of their pajamas.

Along with her partner, Michelle Johns started a precise log listing every person who entered the Corbins' house—the time they walked in and the time they left. It began at one minute after 8 A.M., and would not end until 4:26 P.M. as the sun set.

The 911 operator contacted Forensic Investigator Ray H. Rawlins at the Gwinnett County Medical Examiner's Office, who jotted down the sparse information that was available so far. Then Rawlins called Sergeant Edkin to assure him that the medical examiner would accept jurisdiction.

"I'm en route now," Rawlins said, as he headed out from the ME's office.

The Gwinnett County Police Department would be the chief investigating agency into Jenn Corbin's death by gunshot, although District Attorney Danny Porter was also notified because he and his staff would work alongside the police detectives.

All sudden and/or unattended deaths are worked first as homicides, next as possible suicides, third as accidental, and only then as a natural occurrence. Nobody yet knew where the dead woman would fit, but they had to start at the top of the list.

At this point they did not yet have positive identification of the woman who lay on the bed. Kelly Comeau had been too horrified to take more than a cursory look before she ran back to her house with Dalton and Dillon. She had been sure it was Jenn, but they would have to get an official identification. Still, there was little doubt that she was, indeed, Jennifer Corbin.

Seven-year-old Dalton Corbin had been positive that it was his mother lying there without moving. But he was far too young to be listed as the identifying person.

By the time Rawlins arrived, Gwinnett County Police Department Colonel "Butch" Ayres, Detective Sergeant Vic Pesaresi, and Detective Marcus Head had already joined Edkin and the uniformed officers at the scene. Assistant District Attorney Tom Davis was on his way.

It was still early in the morning as the official vehicles lined the street in front of the Corbins' house. They contrasted grimly with the Christmas lights that glowed in the dim winter light. Almost all the homes in the Bogan Gates subdivision had some kind of Christmas decoration, their front yards displaying Santa Clauses, reindeer, angels, and nativity scenes.

A few neighbors were gathering in small knots, many wearing bathrobes, and speaking with hushed voices as they watched the lawmen park and enter the Corbins' house. All of the law enforcement officers and the paramedics looked grim, their jaws set as they moved slowly. If only the medics would hurry in with a gurney, and then carry someone out to be rushed to the hospital in Lawrenceville, there might be some hope.

But none of them did.

Chapter Two

December 4, 2004

There was no hurry. When a victim is beyond saving, an investigation slows to a crawl. Detectives, CSI units, and medical examiner's investigators hasten only to be sure that every possible scintilla of physical evidence is gathered up and then sealed carefully into plastic bags or brown paper sacks. Body fluids and blood are swabbed onto slides. All the corners of a death site are photographed or videotaped. Or both. In this case, it would be both.

One timeworn tool is a measuring tape, just as important as any modern-day advance in forensic science. By triangulating certain points at the scene with accurate measurements, the scene can be reestablished long after it has been dismantled. How far away from the deceased had the gun been when it was fired? How close together were blood drops or spray . . . or splashes? Sometimes even a swipe of blood located where it should not be is vital in an investigation. To a skilled forensic technician, the tape measure can be a powerful tool, revealing things a killer meant to hide forever.

In this jurisdiction, no thorough search of the Corbins' home could begin until a search warrant was obtained. For now, Detective Marcus Head spoke quietly to the Corbins' closest neighbors. Head was a sometimes somber man in his thirties, with dark—almost black—hair and an open face. He grew up as the son of a funeral director.

"He often took me along with him," Head recalled. "When we went out together to pick up deceased people, death didn't seem unnatural to me, and I think it helped me learn how to talk with those who have been recently bereaved."

Head's decision to go into law enforcement certainly came via a different route from most detectives', but his ability to stay calm in the face of disaster was an important part of who he was.

It was difficult for Head to determine which close relatives of the Corbins had been notified, and where they were. Kelly Comeau, still in shock, hadn't known how to reach Jenn Corbin's parents. She thought she might have a phone number for Jenn's younger sister, Heather. Neither she nor Steve knew where Bart was, but Kelly did manage to find a number for his mother, Connie Corbin, who lived in nearby Snellville. Steve called Bart Corbin's mother at a quarter to nine that morning to tell her, "Jennifer's been shot."

"She was in complete tears," he told police.

Connie Corbin called her younger son, Bobby, and

told him what had happened. He said that Bart was with him, and that he would break the awful news to him. After that, it was hard to figure out who called whom to tell them that Jenn was dead. It was probably Bobby who called Heather, who lived with her husband, Doug Tierney, in a house they had recently bought in Dawsonville.

Heather answered their phone, and collapsed in tears, crying out "Jenn's dead!" to Doug.

"We ran through the house, collecting our kids and headed for Jenn and Bart's," Doug said. "As soon as I got in the car, I called Bobby and asked 'Where's Bart? Is Bart with you?' and he said, 'Yes, he's here—but he's in the bathroom, really, really upset. Are you going over?' "

"Yeah, we are—we're on our way," Doug Tierney told Bobby Corbin. He asked Bobby if he and Bart would be there soon. But Bobby avoided answering.

"Bobby wouldn't tell me, and I never talked to Bart," Doug recalled. "Heather kept saying, 'Go! Go! Go! We have to take care of the boys!' And we did. Heather knew Kelly Comeau had them for the moment but they needed to have their family there."

"Are you on your way?" Doug asked Bobby Corbin again.

There was no response.

Doug couldn't believe it. He turned to Heather and said, "I don't know if they're going over or not."

No one answered Doug Tierney's subsequent phone calls to Connie Corbin's house or to Bobby's house. Maybe they had left to go to Buford. Surely Bart would realize that Dalton and Dillon needed their father, and needed him fast.

Heather called her parents in Lawrenceville and told them what had happened. When Max and Narda Barber learned that they had lost their daughter, their first thoughts were also about their grandsons. Who was taking care of them? Had the boys been injured, too? Jenn's parents were on automatic pilot; nothing could have prepared them for the news that she was dead.

What could have happened? Random thoughts darted through their minds as they fought down panic and disbelief. Max and Narda got in their car and headed toward Buford, where their precious Jenn lay dead. Max drove as fast as he safely could to get to Bogan Gates Drive.

Still, no one knew for sure where Bart Corbin was. Surely he and his brother Bobby would be arriving at any moment.

The Corbin family had gathered at Connie's house in Snellville. Asked later by investigators why they hadn't gone to Buford to check on Dalton and Dillon, Bart's mother said that Kelly Comeau kept assuring her that the Barbers and the Tierneys were on their way to look after the boys. "It was closer for them," Connie said later.

But it wasn't a long way for any of them! Maybe twenty miles from Connie's place in Snellville, twenty-five from Heather and Doug's in Dawsonville, and about sixteen from Max and Narda's place in Lawrenceville.

Detectives at the scene of Jenn Corbin's death kept expecting her widower to drive up, wanting to learn more about what had happened, and, almost certainly, anxious to comfort his small sons. They assumed he would be crying and upset, but like most fathers, would pull himself together enough to race to his children in a time of crisis.

But Bart Corbin apparently could not. He may have been reluctant to encounter his in-laws because their relationship, once loving, had been strained in recent weeks. He may have been totally grief-stricken to hear that his wife was dead, too distressed, as his brother said, to know what to do.

Max Barber parked in the driveway of his dead daughter's home for a very long time, waiting to talk to his son-in-law. His daughter Heather was afraid he was so grief-stricken that he was going to have a heart attack—but he wouldn't leave.

Heather was also upset as she called 911, determined to get word to Sheriff "Butch" Conway, who was a family friend, that she believed Bart had murdered Jennifer.

"The woman who answered at 911 was already convinced that Jenn had killed herself," Heather recalled. "I kept trying to tell her that Bart did it," and she kept saying to me, 'But, Ma'am, you don't understand what happened.'

"And I knew I did understand and she didn't."

They were all in deep and chilling shock; no one could be held accountable for what they thought and said at such a moment.

*   *   *

MARCUS HEAD HAD DONE a "cursory survey" of the shooting scene. He studied the woman lying on the bed, the dried blood beneath her nostrils and on the right rear of her head, the gun tucked beneath the comforter, and the many-paged document beneath her shoulder. He could make out enough of the printing to see that they were divorce papers from her husband. Given the placement of the gun and the wound behind her right ear, he jotted down notes: "Due to the position of the victim's hands and the revolver being in a place that is contrary to gravity . . . we decided to treat the matter as a suspicious death."

It was a very broad category. It could mean anything. Head was just stepping into a case that would dominate much of his life for almost two years.

At this point, Max Barber approached Marcus Head. Distraught as he was, Barber wanted Head to understand that Jenn and her husband Bart had been having marital problems. "They had a fight at Thanksgiving," Barber said. "He hit her in the face. There was another incident three or four days ago. Jenn had to call the police on Bart. He stole her journal or something."

"Do you know if either your daughter or Dr. Corbin own a handgun?" Marcus Head asked.

"I don't know of any," Max Barber said, "but Bart had a shotgun. Jenn was worried because he took it out of their house on December 1."

The two men—a bereaved father and a detective who had just begun an investigation—agreed to talk in more detail later in the day.

While detectives continued to work the crime scene, Gwinnett County Deputy Sheriff M. Brooks drove up to the Corbins' house. He was surprised to see all the police activity there. Brooks told Marcus Head that he was there to legally serve Jennifer Corbin with the divorce papers her husband had filed on November 29. Told that she had died of a gunshot wound a few hours before, Brooks offered to make copies of the no-longer-necessary divorce papers and give a set to Marcus Head. The copy that was still beneath her shoulder was stained with blood, and would be retained as evidence.

Head talked more with Jenn's stunned family. The thought of Jenn being gone was impossible for them to accept. Not Jenn, who had always embraced life with enthusiasm and optimism, who had never hurt a living thing.

Although he doubted it, it was still possible that Jenn Corbin had committed suicide, and Marcus Head tactfully questioned her family about her state of mind. Had she been disturbed lately, depressed? Maybe enough to take her own life?

They stared back at the detective, shaking their heads. Suicide? Jenn a suicide?

Never. Never. Never.

Jenn's parents and her sisters were adamant. "First of all," Narda said, "she would never have left the boys. She would have gone through hell, but she would never have left her boys behind."

Heather was just as sure that her sister would not have killed herself. "There was no letter to the boys, was there?" she asked, and then continued without getting an answer. "She wouldn't have left without saying goodbye to them."

"She would never leave them at all. Not voluntarily," Max Barber said flatly. "She did not commit suicide."

Head scanned the divorce petition. It was a Gwinnett County Superior Court Civil Action warrant: #04-A-13086-5, dated November 29, and filed on November 30, 2004. And there was no question who had filed it: Dr. Barton T. Corbin. Apparently, someone had given Jennifer Corbin a copy of it before she was officially served.

Would the news that her husband wanted to divorce her have been enough to make her commit suicide? Although Head hated to question her family further when they were trying to cope with the reality of her sudden death, he asked again about her frame of mind. Had she made any suicidal threats, even obliquely?

No! Max Barber insisted. If either Bart or Jenn had truly wanted a divorce, it would have been Jenn. Her father said that they all knew Jenn and Bart were having a rough patch in their marriage. Jenn was usually the peacemaker, knowing what to do to calm Bart down or cheer him up. Until recently, she had managed to hide her problems from her family. But in the preceding eight days—ever since Thanksgiving—even she had trouble pretending there was nothing wrong. She seemed to them alternately angry and frightened as she dealt with Bart. Yes, she was miserable, caught inside the marriage.

"As I said," Barber repeated, "Jenni even called the police for help a few days ago."

"Tell me more about that. Why did that happen?" Head asked.

"He was acting crazy."

"Bart ruined the Thanksgiving because he was in such a bad mood," Max said. "He was either sulking or angry about something all day long. And it got worse after that."

From Thanksgiving to December 4 was only nine days, and Head had been a cop long enough to know that more family fights erupt around the holidays than at any other time of the year. But filing for divorce was certainly a radical position for the dentist to have taken. An eight-year marriage wouldn't disintegrate in eight days! There had to be something far deeper, simmering for months or even years. Either Jennifer Corbin had been hiding a great deal from her family, or something catastrophic had happened suddenly, bringing about a sea change in her relationship with her husband.

But Head realized that this wasn't the time to question Jenn's grief-stricken survivors in depth. They had lapsed back into such deep shock that they could barely speak.

All that Head and the other investigators knew for sure

at this point was that Jennifer Corbin was dead. Her husband had not shown up at their home, and no one seemed to know where he was. If Bart Corbin had been trying to prove some kind of point by seeking a divorce so precipitately—perhaps to shock his wife into taking him back—he would be appalled to learn that she had killed herself.

Or that someone had murdered her while he wasn't there to protect her—or their small sons.

Steve Comeau came across the street and told Marcus Head that Bobby Corbin had called him to say that Bart was still at Bobby's house. Comeau gave the detective Bobby's phone number.

Head immediately called Bobby and determined that both he and Bart had been informed of Jennifer Corbin's death. Head asked to speak with the widower, hoping to get some information from him that might explain what had happened.

"He can't talk right now," Bobby Corbin said. "He's very, very, upset. But we'll be coming over there soon."

While he waited for Bobby and Bart to arrive, Marcus Head spoke very briefly to Dalton and Dillon Corbin, who were still at the Comeaus' house. Dalton told him he had gone to wake up his mother to fix breakfast and he had seen blood coming from her mouth. He had also seen the gun close to her hand.

"I tried to call 911 from our phone," he said, "but it didn't work. So I ran over to Kelly and Steve's to get help. My father shot my mother."

Head looked up startled. Had he heard the little boy right? Dalton had said it almost matter-of-factly, as if this was a fact that everyone knew. He would have to be questioned carefully before his memory grew contaminated by remarks he might hear around him. Dillon didn't appear to know what had happened. But Dillon was only four or five.

As much as Head hated to do it, he knew that it was imperative to have Jennifer Corbin's small sons interviewed as soon as possible. They had been alone in the house with their mother and they had found her body. Children often have trouble distinguishing fact and fantasy, particularly when they have undergone a profound shock. The more time that passed before they were questioned, the more likely they would be to slip away from the awful reality of what they had seen.

Corporal Curtis L. Clemmons, a senior member of the Special Victims Unit in the Gwinnett County Police Department, was especially well trained in questioning children. A father himself, Clemmons was a big bear of a man with a gentle voice. He sighed as he was notified of the death. Head asked him to talk with Dalton and Dillon Corbin.

The little boys would leave Bogan Gates Drive soon with their Grandpa Max, but Barber promised to bring them to headquarters later in the day so Clemmons could talk to them. It had to be today; like Head, Clemmons knew that children's memories are so fragile that they can blow apart like dandelion fluff in a short amount of time.

It was difficult for Jenn's family to realize that her lovely home was now a crime scene, cordoned off from everyone but the investigators. The Barbers and Tierneys were told they could not go into the house, not even to get more clothing for the boys. That seemed wrong, too; everything seemed wrong to them. They were both grief-stricken and angry, but they knew they had to get Dalton and Dillon away from there.

As the Barber family drove away with the boys, they

were unaware—everyone was unaware—how long it would take to find the answers to what had happened here . . . and why.

*   *   *

THERE WAS STILL NO SIGN of Barton Corbin.

Marcus Head glanced at his watch—and he placed another call to Corbin's brother to see if they were on their way to meet with him. He hadn't talked to Bobby Corbin for half an hour.

Bobby Corbin wasn't as cooperative this time. He was reluctant now to bring Bart to Bogan Gates Drive, saying that Jenn's relatives had been calling him, claiming that Bart had killed her. Perhaps they had, Head thought; emotions were running high. The victim's parents and sister had certainly been angry and ravaged enough with grief to make accusations—particularly since it appeared that the dentist and his wife had been having violent arguments.

"I haven't drawn any conclusions," Head said quietly, "or formed any opinions. But I do need information from Dr. Corbin so I can conduct my investigation."

"Well, I'm concerned about my brother," Bobby said. "I'll call you back soon."

Marcus Head talked further with Steve Comeau, asking him what he had observed in the early morning hours of this bleak day. Comeau said he had arrived home about a quarter to two, and spent a short time in his garage, unloading tools from his truck. It was then that he had heard a vehicle coming down the street.

"This would have been about what time?" Head asked.

"Maybe about two A.M.—I'd been home about fifteen

minutes when I heard it. I recognized it as the sound of Bart's truck."

Comeau said that he hadn't really paid much attention, since he was so used to hearing Bart come down Bogan Gates Drive and turn into his driveway.

"Did you actually see it—look over there to see if it was Dr. Corbin?"

Comeau shook his head. "I didn't look."

And he couldn't recall if he'd heard one of the truck's doors open and close—or two. As close as he could remember, the truck he believed was Corbin's had stayed only "ten or fifteen minutes" before he heard it leave again, roaring up the street.

"The truck's engine noises made it sound like the driver was in a hurry."

As far as his neighbors knew, sometime in the past few weeks, Bart had moved out of the master bedroom he had shared with Jenn. Jenn had come and gone, sometimes staying at Heather's house. Things were up in the air in her marriage, but the Comeaus said they had still felt that the couple might simply need some time apart to sort out their feelings. And they probably needed to see a marriage counselor. Jenn would have had them go sooner, but Bart had told Kelly Comeau that he didn't want to talk about his private life with any counselor.

Slowly now, the awful, immutable truth had begun to sink in with the Comeaus. There was no longer any reason to sort out feelings or to see a marriage counselor. There was nothing left of the marriage that had begun with so much hope and happiness. And there was nothing left of Jenn; her essence, her soul, no longer warmed their lives. Ironically, it was always Jenn who brought order out of chaos, who solved problems and promised that "every-thing will be OK"

Now Jenn Corbin lay dead across the street; her sons Dalton and Dillon had left, looking lost and confused, oc-casionally crying inconsolably: and no one knew where their father was.

None of Jenn's family and close friends would budge on their insistence that she would not have chosen to end her life. Those who loved her kept repeating it like a mantra: "Jenn would never, ever, kill herself," Heather said. "She wouldn't have done that to the boys, knowing how much they needed her. She would never leave her sons. Never. Even if she was depressed and we didn't know it, she wouldn't shoot herself, knowing that Dalton or Dil-lon would be the ones to discover her body.

"She loved them too much."

CHAPTER THREE

DECEMBER 4, 2004

ONCE THE SEARCH WARRANT arrived, the CSI team who waited on Bogan Gates Drive moved through the silent brick home, gathering anything that looked as if it might be evidence. Crime Scene Technician Amber Roessler and Forensic Investigator Ray Rawlins photographed the bedroom and Jenn Corbin's body, while other technicians took more photos of the house, videotaped the scene, and took measurements that would allow them to triangulate the position of vital elements later. Whatever was there now would never be exactly the same again. It was absolutely essential that they photograph the master bedroom and the entire interior and exterior of the Corbin home. They would bag even the most unlikely items into a chain of evidence, labeling and sealing everything separately so it would all be sacrosanct, no matter how many hands the possible clues passed through. And each person who touched them would initial them.

At 3 P.M., almost eight hours after Dalton Corbin ran across the street to get help for his mother, the CSI crew secured the scene. Jennifer Corbin's body still lay where it had been found many hours earlier. It seemed somehow callous to leave her there, but the investigators had no choice; all they could do for her now was find out how she had died, and every detail about her death, no matter how seemingly inconsequential, was important to them. If she had taken her own life, they would be able to verify that. But if someone had killed her, they would know that, too, and if that was the case, they were determined to find that person. In a homicide investigation, nothing can be taken for granted, and things are seldom what they seem.

Reporters monitoring police calls in Gwinnett County notified their editors about a death on Bogan Gates Drive, noting that it seemed to be a suicide, and that was the way it appeared in local papers and television news. Although those who really knew Jenn shook their heads in denial, strangers in the greater Atlanta area heard "suicide" and accepted it.

Marcus Head and Ray Rawlins hadn't known Jenn Corbin when she was alive. Now, they would meet her in death. Head would work backward to trace what events, if any, could have made her desperate enough to take her own life. Or what secrets lay hidden in her life—or in a killer's life—that might have marked her as a murder victim.

But all of the Gwinnett County investigators' minds were open; they would consider every eventuality. And hopefully they would come to know Jennifer Barber Corbin almost as well as those who had known her in life. Maybe even better.

Once the crime scene technicians had finished their work, Rawlins and Head entered the house again. The front door opened into a foyer, with a formal dining room to their left and an office on their right. They noted that the Corbins' house was very clean, and decorated by someone who had been proud of it, someone who had the creativity and ability to blend furnishings that were both expensive and practical into a warm and welcoming home. The two men tried to ignore the Christmas decorations. It was bad enough that two little boys had lost their mother, but to lose her at Christmastime made it even worse. Those kids would undoubtedly think of this day and feel their loss every Christmas for the rest of their lives.

Rawlins and Head crossed the foyer and headed toward the back of the house. A hallway led off to the right, and they followed it to the master bedroom. It was a rather grand suite with dark wood furniture, bedside tables with marble tops, and a king-sized canopy bed with massive carved posts and an ornate design in the headboard. The drapes and bedding were a Tommy Hilfiger design, with a pattern of cabbage roses and paisley shapes.

Next to the bed, somewhat incongruously, there was a jeroboam-sized Absolut vodka bottle, now serving as a bank for coins. The lights were on, and so was the television set.

Jennifer Corbin lay diagonally across the bed, her tall form graceful, her face calm. She rested mostly on her left side. There seemed to be no sign at all of a struggle, although her position wasn't that of someone prepared to sleep. Her upper back was parallel to the headboard and her feet angled off to the far side of the bed. There were three pillows on the bed; the comforter covered her only from her waist to her ankles. One of the pillows was fluffed up, but there was a deep oval indentation in the middle.

Jennifer's left arm was underneath her body, except for her hand, which was near her left breast. Her right arm was bent at the elbow so that her forearm rested across her waist. The grips of what looked to be a .38-caliber revolver were beneath—and a few inches away from—her right hand. It rested on the comforter. However, the barrel was almost hidden beneath the comforter.

The two investigators frowned, wondering again how the gun could have ended up in that position. It didn't seem probable—or even possible—that it had dropped from her hand at the moment of firing and ended up underneath the covers. Certainly, she would not have been able to slip it there. It would take the autopsy to say definitely, but, with her head wound, they believed she had died instantly.

Because they did not know the actual manner of Jennifer Corbin's death, it was essential that her position and the position of the gun and the path of blood flow be noted. Her head was tilted a little to the left. Blood had drained from her nostrils and traveled in an uninterrupted line slightly upward to cross her left lower eyelid and then drip down onto the mattress. There was no other blood on her face or mouth. This would indicate that she had not moved or, more accurately, had not been moved after she was shot, unless she had lain in one position until the blood had dried, and that was unlikely. The blond hair on the right side of her head and across the rear of her head was stained scarlet.

It would now take experts in blood patterns and ballistics to determine the angle of fire, how far the gun had been from her head, and whether Jenn or someone else had fired the gun.

Inexorable postmortem indicators would help them

narrow down the time of her death. Those portions of her body that were uncovered were cold to the touch now, and rigor mortis—that stiffening that comes soon after death—had already begun. It would render her body completely rigid for forty-eight hours or so, and then slowly dissipate.

Ray Rawlins saw that livor mortis, or "lividity," had begun. This phenomenon of death is a reddish-purple, mottled stain that occurs when blood settles in the lowest part of a body after the heart stops pumping. There was no secondary shading, no lighter pink blushing. (If a body is moved after lividity begins, the darker marking will remain fixed, but a lighter mottling will show that someone changed the victim's position some time after death.)

The entry wound of the single bullet was on the right side of Jenn Corbin's head—toward the back—and there was a "near-exit" wound on the left side with a small piece of bone protruding from the skin there. The bullet itself was apparently still lodged in her brain, just short of exiting. Jenn's eyes and the tissue around them were bruised and swollen, the "raccoon eyes" that are expected after a bullet wound in the head. This was not a sign that Jenn had been beaten, although it might appear that way to a layperson.

Her hands showed no evidence of defense wounds; her nails were well kept and unbroken, the skin smooth, and without scratches.

Either Jenn had committed suicide, or, if she had been murdered, she never saw it coming. This might offer some faint comfort to her family. She had not died afraid.

Ray Rawlins carefully removed the revolver from where it lay partially under the comforter. He marked the cylinder on both sides of the frame, and then released it.

There was a spent shell casing beneath the hammer; it would prove to be just like the three unfired cartridges—all round-nosed projectiles. One chamber held neither a spent cartridge nor a jacketed slug. This method of loading a weapon is sometimes used as a safety measure. If the trigger should be accidentally pulled, there would be no bullet in the chamber.

The gun was a Smith & Wesson .38-caliber blue steel revolver. The serial number was 397676. With any luck at all, this number would let them trace ownership of this weapon back to the day it first left the Smith & Wesson factory. There were no visible fingerprints on the rough-textured grips, or the barrel.

At 3:15 P.M., Ray Rawlins officially pronounced Jennifer Corbin dead. It was a mere formality. The paramedics from Fire District #14 had already examined her body and told him that she was deceased.

Marcus Head helped Rawlins slip paper bags over both of Jennifer Corbin's hands, which they then secured with evidence tape. If there was GSR (gunshot residue) there, or any skin from a killer under her fingernails, the bags would ensure that no evidence would be lost between her home and the Medical Examiner's Office.

Carefully, they wrapped Jennifer's body in a new linen sheet and then slipped it into a brand-new "disaster bag." This was a preventive measure so that there would be no loss of fibers or residue before she reached the Gwinnett County Morgue.

Quietly, Jennifer's neighbors watched as she left her home for the last time. The home she had loved was surrounded now by yellow police tape.

*   *   *

EVEN AS their mother's death investigation was in its first hours, Dalton and Dillon Corbin waited nervously beside their grandfather Max at the Gwinnett County police headquarters at 770 Hi Hope Road in Lawrenceville. It was an ironically cheerful address for an agency that dealt with so many tragedies.

It was still only early afternoon on December 4, but the day seemed to stretch on endlessly for Jenn's family, especially for her sons.

Investigator Curtis Clemmons led Dalton into an interview room that was designed for children. There was a small round table there, a wooden chair scaled just right for an almost-seven-year-old boy.

A hidden camera caught every nuance of this interview. Dalton looked so young and vulnerable, but he was clearly trying to answer Clemmons' questions the best he could. He gave his name: Dalton Fox Corbin. And his address: 4515 Bogan Gates Drive in Buford, Georgia. He knew his birthday, March 12, 1997, and his phone number.

Clemmons wasn't nearly ready to ask Dalton the hard questions that must come later. First, he had to create an ambiance of trust and approval. He kept his voice soft and encouraging, complimenting Dalton on his intelligence. He meant it sincerely: Dalton was obviously very smart. Dalton seemed to be enjoying this part of their conversation, and yet he sat perched like a little bird on his chair, alert and ready for flight.

"Do you wear glasses or contacts?" Clemmons asked. It wasn't a necessary question, but each query that didn't remind Dalton about what had happened seven or eight hours earlier seemed to make him feel more secure with Clemmons.

Now the investigator held out a series of colored slips of paper. Dalton easily identified them all, as he did with the drawings of animals that came next.

"Good . . . good," Clemmons said.

"What class did you like best at Harmony School?" Clemmons asked.

"Kindergarten!"

"What's your favorite food?" Clemmons asked, knowing the answer already from having talked to scores of children.

"Pizza!"

He asked Dalton if he knew the difference between a "good touch" and a "bad touch," giving examples of being punched in the nose, or being hugged by his grandfather.

Dalton knew. His mother had taught him carefully how to protect himself. And he knew the difference between the truth and a lie.

He also realized what questions were coming next. Suddenly Dalton dropped his head and rested it on his folded arms. Neither Clemmons nor the little boy in front of him wanted to broach the subject of Jenn Corbin.

"Do you know why you're here today?" Clemmons finally asked.

" 'Cause my mom got killed this morning," Dalton said. "When I woke up, I went to go see my mom, and I was right by her and there was blood right here." He pointed beneath his nose. "I couldn't wake her up so I wanted to call 911."

There, it was out, and like Pandora's box, the bad things could not be put back. And even with that, it was heart-wrenching to watch. A child cannot grasp the permanency of death. Dalton came as close as any seven-year-old could, but he could not imagine all the years ahead without his mother. He spoke calmly, as he answered Clemmons's questions. He knew it was 7 A.M. when he went to wake his mother, and that his brother Dillon was asleep. "He woke up," Dalton said, "when he heard me saying 'Mommmmm!' "

He knew the TV in his mother's room was on, and that Dillon had come into her room, too.

"Anyone else there?"

"My dog. Zippo."

"Did you hear any noises last night?"

"Uh-uh. [No.] I went to sleep about ten o'clock. And my dad killed her."

Clemmons was careful not to betray any shock at this answer; he didn't so much as move his hands or shift his body. He asked Dalton why he thought his father had killed his mother if he hadn't seen it happen. Dalton explained that it was because his father's car was usually at their house every morning, but on this morning it was gone.

"Who told you that?"

"I figured it out myself."

"Did you see your dad?"

"No."

Dalton said that his parents had been fighting a lot, and he repeated that his father had killed "my mom" and then left, and went to his Uncle Bob's house.

But was Dalton describing what he had seen and heard, or was he confabulating? Could he really separate one day from the next as he tried to recall the interactions in his family over the past nine or ten days?

"All I heard was my mom, dad, and my brother eating supper at six o'clock," he told Clemmons. "We ate steak and ice cream, and my mom went to bed and my dad went to work. He's a dentist."

"He works at night?" Clemmons asked, with just a touch of surprise in his voice.

"He's been stealing things from my mom—like her new cell phone and records."

"After dinner, you went to bed at ten? Did you hear your mom or dad fussing?"

"No. The last time they argued was last Wednesday."

"When you went to bed, was your dad still home?"

"Yeah, he was sleeping right next door to me. My mom and dad sleep in different rooms."

"For how long?"

"Mmmm—since last weekend."

* * *

CAREFULLY, CLEMMONS REVIEWED what Dalton had told him. The investigator knew what Marcus Head had learned so far because Head had briefed him, but he was scrupulously careful not to suggest anything at all to Dalton.

"You, Dillon, your mom, dad, and Zippo, your dog, were home? You ate dinner at six, and you went to bed at ten. You watched TV for four hours and went to bed?"

"Umm-hmm. [Yes.] Sometimes I sleep in my bedroom, and sometimes in the toy room with Dillon."

Dalton was sure that his father was home when he went to sleep. But when he woke up, he was gone. He said he had seen the gun in his mother's bed, but he didn't touch it.

"That's good," Clemmons said fervently, knowing that the gun was still loaded at the time.

Dillon had wanted breakfast, too, but their mother couldn't hear them. Dalton knew that she was dead. And that was when he ran over to the Comeaus across the street. He had tried to call 911, but the phone wouldn't work.

"Did you wonder why the phone wasn't working?"

"Maybe my dad cut it off."

"Has your dad been mad at your mom?"

"Yes."

"Why?"

"He thinks my mom is a liar. They argued all the time from last Wednesday until today. They talked about living in separate houses and getting an attorney. Yelling at each other."

"How did that make you feel?" Clemmons asked quietly.

"I felt sad."

Dalton said his dad had talked to him about the possibility of a divorce. "He said 'I love you, and I always will love you.' "

This was a tough interview for a man who was a father himself. Clemmons asked Dalton again if he had heard anything strange during the night just past. The little boy thought his parents were talking about his father taking Dalton's computer away, and there was something about his mother's taking his father's bank account away.

"There was an argument last night?"

"Yeah."

"How did you feel?"

"Scared. My mom was holding my hand. She always holds my hand when I'm scared, and it makes me feel better." He said he'd asked his mother to eat dinner right next to him. "I do that when I'm scared. And she does."

Dalton Corbin had tried to figure out exactly how his mother got killed, but he wasn't really sure. He hadn't actually seen anything happen, but he had been an observer of a marriage that was clearly disintegrating. He studied his hands now and crossed one finger over another until they were all crossed. Did this make him feel safer, or was it only a nervous habit? Probably a little of both.

His memory was uncertain. He hadn't heard anything during the night. No, his father never *said* he would kill his mother. Nor had Dalton ever seen his mother with a gun. He didn't see the murder, or hear the murder, but he knew . . . this small boy believed his father came home to sleep and then he got a gun and killed his mother in the morning.

"How do you feel about your mom?" Clemmons asked gently.

"I'm really sad."

DILLON WAS ONLY FIVE, but his turn was next. The camera caught him as he sat at the little chair in front of the round table. He swayed back and forth, muttering to himself: "Ummm. Ummm. Some. Some."

While he waited for Curtis Clemmons to come back into the room, Dillon laid his head down on the table, and then he dotted the tabletop with each finger in turn, as if he was leaving little circles there. He looked so tired as he rested his head on his arms like Dalton did. He seemed nervous.

When Clemmons came back into the room, Dillon looked up politely. He was just as bright as his older brother. He knew his middle name, "Avery," his phone number, address, colors, and animals. But he was totally confused about how his life had changed in one horrible watershed moment. He knew his mother was dead, but he was not at all sure about the sequence of events. He parroted a little of what Dalton had said, but Dillon often contradicted himself.

He was sure his kindergarten teacher's name was "Miss Donna," and he liked her. Pizza was his favorite, too. But Dillon could not remember if he had eaten breakfast or not. He had seen his mother lying in her bed with blood on her nose, but he also thought she probably fixed breakfast.

Dillon said that he had gone into his mother's room before Dalton did—which was doubtful—and then he said that he had seen his father kill his mother.

Gently, Clemmons reminded the five-year-old about the difference between the truth and a lie—and Dillon admitted that he hadn't seen his mother killed. He could not possibly know that he would never see his mother again. Or that his father had still not gone to their house nor asked to see him or Dalton.

Detectives grow accustomed to tragedy and to violent death, and they learn to protect their own emotions. But none of them ever becomes immune to the sadness of children caught in the web of adults' problems.

CHAPTER FOUR

DECEMBER 4, 2004

BART HAD NOT CALLED detectives back for eight hours on this long December 4. Neither Bobby nor Bart Corbin responded to messages from the family or from the detectives. Bart knew that Jenn was dead. Bobby had said Bart was very upset when he heard she had been shot, so upset he was in the bathroom vomiting.

Was he watching television now or listening to the radio? If his filing for divorce was meant to scare Jenn into coming back to him, and if he still loved her, he wasn't acting like a grieving widower.

Whatever Bart's true feelings, Marcus Head learned from Bobby Corbin that Bart would not be coming to his home on Bogan Gates Drive. And Bart Corbin had "lawyered up." Gwinnett County Police Investigator Fred Mathewson had obtained a search warrant to swab

Corbin's hands for the presence of gun residue. If he wasn't coming to talk with them and to submit to the tests willingly, they would have to do it the hard way.

Head received a phone call from Steve Roberts, an attorney who said he had been retained to represent Barton Corbin. "I informed Mr. Roberts," Head wrote in the growing case file, "that I had a search warrant to seize Barton Corbin for the purpose of swabbing and wiping his hands to conduct a gunshot residue test."

Senior Assistant DA Tom Davis was with Head at the Corbins' house and he took the phone to speak with Roberts. The two attorneys agreed that Roberts would bring Corbin to police headquarters at 4 P.M. that day.

Bart Corbin, accompanied by his brothers, did arrive at police headquarters as agreed. As Bart, Brad, and Bobby walked toward the room where Bart's hands would be tested for gunshot residue, Marcus Head told him that detectives and CSI personnel were just about to finish processing the death scene at his home.

"Are there any special instructions or details that I should know?" he asked Bart. "About how to secure your house before we all leave?"

Bart informed him that he would answer *no* questions—not even that one.

CSI Investigator M. Briscoe swabbed Corbin's hands, using the Georgia Bureau of Investigation's gunshot residue kit while Head and Davis watched.

The test was negative for gunpowder or barrel debris. That wasn't necessarily proof either way about whether he had fired a gun. Simple handwashing would wash gunshot residue away, just as touching such varied things as toilet paper or paper towels could create a false positive result. But the GSR test was an important step nonetheless. And the mere administration of a residue test often made guilty suspects nervous. Corbin seemed calm. Annoyed—but calm.

Next they inspected his clothing, but they found no bloodstains or other signs that would indicate he had fired a gun.

Except for his initial exchange with Marcus Head, Bart Corbin remained silent, refusing to speak at all during the entire time he was in the room with the law enforcement personnel.

Head asked Bobby Corbin how his brother had learned of his wife's death, but Bobby didn't want to answer any questions, either.

Were all the Corbin brothers gripped by shock, or were they only closing ranks to frustrate the detectives who were trying to determine how Jenn had died? In the end, Head could do nothing more than give Bobby a copy of the search warrant for the procedure.

And then he escorted Bart, Brad, and Bobby out of the building and watched them drive off.

Finally, the sun was setting on an endless day. Now the Gwinnett County team would try to follow the tangled skein of an unraveling marriage back to the point where Jenn and Bart began to veer from their design for happiness. If the detectives could isolate the catalysts for the apparently sudden decision to divorce, they could probably identify Jenn's killer.

Yet they were about to plunge into an investigation that was far more intricate than any of them could imagine. They would walk into a virtual hall of mirrors. And even when a way through was found, they would discover passageways into further mysteries. It was a maze of relationships and events that had brought two loving extended families to their knees in a morass of tragedy.

CHAPTER FIVE

DECEMBER 5, 2004

DR. CAROL A. TERRY rose early the next morning, even though it was Sunday. She was scheduled to perform a postmortem examination of the body of Jennifer Corbin. As far as the public knew, this young woman had taken her own life. But neither the Gwinnett County police investigators nor District Attorney Danny Porter and members of his staff were satisfied with that assumption. Before anyone could be officially declared a suicide, there were always tests and an extremely thorough autopsy to be done. There were also "psychological autopsies" of the deceased to be explored. From what little was known of Jennifer Corbin's life, she seemed a most unlikely candidate for suicide.

The manner of her death was odd. Even if fatally depressed, few females kill themselves with a gunshot to the head. They want to look attractive when their bodies are discovered, whereas males don't seem to care. Women tend to take their own lives with sleeping pills or by cutting their wrists. Many even put on makeup and wear their prettiest outfit or nightgown.

But Jennifer had worn an old sleeveless green satin shortie nightgown. Both its straps were torn off in the back, and she had them secured with safety pins. It was the sort of quick patching job that women do on clothes that no one is going to see. Underneath, she wore pink panties. Dr. Terry noted that they were in place with no sign that anyone had tried to remove them.

The clothing and possessions worn by the dead are somehow more "alive" than the body shell left behind, and tell their own small stories. The jewelry on Jenn Corbin's body seemed intact: clear, square diamond earrings; a "brownish-red" teardrop-shaped pendant on a thin gold chain encircling her neck, with a ring that matched it on her right hand; a gold nugget bracelet on her right wrist; a gold wedding ring and an engagement ring with a rectangular diamond; an Aquatech watch with a digital display reading 6:42:21. The watch display did not change as real time passed—the battery had apparently failed a few hours after she died. On her right wrist, Jenn wore a white and pink beaded bracelet with the beads spelling out "Kylie." The childish bracelet was in support of a friend's child who was fighting cancer. The "brownish-red" stones in Jenn's necklace and in one of her rings were garnets, her favorite semiprecious stone, which she had worn constantly for many years after her late grandmother, "Nana," gave them to her.

Jennifer Corbin had a small tattoo on her right ankle—the familiar mask of tragedy and comedy. She had been a true fan of the group Mötley Crüe, and the masks were from the cover of one of their top albums.

Forensic Technician Zubedah Mutawassim, Assistant DA Tom Davis, and DA's Investigator Kevin Vincent joined Ray Rawlins and Marcus Head to observe the post-mortem exam. Perhaps Dr. Terry would find something that would end this death investigation once and for all. More likely, there would be small things that didn't mesh with suicide.

Jenn Corbin was a good-sized woman, but not at all overweight. She lacked perhaps a half-inch of being six feet tall, and she weighed just over 170. Jenn would have been capable of putting up a good fight had she had any warning at all of danger. But the investigators at the death site hadn't noted anything that suggested a struggle—no overturned lamps or chairs, nothing broken. When the brown paper bags that covered her hands were removed, Dr. Terry found not even a minuscule cut or scratch. If Jenn had been murdered, she would have to have been taken by surprise or she might even have been asleep.

If she was murdered. That was the biggest if. All the suspicions in the world wouldn't help in a courtroom unless the Gwinnett County detectives and prosecutors could prove their theories to a jury.

The woman before them was wearing a little makeup: pale pink lipstick. She had three piercings in each ear, although she wore only the two small square diamond earrings now. They were removed along with her other jewelry, her greenish-blue satin nightgown with the black "frog" fastenings, and her pink panties, and bagged into evidence. Someday, they might be used as evidence in a trial, or if not, they would be given to her family.

The single, fatal bullet wound was to the right side of

her head—behind her right ear. The wound path was from the right side of her head to the left, and upward. The bullet had effectively cut her brain stem in half and fractured her skull in several places.

Death would have been instantaneous.

The entrance wound was round and only three-sixteenths of an inch in diameter. There was soot from the gun barrel near the wound, but no stippling—the tiny burned specks that "tattoo" the skin around the hole where a bullet fired from a short distance goes in. The edges of this entrance wound were not seared or torn by the force of the heated gas in a gun barrel. A contact gunshot wound usually leaves a "stellate," or star-shaped, wound. This was not a close-contact wound.

After establishing the path and angle of the deadly wound, Dr. Terry carefully examined the other organs in Jenn Corbin's body. Was it possible that she was suffering from some fatal disease—something that no one who loved her knew about? That could have been a motive for suicide. But the forensic pathologist found every indication that Jennifer Corbin had been in excellent health.

Somehow, normal findings in an autopsy make the subject's death more tragic. That was true in this case. All things being equal, Jennifer Corbin would have lived to be a very old lady. Her lungs, heart, arteries, liver, kidneys, and reproductive organs were all completely normal. Sometime in the past, she had had her gallbladder removed, and surgical clips remained—which was a normal procedure. She had a small bruise on the right side of her lower abdomen, but it had faded into the yellow-greenish hue of a healing contusion. It was probably not significant; mothers of small boys often have bruises from riding herd on them and usually can't even remember when they got them.

Jenn Corbin's last meal had included green beans. When that information was added to her body temperature when she was found, and the degree of rigor and livor mortis now, it would help to mark the time of her death. In some instances, pinpointing the exact time a victim died isn't important, but in others it can be vital. This would be one of those cases. Jenn's death had probably occurred between four and five hours before her body was discovered: somewhere around 2 to 3 A.M.

The official cause of her death was listed at the beginning of the "Summary of Findings" derived from her autopsy. It read: "Penetrating gunshot wound of head. Loose-contact range entrance wound on right side of head (posterior to right ear, in right posterior temporal/anterior occipital region)."

The observers at the autopsy looked grim. This was definitely not a contact wound where the gun's barrel had been placed against her head. There was no muzzle impression, no tears around the edges of the wound itself, and no stippling. The gun would have to have been fired from several inches away. While it was remotely possible that Jenn Corbin could have twisted her right hand into an awkward position that would have allowed her to place the gun barrel against the skin behind her ear, it wasn't likely. And it was clearly impossible for her to have held the weapon inches away from the entry point behind her right ear. Her arm was simply not that long.

Nevertheless, the first media reports in the Atlanta/ Gwinnett County area would report that autopsy results were "inconclusive," reinforcing the impression for many viewers and readers that Jennifer Corbin had committed suicide.

The news that Jenn Corbin's husband had filed for divorce would have been a great shock, except, perhaps, to those who were close to her. The information that she had died violently by her own hand was almost impossible for her friends and co-workers to absorb. And for her immediate family, it continued to be unthinkable.

*   *   *

JENNIFER CORBIN'S SECRETS would be opened up for the world to see, but, inevitably Bart Corbin's own private life would also be held up to the light—all of his secrets, his misdeeds, his past, and his present. That's what a murder investigation was, is, and has to be—an ongoing invasion of privacy, not just for the victim and the suspect, but for those who worry about friends on both sides of a case, strangers who have some kind of connection, and witnesses. The net spreads out and they are all caught in it, their private thoughts and actions explored relentlessly.

It's the only way a death investigation can proceed. When a life is stolen prematurely, truth is the one path to justice.

Jenn and Bart Corbin's scrapbooks and picture frames were full of happy family photographs: the two of them dancing at their wedding, looking totally in love; Jenn and Bart rafting through a deep canyon; Jenn, happily exhausted after Dalton's birth; Bart holding Dalton minutes after he was born; Bart helping two-year-old Dillon blow out the candles on his birthday cake; a tan Bart, barechested and broad-shouldered on their own houseboat on Lake Lanier, and proudly holding two-month-old Dillon;

the couple, both a little heavier than at their wedding reception, dancing somewhere at a charity dinner; all four Corbins posing happily at Disney World; Bart and Jenn beaming happily at a Corbin family wedding. And so many photos of Bart and Jenn with her family, usually laughing with Narda and Max, Heather, Doug and Rajel.

It seemed perhaps too perfect, happy moments caught forever on film but somehow evaporating in real life.

Chapter Six

December 6, 2004

At thirty-three, Jenn Barber Corbin was the personification of what most young wives and mothers strive to achieve. She wasn't conventionally or "cookie-cutter" beautiful, but she had lovely and expressive brown eyes, golden-blond streaks in her thick hair, and a voluptuous figure.

Jenn was always smiling, no matter what troubles she might be dealing with. It was that luminous personality that people remembered about her now.

Jenn's part-time job as a preschool teacher allowed her time to take care of Bart and her little boys. She worked a few hours on weekdays at the school in the Sugar Hill United Methodist Church. On Sunday her family attended services there.

"Before any of this happened," Jenn's good friend and

fellow preschool teacher Jennifer Rupured observed, "I would have said Jenn would have made a great character in any other type of book [rather than a true crime book]." Rupured listed possible books that were more in Jenn's genre: " 'Martha Stewart Cannot Outclean Jenn Corbin!' or 'Mom of the Year: How to Bake Six Pies and Clean House at the Same Time You Drive Your Kids to Baseball.' Or even 'Die-Cutting with a Passion: How to Create Preschool Bulletin Boards Using Only 700 Handprints Individually Cut Out.'

"Jenn had the kind of a personality an author could absorb and understand because it was so large and lovely," Jennifer Rupured said, remembering how Jenn had dug little pots of shamrocks on St. Patrick's Day for her students, and kept "lucky" pennies to hand out when someone needed to have a wish come true.

No matter how busy she was, Jenn Corbin would stop and listen to someone who needed an attentive ear, having that rare ability to focus entirely on the person who was speaking. That was undoubtedly because she truly was interested, and she did care about other people—whether it was one of the preschoolers she taught or an adult friend. Or even a virtual stranger.

But she was definitely not a sweetie-sweet kind of woman, and she was known to use four-letter words on occasions that called for them. Her sense of humor could be ribald at times. Neither she nor her sisters nor their mother fit into the stereotype of the genteel Southern belle. Still, there remained in Jenn a suspension of disbelief that made her have faith in happy endings, no matter how many times life rose up and smacked her in the face.

If Jenn had flaws—and of course she did because she

was, after all, only human—one was that she trusted people too much before she fully knew them. That would include those on the periphery of her life and even a few who were part of her innermost circle. She had forgiven much, overlooked things that most women would not, and always tried to keep her own problems to herself to spare her family worry. At the time Jenn died, she was struggling with seemingly insurmountable decisions. She who had always believed in marriage wanted nothing more than to break the vows she had made eight years earlier.

She had fallen in love with someone else.

But very few people knew about it. In most people's eyes, Jenn Corbin was a paragon, above reproach, incapable of reaching out for the happiness that might be achieved only by flouting conventional morality.

"She was a wonderful teacher, fabulous mother, and true friend," one of her students' mothers wrote about her. "There was no way she would have committed suicide. She was not the type. And she lived for her boys, whom she completely adored! She had a great support system of family and friends and would never have left them of her own accord. She loved her boys with her whole being and all the kids she taught, too. She would never have let them [her sons] find her with a bullet in her head. She was upbeat, fun, and someone everyone wanted to be around."

This opinion was repeated over and over as reporters and detectives fanned out to learn everything they could about her. And even while Georgia media outlets carried the news that Jennifer Corbin had apparently committed suicide, forensic pathologists knew that ballistics and physical evidence ruled out the possibility that she had shot herself. And those who knew her in life believed in their hearts and guts that someone had deliberately wanted her dead.

To bring her the justice she deserved, events in her life would have to be peeled away layer by layer, exposing what should have been her secrets, her dreams, and her hopes for the future. There is perhaps no human being without undisclosed desires and even sins—or things they consider sinful—that they would never want others to know about. What things would Jenn Corbin have been hiding?

Her life was gone in an instant, snuffed out by a single bullet. And now Jenn's inner world would be put under a microscope and picked over for possible clues. No one was eager to do that, not the Gwinnett County police nor District Attorney Danny Porter, and certainly not her family.

Now that the Gwinnett County investigators knew Jenn's marriage had, for all intents and purposes, ended, they understood why Bart Corbin might not have been in their home when she was found. That was to be expected.

CHAPTER SEVEN

1964–1996

JENN CORBIN GREW UP as Jenni Barber, the second daughter of three, in a family so typical of middle-class America that their losing her to murder could chill the heart of any parent.

Thomas Maxwell "Max" Barber and his wife Narda both came from strict families. Max was born in Logan, West Virginia, the youngest of four handsome sons. His father was a coal mine engineer, who taught his sons respect toward their elders and gallantry toward women.

"My mother was a wonderful cook," Max remembered, "but I always wondered if I would get enough to eat. My dad would serve my mother first, then himself, and then my brothers, starting with the oldest. Being the youngest, I always hoped there would be something left."

It was a family joke, and Max Barber did get enough;

he grew to be six feet three inches tall, a star athlete who was offered a basketball scholarship to Florida Southern University in Bradenton, Florida, where the elder Barbers eventually settled.

Although Max extolled Narda's cooking, he would always tease her that she couldn't equal his mother when it came to banana pudding and lemon meringue pie.

Narda Upton was the only child born to career Army Colonel William F. Upton and her mother, Sylvia. Her father was forty-five and her mother thirty-three when she was born. Home base for them was a farm in Derry, New Hampshire, but the service family traveled a great deal, and both Narda's parents were assigned to the Pentagon when she was a small girl.

"My dad retired when I was quite young," she remembered. "And then we really traveled. They bought an Airstream trailer and we went all around America, so I got to see a lot of the country. Eventually, they bought our home on Lido Quay in the Bay of Mexico off Sarasota, Florida."

It was in January 1964 when Max first met Narda. He was two years older and about nine inches taller than the bubbly girl with lovely eyes and thick wavy hair.

"The first time I saw her, she was dancing with someone at a sock hop in Bradenton, Florida. I had a date that evening, and she was a friend of Narda's and she introduced Narda to me. It was like magic immediately! The beauty, the voice, the composure she possessed. Narda, her date, my date, and I left the dance together. I believe we went to McDonald's in Sarasota. I was the driver that night, and I deliberately drove Narda home last. I remember well walking her to the front door of her home and thanking her for the company. The following day, I had plans to drive to Tampa to watch the cars race at the Tampa Dragway, and I was already planning how to see her again."

Narda had mentioned on the night of the sock hop that she would be taking the bus to St. Petersburg, where she was attending college.

"I wanted to know more about her," Max said, "so I looked up her phone number and called her. When she answered the phone, we made small talk and then I asked if she would like to accompany me to the races and said I would take her to school from there. She told me that her parents would have to approve, and that she would ask them. They agreed to meet me and talk with me about driving Narda to school by way of Tampa."

Narda's father was very cautious about who his daughter dated. Max Barber remembered the grilling he got from the colonel, who virtually interrogated him military-style about his intentions toward Narda. Her father wanted to be sure Max was a safe driver, and an honorable young man.

Max barely remembered answering. "I was so smitten with Narda. As I recall, we had a wonderful day."

Narda felt a strong attraction to Max from the moment they met, just as he was captivated by her. Neither of them wanted to date anyone else. They continued to date for several months before marrying, on January 28, 1964. They were young and the whole world lay ahead of them.

Max had a good job, and despite his gentle manner, his sincerity shone through, making him a great salesman. He moved up through increasingly prestigious positions at Sears—specializing in "hard merchandise," big-ticket appliances like refrigerators, washers, and dryers. Sears transferred its managers frequently, and the Barbers would live in many cities: Sarasota, Florida; Augusta, Georgia; Bowling Green, Kentucky; High Point, North Carolina; Columbus, Cleveland, and Westerville, Ohio.

Shaun Rajel, their first daughter, was born in Sarasota in 1966. Five years later, Jennifer Monique arrived in Bowling Green. She was born on January 25, 1971, and then Heather Nicole came along in High Point, North Carolina, in September 1974.

After so many years and so many cities, the Barbers moved to Gwinnett County, Georgia, to a neighborhood of young families in Lawrenceville. Their split-level home was new, built with similar houses on what had recently been acres of woods. The lots there radiated from the center of a circle, most of them narrow in front, widening in back so that their backyard fences touched. It was an ideal place to raise children. The Barbers could talk over their back and side fences to four other families.

"We shared our good news and not-so-good news over our fences," Narda recalled. "Our neighbors have always rallied around each other for years, some thirty years now."

Pine trees, oaks, and poplars grew from saplings over those decades. Narda planted a garden every year, full of the sweet potatoes Max liked, along with peas, okra, tomatoes, and pole beans.

Kids in the area played in each other's yards and swam in the country club pool just beyond their fences. It wasn't a fancy and expensive country club—but it, too, represented the solidarity of longtime friends who grew older together, scarcely noting the years that passed.

Rajel was a brunette, and petite like her mother, but Jenn and Heather took after Max; they both grew tall enough to be models; their wavy hair was as thick as Narda's.

Narda is an artist, and her paintings and other art projects were hung throughout the Barbers' home. She had a studio at the rear of the property, where she experimented with many different techniques and media.

As most parents do, Narda and Max Barber cherished memories of their girls when they were small—especially Jenn. "She was sweet and kind—always—but there were moments," Narda recalled. "One time, I had left several cans of spray paint on the back porch, and I warned the girls not to touch them. Of course, they all promised they wouldn't. Well, some time passed and I heard Jenni sobbing her heart out. I went to check on her, but she wouldn't look at me. When she finally looked up, I could see that she had sprayed herself in the face with red paint and her little nose was solid red. I think she thought it was going to stay that way forever."

And then there was the episode with Hershey's chocolate syrup.

"Max liked chocolate syrup on ice cream, and the girls all did, too. I explained to them that it was for special occasions, and that they weren't allowed to take it out of the refrigerator without permission.

"One day, I went to get it, and it wasn't there. Nobody admitted that they had taken it. I noticed that Jenni was wearing a jacket all zipped up the front—and it really wasn't cold enough for a jacket. When I asked her why, and suggested she unzip it, she kept coming up with reasons not to. Well, she didn't have a single drop of chocolate on her—not that I could see—but when we unzipped her jacket, that little girl had chocolate syrup from just below her chin down to her waist! It was hard not to laugh."

*   *   *

ALL OF THE BARBER GIRLS attended Central Gwinnett High School. Rajel graduated and married young, giving birth to a daughter who would be a decade older than her cousins born to Jenn and Heather. Rajel moved out west for a while, where she invited a small boy into her home after she realized he lived with a huge, motherless family in her California neighborhood. When Rajel and her husband had to move away, she knew she couldn't leave Joey behind. He became part of the Barber family.

Rajel joined a congregation much stricter than the Methodist church her parents attended. Her life was quite different from those of her younger sisters, who were still teenagers while she was a married woman. It was natural that Jenn and Heather grew closer in their high school years. Both of them were recruited for the basketball team; at their height, they were the most sought after for the squad.

Jenn dated off and on in high school. She tended to be the loyal half of any relationship. The son of a couple who were close friends and neighbors of Max and Narda loved Jenn from afar for years, but they were never closer than buddies who had grown up together.

Jenn Barber took after her mother in artistic talent. While Narda was the professional artist, who painted with sweeping free-form technique, Jenn was far more precise, drawing and painting with exquisite balance and straight lines, angles and intersections that fit neatly.

When Jenn went off to college, she headed for Savannah, that picturesque and sultry city—rife with history and live oak trees dripping with Spanish moss—that sits far south of Atlanta, almost on the Georgia-Florida state line. Jenn enjoyed her years at the Savannah College of Art and Design. Established in 1978, SCAD, as it is commonly known, is a relatively new college, but the site harks back to the nineteenth century. The private college purchased and renovated many of the dilapidated red-brick edifices of another era that were located on the famous "twenty-four squares" of the old town section. Where there was once an armory for volunteers, cotton warehouses, and even coffin factories, classrooms blossomed.

Jenn Barber had wonderful years in Savannah. She wasn't sure what she wanted as a career because she enjoyed and was interested in so many things. She liked photography, but she also was happy with interior design. One day she hoped to have her own house, and she knew it would be a masterpiece of balance and good taste. She loved anything that called for her creative side, and she was skilled in many areas. It was difficult for her to choose one.

When she returned to Gwinnett County, Jenn was still waffling a little about what she wanted to do. She stayed in touch with many friends she had met in Savannah, but in the end she signed up to take classes in pre-nursing at Gordon College. The one thing Jenn did not want to be was a housewife without a career. She was too confident and independent to walk a few paces behind a man. She did hope for love—romantic love.

But then, most women do.

Jenn thought she had finally found that when she was in her mid-twenties. She shared a small bungalow in the Virginia Highlands area of Atlanta with a man she had dated for months. It was the perfect house for romance, situated next to a charming little park. But their relationship didn't last, and they both moved on without hard feelings.

After the breakup, Jenn moved home to Lawrenceville for a while. She didn't intend to have her parents support her while she figured out her life. She took a job at Barnacle's Oyster Bar in Duluth, Georgia, where she made good tips as a waitress and more as a bartender. She was known for her White Russians. The management noted her unfailingly gracious connection to patrons and her concern for their comfort. Jenn's smile and her height made her a standout. More than that, her bosses saw how efficient she was and how quickly she learned the way the restaurant worked. She was soon promoted to shift manager.

Jenn wasn't really looking for a permanent relationship. She dated casually, and she had many friends. She liked her job at Barnacle's, content that whatever was meant to happen in her future would happen. Rajel was married, and Heather was off at college. The Barber family was in a good place.

*   *   *

BART CORBIN HAD FINISHED dental school. He filled in for Dr. Richard Huey in Huey's dental practice in Lithonia in 1991 when the older dentist recovered from a hand injury. He was looking forward to having his own practice as soon as possible, but he had to work for several other established dentists until he saved enough money to open a dental clinic. For a few years, he volunteered his services one Friday a month at a free clinic for the indigent: the Ben Massell Dental Clinic, where Barbara Jones, the clinic supervisor, recalled, "We only saw his giving side here."

One day far in the future, Jenn would ask her sister Heather, "Do you ever wonder about what your husband did or who he knew before you met him?" And Heather would answer, "No, I know what Doug's life was like."

"I don't," was Jenn's reply. She knew virtually nothing about what Bart had done and with whom he might have been involved before she met him. It hadn't seemed to matter at first.

In retrospect, it was easy to see what Jenn Barber saw in the man she fell in love with. Bart was handsome and muscular, with chiseled features, a man who knew precisely how to dress and how to approach women. As far as Jenn knew when she met him, he had had no serious relationships since he finished dental school. That was true enough—he had had no important public relationships. Sometime in his early career as Dr. Bart Corbin, however, Bart had begun a clandestine affair with a woman who worked in the business side of a dental practice where he occasionally moonlighted. It was a dangerous liaison. The woman was married, with two small children, and she was torn between her husband and Bart—who had led her to believe that she was very special to him, so special that he suggested that their lives would always be closely connected.

Jenn knew nothing about this woman when she first met Bart. Almost certainly, she didn't know about a different woman decades older than Bart who some would say was also engaged in a physical affair with him.

No. Dr. Bart Corbin appeared to be a most eligible bachelor, and his meeting with Jenn Barber providential. He was a frequent customer at Barnacle's; he made it a regular stop after he finished a day of treating dental patients. His younger brother Bobby worked at Barnacle's as the doorman, and Bobby's future wife, Suzanne, worked there, too. It was 1995 when Bobby introduced Bart to Jenn. She liked the fact that he was very tall. At six feet three inches, he could actually look down on her, something that didn't happen very often.

Bart was sometimes a bit inscrutable, but that made him more interesting, and he was certainly fun to be around. Like almost everyone who described Bart's best trait, Jenn was drawn to his wittiness. He could offer a quick and hilarious comment on almost anything that came up in conversation.

And Jenn knew that Bart stared at her when he didn't know she was looking. That was nice.

They began to date, and Jenn was in high spirits. Bart appeared to be happy, too, and falling as much in love with her as she was with him. When Jenn brought Bart home to meet Max and Narda, they were pleased. Although he was seven years older than Jenn, she and Bart seemed to be a good match. Max Barber watched Bart's interaction with Jenn, and he was gratified to observe that the tall dentist seemed to care a great deal for his daughter. That was the most important thing to Max, who was very protective of his three daughters. As many fathers would, he liked the fact that Bart was a dentist, a professional man. He would make a good living in a "helping" profession.

There was only one thing that Max found off-putting: Bart's conversation was sprinkled with profanity. That wasn't the mark of a gentleman, and it grated on Max. Still, as he came to know Bart better, he no longer noticed his swearing. He liked Bart as a future husband for his

"Jenni," and the two men had a lot of interests in common; they often went fishing or boating together.

Of course Jenn's parents didn't know about the other women in Bart's life. He kept that side of himself completely obscured. But he certainly did not give up his younger paramour. As it turned out, the older woman wasn't around long enough to cause any waves.

Jenn often confided in Narda, her father Max, and her sisters. But she tried never to tell them more than she thought they could handle easily. During her early courtship, there was nothing untoward to tell them.

Narda was anything but judgmental. After Jenn and Bart had dated for a few months, she assumed that Jenn had probably stayed over with Bart on occasion, spending the night. Although Jenn currently lived at home with Max and Narda, she had lived with her former boyfriend.

"Jenn was not a kid," Narda recalled. "She'd been to college, tried nursing school, and now she was home with us and working a lot. She wasn't a teenager—she was twenty-four when she began to date Bart. She had lived apart from us. All three of our daughters were constantly coming and going.

"Eventually, Bart had to go on a dental seminar that was held in a ski resort in Colorado, and he invited Jenn. But she was working and couldn't go. Still, they stayed in very close touch all the time he was gone. When he came back, they saw each other more and more. Then there was another meeting that was built around a trip to Italy. This time, Jenn went, and they were together almost all the time after that."

They went everywhere with another couple on the Italy trip, Mary and Gary Lands. Mary, six years older than Jenn, was a striking brunette, as friendly and warm as Jenn herself. Bart got along very well with Gary Lands. They would remain close friends after they got back to the Atlanta area.

After they had been back from Italy a few weeks, Jenn called her mother and said she needed to talk. "She asked me 'Was I sitting down?' And I told her 'yes.' "

"Well, Bart and I have made a decision—and I'm pregnant," Jenn said in a happy voice. "Bart and I have decided we're going to get married and have the baby."

Apparently they had considered other choices, including ending the pregnancy or adoption, but Jenn hadn't wanted either of those alternatives.

Narda recalled being thrilled. "I had never seen—or thought of her—being a mom before. Jenn was more career oriented. But now she was asking me how quickly could we plan a wedding? Could they have a big wedding? Jenn wanted it. And somehow we did it in six weeks—an outdoor wedding at The Pottery in Commerce. Violins and all of that."

Max and Narda were pleased about Jenn and Bart's marriage, and they gave her that lovely garden wedding in Commerce, Georgia, on September 1, 1996. Jenn eschewed a traditional pastel color scheme for her wedding, and chose bridesmaids' gowns of black and white instead. They carried red roses.

The new Mrs. Bart Corbin was radiant with happiness, and wasn't at all disturbed when her gown swept the damp red clay of Georgia and the hem ended up smudged by the soil. Jenn and Bart made a very handsome couple. When she wore high heels—which she usually did—they were the same height, a few inches over six feet tall. When they danced cheek-to-cheek at their reception, they seemed such a perfect fit. He kissed her as they danced and they appeared to be in a world of their own. Many of the women in the crowd secretly wished they had a man like Bart in their lives.

Jenn looked absolutely beautiful.

They didn't go away on a honeymoon. They spent the weekend at Max and Narda's houseboat on Lake Lanier. As Jenn sometimes said, laughing, "We had already had our honeymoon—our trip to Italy!"

"It was great," Narda remembered. "And we got a baby!"

PART TWO

Barton Thomas Corbin

"DR. BART"

Chapter Eight

1963–1987

BART CORBIN'S FAMILY BACKGROUND was not nearly as tranquil as Jenn's. Although Bart's father, Gene Corbin, attended Bart and Jenn's wedding, he and Connie were divorced by then, and he was living with another, much younger woman. While the Barbers had three daughters, Gene and Connie Corbin had three sons. Bart and his twin brother, Brad, who were born in Jacksonville, Florida, on December 22, 1963, were the oldest, with Bart arriving three minutes before Brad. They were fraternal twins. Bart was the more outgoing and popular, while Brad's personality was quieter. Actually, Bart was often closer to his younger brother, Bobby Corbin, who was born four years after the Corbin twins.

Eugene Adams Corbin had once been a military policeman in the service and a police officer in Jacksonville.

He was twenty-six when Bart and Brad were born, and Connie was twenty-three. She worked in retail sales. One woman who knew her said, "Connie Corbin's entire conversation was about the bargains she scored. If I had to describe her in one word if would be 'Shopper!' " The elder Corbins' marriage had been fairly tumultuous, and their boys were all very supportive of their mother, particularly after Gene's common-law wife became pregnant about the same time that Jenn did. Bart had both a son and a half brother the same age.

The Corbins had moved from Jacksonville when Bart and Brad were seven years old—first to Atlanta, and then to Snellville in Gwinnett Country. They settled for good in Snellville, about fifteen miles from Buford.

The Corbins' home was also in a neighborhood used to the sound of kids shouting and playing. Snellville had a population of about 10,000 when Bart, Brad, and Bobby were growing up. Their house was a fairly large ranch-style structure built on a cul-de-sac. Old-growth trees shadowed the sidewalks and streets where they lived, and they had their own swimming pool, which was the envy of the neighborhood kids. When the Corbin boys were old enough, they spent a summer or two digging out dirt under the house so a basement and a recreation room could be added.

Gene wanted his boys to star in athletics. He donated money to the junior high school they attended for sports facilities, and at least one parent wondered out loud if he was trying to buy a first-string spot for his sons on the school's teams.

*   *   *

BART, BRAD, AND BOBBY all attended South Gwinnett High School in Snellville. It was a typical conservative Southern small-town school where the emphasis was far heavier on football and other sports than on sex education. Rather than discussing birth control and individual responsibility, Bart and Brad had a health teacher with decidedly puritanical views. They were taught that "girls don't like sex," and that if boys were thoughtful and considerate of the girls they liked, they would never cajole them with persuasive arguments or force them to have intercourse because, according to their health teacher, "They would hate it! No woman enjoys sex."

It may have been a moot point for Bart Corbin, anyway. He didn't have a girlfriend in high school. He acted in a play at school, while Brad was in the French Club. More important to their father, however, was that his boys excel at football, and he rode them pretty hard. They all turned out for the sport in high school and college. Concentrating on athletic competitions, combined with the "Do not touch girls" edict they learned in health class, they appeared to remain "good Southern boys" in high school.

When Bart went off to the University of Georgia in Athens, he was apparently a virgin. The young women who knew him then recall that he certainly acted like one.

Gene Corbin had his own company, called Gecor, and all of his sons worked for him during their school vacations. Even friends close to the Corbin family weren't sure what the main product or service Gecor offered was. Some said that Gene had business "offshore," and others believed it involved chemicals in some way. It wasn't really that mysterious; Gecor manufactured common household chemicals used in everyday products like cleaning solutions and lawn fertilizer.

Gene ordered rather ugly blue "gimme" caps with his company logo on them and handed them out to employees, including his sons, and a young man who worked for him—Richard Wilson—who hung around with Bart. Bart never wore his cap.

The family business was successful enough that Gene could give all his sons cars when they went off to college. In Athens, Brad drove a secondhand Lincoln Continental, and Bart's pride and joy was a yellow and white Chevy pickup with a massive roll bar on top and dual foglights above that. Bart added a screened Confederate flag across his rear window. Bart's truck had the requisite gun rack, although it was empty.

Bart had already reached his full height, of six feet three inches, and he weighed about 240 when he graduated from high school in 1982. He didn't have well-defined muscles then—he was actually a little chubby. Bart was a good enough defensive lineman at South Gwinnett High that he probably could have gotten a scholarship to a small college, but he and Brad chose the University of Georgia in Athens instead. Although the Corbins' income from Gecor was substantial, Bart, Brad, and Gene Corbin occasionally gloated about their cleverness to acquaintances, saying that they had managed to receive considerable financial aid from UGA.

Athens was less than fifty miles from Snellville, but it was a new world to the Corbin twins. Both of them followed a pre-med curriculum, with the requisite heavy emphasis on science.

As he started college, Bart was a walk-on for the Georgia football team, the Bulldogs. He hadn't been recruited by the coaches, and he certainly wasn't a star, but he played all season and was rewarded with a letterman's jacket and a watch. He gave the watch to his father.

The Corbin twins didn't let athletics get in the way of their ambitious goals; Brad wanted to be a brain surgeon, and Bart wanted to go to dental school. He often said he had settled on being a dentist way back when he was a little boy watching *Rudolph the Red-Nosed Reindeer*. He had become fascinated with Herbie, one of Santa's elves, whose ambition was to be a dentist.

Bart and Brad roomed together at Myers Hall on the UGA campus. They were big men who dwarfed the small room they shared, although they cleverly designed and built bunk beds with spaces for their desks to fit in below, and made the most of what space there was.

Despite his dentistry ambitions, Bart was not a particularly gifted candidate. However, he developed an enviable work ethic and studied hard to make up for whatever he lacked in natural ability and dexterity. When he wasn't in class, at football practice, or studying, Bart hung out with other guys in his dorm. And he was popular. His sometimes scathing sense of humor made them all laugh.

There was no girlfriend back home for him, and he was apparently hesitant to approach coeds at UGA. Indeed, the Corbin boys didn't trust women very much. Gene Corbin was said to be somewhat scornful of women, and he may have passed that attitude on to his sons.

Bart might not have started dating if a pretty brunette sophomore from a small town in New York State hadn't made up her mind to meet him. That fall of 1982, both Bart Corbin and Shelly Mansfield* were taking a required

* The names of some individuals have been changed. Such names are indicated by an asterisk (*) the first time they appear.

class in American history in a large lecture hall in the
School of Journalism. Virtually hidden in the crowded au-
ditorium, Shelly watched the tall, beefy freshman with the
deceptively cherubic face, and she liked his dark eyes
under their thick eyebrows. She decided she wanted to
meet him. Despite his size, he seemed somehow innocent,
like a junior high kid in a man's body.

"He sat down in the front," Shelly recalled a long time
later, "and I can't say exactly why, but I just thought he
was cute."

He seemed to be oblivious of her, but she was determined to change that. "Most days after class," Shelly said,
"I would let him leave before me, and then follow him to
the elevator. I would always sort of look at him, and he
would sort of look at me, but both of us were too shy to
say anything. This went on all quarter and I never screwed
up enough courage to talk with him. So the quarter was
over and I figured I'd lost the opportunity to meet the cute
boy in the camouflage pants."

That freshman year, Bart and Brad turned nineteen
during their Christmas vacation. Shelly had no classes
with Bart during winter quarter. But she didn't forget
him, and she was happily surprised to run into Bart on a
bus to the building where they would register for spring
quarter.

"There he was!" she recalled, laughing. "So I kind of
shadowed him when we got to the Registration Center and
I found out what his name was: Barton Corbin. I was still
afraid to say 'Hi' to him though heaven knows why—he
was not intimidating."

But Bart's twin, Brad, was with him in the registration
lines, and Shelly didn't want an audience if she approached
Bart and he rejected her. She went back to her dorm,

Creswell Hall, and pondered what she could find out about Bart now that she at least knew his name. Shelly was a "Northerner," six months older than Bart, and she had considerably more dating experience than he had.

"What I did," she remembered, "was look up his address in the student directory and I sent him a note, telling him I thought he was cute."

She scribbled that she would like to meet him, and added her phone number to the note. Of course, once she had done that she regretted it, sure that he would think she was weird, and would never phone her.

But he did, and Shelly was relieved to find him quite friendly on the phone, even though she realized that he had no idea who she was. "I've never liked talking on the phone," she said, "to anyone that I can easily see face-to-face. We arranged to meet the following evening in the lobby of my dorm."

Shelly was a very pretty young woman, with abundant long, almost-black hair. She was about to become Bart Corbin's first serious girlfriend, and she would have a great impact on his life, more than she could possibly realize. One might even say that Bart would hold any woman who came after her up to Shelly's image.

Shelly had no aspirations toward marriage. She intended to become a writer or a reporter. She was remarkably bright, although she was a somewhat capricious student who sought out only those classes that interested her, and even then didn't mind playing hooky from time to time.

More than two decades later, she would recall meeting Bart in her dorm lounge in vivid detail. "It's funny," she commented, "how I can remember that night like it was just a few months ago. I was wearing a ruffled, hot pink minidress that accentuated the tan I had already, despite the fact that it must have been only March. I was leaning against a pinball machine when he walked up. We just clicked right away. I thought he was really sweet and funny. We sat in the lobby and talked, then went outside and sat on one of the planters between Creswell and the dining hall.

"We were there a long time, yet the hours just flew by. Despite the strange circumstances of our introduction, we were immediately comfortable together, chatting away like old friends.

"We had a couple of beers, and by this time I had a bit of a buzz. I was sitting in his lap, and my skirt kept hitching up. He was very careful to smooth it back down—repeatedly—and preserve my dignity.

"Most nineteen-year-olds would not have been so chivalrous. It really made an impression on me. I thought he really was the 'Southern gentleman' that we coeds were always hearing about—but not seeing much evidence of. So we just started dating, and it was totally natural."

Bart was soon entranced with Shelly. Three months later, at the end of his freshman year, the men in Myers Hall voted him "Most Likely to Fall in Love Through the Mail" at their year's-end party.

Shelly was in love, too. They had both fallen hard very rapidly. It was spring, and they spent all their free time together during the week as well as on weekends, if Bart didn't go home. Very early on, he bought Shelly a bright yellow T-shirt at the Kmart in his hometown, with "Where the Hell is Snellville?" emblazoned on the front. When Shelly went home to New York State, she wore that T-shirt proudly, although no one in her hometown had any idea—or any interest in—where Snellville was.

During the school year, Shelly had worn Bart's letter-man's jacket on campus. It was a status symbol as well as a reminder of him.

Their relationship grew closer. Early in their court-ship, Shelly had once asked Bart why he wanted to be a dentist, joking that "I think it's gross to stick your fingers into somebody's mouth to make a living!"

"I'm not doing it for any altruistic reason," he said. "My interest is in the deep-pockets theory."

"You mean for money?"

He nodded. "Dentists get paid a lot of money."

His avarice didn't bother her at the time. She knew money was very important to Bart, and she was caught up in the first, nonjudgmental stage of being in love. When they went out, they went Dutch. Shelly didn't view Bart as stingy in a mean-spirited way, but she admitted to herself he was definitely parsimonious.

The Georgia Bulldogs–Florida Gators football game was arguably the biggest event of every school year at UGA. The game and attendant celebration in Jacksonville, Florida, was famous for being "The World's Largest Out-door Cocktail Party." Between the rivalry that grew each year and the opportunity to socialize, every student in both colleges wanted to attend.

"Most of us would have sold our blood for plasma and the family silver to be part of that," Shelly recalled. "And we could have gone the year Bart was a sophomore! I would have been thrilled if I'd known that Bart had actu-ally won the student lottery for some prime tickets."

But Bart didn't tell Shelly he'd won until after he sold the tickets for a steep price. "I almost blew a gasket," she said. "And he knew I would. That's why he didn't tell me until it was too late. He said that it was just too expensive

— to go, and he didn't even think about what a once-in-a-lifetime experience it would have been for both of us, something beyond price. I thought his decision was idiocy, and I didn't forget it even though I forgave him."

The money from those tickets was the most important thing to Bart then, just as money would almost always come first with him. Indeed anything he owned belonged only to him and he would let it go only when he was ready.

Later, Shelly reasoned that Bart's parents were probably struggling to put three sons through college at once, even though she knew the sons were getting financial aid from the school.

The elder Corbins lived well—but not lavishly. She had seen that. Bart began taking Shelly with him when he went home to Snellville, and she got to know his family. She really liked Bobby, the twins' younger brother, who enrolled at UGA as a freshman when Bart and Brad were sophomores. She found Bobby to be unfailingly good-natured and always smiling. Shelly watched the family interaction and deduced that Bobby was the family favorite—at least with Gene Corbin—because he was the son who was outstanding in football. She never felt close to Bart's twin, and suspected Brad was a little jealous of the time Bart spent with her. Or it might have been because she and Bart were in love, and Brad didn't have a girl-friend.

"Gene was nice enough to me," Shelly recalled. "I think he was amused that Bart was dating a 'Yankee' from New York. He seemed to feel that I was a phase that Bart would grow out of."

Gene's patronizing attitude didn't bother Shelly. Connie Corbin, however, was another story. Bart's mother struck Shelly as a very moody woman, and Shelly never knew what kind of a reception she would get from Connie. If Gene thought his son's dating a Northerner was just a phase, Connie seemed to view Shelly as "The Enemy," even though she occasionally surprised her by being friendly. "She could be nice," Shelly said. "Once she showed me how to cook chicken planks—which is Southern for tender breast strips that are dipped in batter and deep-fried. Then they serve a bunch of different sauces with them. Bart liked them a lot."

On most visits, however, Connie was "icy," and during one weekend when Shelly came home with Bart, his mother refused to speak to either of them for the two days they were there. Neither had any idea what had made her angry.

Bart was very hesitant to make love to Shelly at the start of their relationship, and she wondered why, because he seemed "like a healthy boy" to her, except for his caution about being intimate. She eventually learned about his Bible Belt sex education classes and his belief that all women were turned off by sex. She convinced him that she wasn't breakable and that women could, and usually did, enjoy intercourse.

And Shelly, this dark-haired, pretty woman who Bart probably sensed was more intelligent than he was, was his first lover. She was sure of it. Shelly was convinced he was faithful to her. "We spent so much time together that he didn't have time not to be."

Shelly found Bart to be even-tempered, with no trace of the labile moods of his mother. He wasn't jealous of the ex-boyfriend in New York who had preceded him. One night, however, Bart was upset when she accidentally called him by the other boy's name. Fortunately, it wasn't during an intimate moment. Shelly believed that, for the most part, Bart resented her former lover because he had treated her badly. "He knew that this other guy was a loser, and he didn't like it that the guy had made me unhappy."

She never recalled seeing a trace of rage or temper in Bart, and as far as she could remember they had only one fight during their years together, and she felt it was her fault.

"We were having some relationship 'hiccup,' " she said. "I don't even know what it was about, but I made some long statement about my feelings. He leaned toward me and said, 'N'yah-n'yah-n'yah.' I was so mad that I reared back and slapped him as hard as I could. So he was being a jerk, but I was the one with the temper. When I think back about his reaction to being slapped, all he evinced was shock. He handled it a lot better than I did, and it never happened again."

In the fall of his sophomore year, Bart was once more a walk-on to the Bulldogs' football practice, but he quit halfway through the season. It was an agonizing decision for him. He didn't want to disappoint his father, but he knew he couldn't keep up with his studies and turn out for practice, too.

Another decision he had made during the summer vacation just past had made him less effective as a defensive lineman, anyway. He knew he had no chance of being on the first-team squad; he was big, but he wasn't "gigantic" like the star athletes at UGA were. And Shelly had encouraged him to lose weight over the summer. He managed to lose thirty pounds, and was striving to look less like a chubby kid from Snellville.

"He became quite confident," Shelly remembered. "He enjoyed dressing in a stylish way when we went out."

Bart bought a white blazer—something that was very popular in an era when *Miami Vice* topped television ratings. Shelly bought him some Calvin Klein tank tops, and he looked good. He was no longer the slightly plump boy in the camo pants she had been attracted to a year earlier.

She was amused to see how often Bart looked at himself in store windows, flipping and patting his hair as he admired his own image.

And still, even though Shelly was only six months older than Bart, she was years older in sophistication. She loved him and they began to talk—if only tentatively—about marriage. Twice she took Bart to visit her family in western New York, and in 1984 they stood against the guardrails and watched the thundering power of Niagara Falls, and then rode on one of the *Maid of the Mist* boats that seemed actually to pass under the falls. They wore the slickers that all tourists do, and posed smiling for a photo.

Shelly's parents liked Bart a lot and encouraged their romance. He seemed to love her, and he was a good-looking young man who was headed for a much-respected career.

Shelly was close to graduation when she began to think seriously about what it might be like to be married to Bart. They were headed that way, and she had actually picked out her stainless-steel pattern and bought one place setting. It was the very ornate "Michelangelo" from Oneida.

But then she began to question the wisdom of marrying Bart—not because of anything he had done, but because she realized their goals were so different. She never thought he would be anything less than kind to her as a husband. Nor did she think he would ever be unfaithful. But she felt too young to be married. She still had so many things she wanted to experience in her life.

Shelly had wanted to be a reporter since she was eight years old. If Bart was accepted into dental school, they would be living in Augusta, Georgia—a city some wiseguy students at UGA called "Disgusta." And, try as she might, Shelly could not picture herself as the young wife of a dental student. "I did not get a degree to be someone else's accessory," she said.

Although Shelly had unconsciously put her ambitions to become a "Crusader for Truth" in the background during the years she spent with Bart, they hadn't gone away. Now they began to resurface. She knew that Bart had no lofty humanitarian goals to achieve as a dentist. His goal was still to have "deep pockets" full of money. It was somehow an odd stance for a man who seemed so sensitive and easily hurt, but she suspected it was another thing that Bart had learned from his father.

Shelly accepted that she was sometimes heedless of Bart's feelings. She knew she didn't love him enough to sacrifice all the goals in her own life for him.

As a journalist, she wanted to place both sides of stories in front of readers so they could make informed decisions that would, hopefully, protect the democratic society she believed in. It was a lofty ambition, and it mattered terribly to her.

Again, marriage to Bart Corbin, whose goal was to make as much money as possible, would not permit that, nor could she imagine spending her life as a dentist's devoted wife in some small Georgia town.

While Shelly wanted to help the disadvantaged, she also hoped to marry a man who was less frugal. Her parents had kept her on a fairly tight allowance in college, but she realized that she had been somewhat spoiled and not very careful with money. If something fun and interesting should come up, she wanted to be able to experience it, and Bart had shown her again and again how stingy he was. She sensed that would be a lifelong habit, no matter how much success he might one day have as dentist.

If she married him, her life would be spent "in distant suburbia," and she would be bored. That wouldn't be fair to either one of them. She realized she wouldn't be happy if she married Bart Corbin.

Shelly began to move emotionally away from Bart, all the while avoiding a major confrontation. Her strategy was to gradually grow distant and hope he took the hint. Sometimes she deliberately picked fights with him about something stupid, deliberately being passive-aggressive, hoping he'd get sick of her. She wasn't in the least afraid of him, but she didn't want to hurt him. If he had only been "a jerk," it would have been easier, but she still found Bart a good person overall, and she was afraid he would be devastated.

Her plan didn't work. Bart didn't react to Shelly's backing away from him. It was if he didn't notice. She felt that she was being a moral coward; she no longer loved him. Oddly—or perhaps not—she has no memory of the moment she told him that she wanted to break up.

She only remembered that he cried, and that he wasn't angry with her.

Bart had seemingly let her go without a struggle. They often ran into each other on campus or elsewhere in Athens, and she was happy to see him. She never felt threatened, or that he was following her or stalking her. She didn't even wonder about how they often seemed to be in the same place at the same time.

Bart Corbin had lost his first girlfriend, the first and perhaps only woman with whom he had ever been both physically and emotionally intimate. And he had swallowed any anger or overt signs of grief. Shelly began to believe that they had both dodged a bullet; it had been a great couple of years and they had successfully broken up without any lasting negative feelings.

*   *   *

SEVERAL MONTHS AFTER they ended their romance, Bart learned that he had been accepted at dental school. Shelly was sunbathing by the pool of the apartment complex where she lived—and where one of Bart's friends also resided—when she heard footsteps crunching on the gravel path. It was Bart Corbin.

"He would have known where to find me," she said. "He was all excited that his hard work had paid off. And I am quite certain that, other than his twin, Brad, I was the first person he told—even before his parents."

Shelly sensed that Bart wanted to impress her, and that seemed perfectly reasonable, but she was surprised that he had told her about his success almost before he had told anyone else. She had moved on from their relationship, and she assumed that he had as well. She was glad to see him, as a friend, and they set up a date; he would come to her apartment that evening—"just to hang out."

They spent several pleasant hours together, and Bart never brought up the subject of their reuniting as a couple. But she knew he still had feelings for her. If she had suggested that they get back together, she was sure he would have wanted to.

"But I put the kibosh on that by rattling on about some guy I liked at the time," she recalled. Later, she was ashamed of her own behavior, sorry that she had been mean to him. Once again, fearful of being tied down, she had hurt Bart and seen tears in his eyes.

He turned and left abruptly and she never saw him again. She had no idea what awesome forces may have been set in motion.

Shelly had hoped to work for a small-town newspaper for perhaps a year, and then move on to a big-city paper. When she graduated in 1987, she did work for a paper in Griffin, Georgia, for six months.

After that, Shelly worked as a journalist all over America, and then in another country. Her decision not to marry Bart allowed her to be true to what she believed in. She worked long hours and received positive feedback from both the public and her colleagues, but she was haunted by the fact that she wasn't contributing to less fortunate people as she had once planned to do. She joined the Peace Corps and was sent to Thailand, where she found "meaning in my life again."

She seldom thought of Bart Corbin. If she did, it was to remember the sensitive man she once cared for, and to feel guilty that she had hurt him enough to make him cry. She was sorry about that. Even so, she knew she had made the right choice.

Bart graduated from the University of Georgia in 1987. When he entered the Medical College of Georgia in Augusta, he was beginning a new phase in his life. Shelly assumed that Bart was on the path to find what mattered to him. If he was angry with her, she didn't know it. At least not for a very long time.

Chapter Nine

1987

WHILE SHELLY TRAVELED far away from Georgia on her adventurous life, Bart began dental school in Augusta. When Bart entered the Medical College of Georgia, he was a long way from both Snellville and Athens—not in miles but in the way his personality had changed. He was a bitter young man who had grown an invisible, impenetrable shell. His sense of humor was still on target, but now there was a meanness about it.

Those who started the first year of dentistry school at MCG would stay together until they graduated. Not surprisingly, the students in Bart's class grew to know each other very well as they studied in a much more intense program than they had followed in undergraduate school. Just as his fellow students at UGA liked Bart, he was fairly popular at MCG.

But that was mostly with guys; women on his new campus were slower to warm up to him.

Bart struck some of women as a rather odd duck. One woman—Lee Reardon*—recalled knowing Bart during the years he spent at dental school, an acquaintance that came about because her brother, Corey*, had initially befriended him.

"He seemed to be a lot of fun," she said. "Bart was very outgoing and always ready for the next party. He was a little rough around the edges, his hair was a little too long, he wore an earring, and his clothes weren't preppy—which was the style at the time."

Bart didn't look like the students who belonged to a fraternity; he resembled a rock star or perhaps a gypsy. Initially, women on campus at MCG weren't drawn to him. Bart looked very different from the time when he first met Shelly. He was still tall, of course, but he was very thin now. He parted his hair in the middle and wore it in a kind of shag that touched his collar. But without Shelly to help him pick out clothes, he certainly wasn't very stylish. Sometimes he affected all black clothing.

He showed some interest in Lee Reardon, but he wasn't her type at all. She considered herself fortunate when he stopped asking her out. Although Bart struck her as "happy-go-lucky," her brother—who was also a dental student—warned her not to get involved. Corey Reardon had perceived two sides to Bart's personality, one with "an edge."

And there was a certain unpredictability in Bart, a sudden flare of anger at times. No one who knew Bart as an undergraduate back in Athens had ever mentioned his temper. Now he was known for having a very short fuse.

Unexpected things could set him off. He would sometimes erupt instantly into a raging tantrum.

Bart had worked to his capacity in undergraduate school and succeeded by studying harder than most of his peers, but the demands of dental school challenged him more, and he was often impatient and testy. One dental student described him as having "an explosive temper," and recalled a time when Bart was so frustrated that he threw one of his own projects against a wall, shattering it. But then they were all under a lot of stress, and most people didn't find Bart's outbursts that disturbing.

Some of his closest friends delighted in teasing him by doing impressions of "the angry Bart."

He didn't seem to mind.

In his first year at dental school in 1987, Bart dated a girl named Eden* briefly, but it wasn't a serious relationship. One of Eden's friends recalled that he was generally considered odd. For one thing, he didn't believe in wearing deodorant, saying that to do so was unhealthy. Since Augusta was often hot and humid, people noticed his body odor.

"The one thing I remember about Bart," she said, "was that he considered himself superior to others. He seemed devoid of empathy or any capability of significant emotional attachment."

This woman, who later became a dental hygienist, commented on Bart's fixation with making a lot of money. She met him a few years later—after he had become a dentist—but before he married Jenn Barber. They happened to run into each other at a restaurant, and had dinner together, talking about dentistry as they ate. She spent just one day working for him, and found that he was still a cold and distant person, particularly with his patients. He was far more concerned with the financial aspect of his practice than he was with the clients in his chair.

"He was very egotistical," she said. "To this day, I'm incredulous that he thought I was interested in him romantically. I was definitely not."

Oblivious, Bart told her not to expect to date him. "He said he was looking for a different 'caliber' of woman. In particular, he hoped to marry another dentist."

Bart Corbin's imperious attitude was a turnoff for a number of women he met in dental school. Where he had been somewhat naïve and socially awkward at UGA, he had learned to hide his emotions inside. Gradually, he began to present a seamless façade. Few, if any, of his new friends had known Shelly Mansfield, and he didn't mention her, nor their breakup.

He was still considered handsome and witty, and he made satisfactory grades in dental school in both classes and labs.

And before too long, Bart would meet a woman who would finally put his memories of Shelly Mansfield in the background. Her name was Dorothy "Dolly" Hearn. Dolly Hearn was one of the secret things that Bart Corbin never discussed with his wife, Jenn.

CHAPTER TEN

DECEMBER 4–10, 2004

CHRISTMAS 2004 was three weeks away, Jenn Corbin had been dead for less than a week, and the Corbin case was constantly at the top of the news in Atlanta. While there were whispered questions about what might have led her to commit suicide, there were also a lot of suspicions about her widower, particularly behind the closed doors of the Gwinnett County Police Department and the Gwinnett County District Attorney's Office. Bart Corbin wasn't acting like a grief-stricken man who had just lost his wife; he was avoiding detectives and their penetrating questions. -

Bizarrely, Corbin refused to give permission to Jenn's family—who were still caring for Dalton and Dillon—to enter the house on Bogan Gates Drive to get clothes for the boys and pick up the Christmas presents Jenn had bought and wrapped for them. Where most families would have shared their grief, that was not the case here. Lines were drawn between the Corbins and the Barbers.

Somehow, Max and Narda Barber pulled themselves together for Dalton and Dillon's sake, and Heather and Doug Tierney and Rajel Caldwell did their best to care for the boys, who, for all intents and purposes, were orphans. Their mother lay in a funeral parlor and their father hadn't come to see them, nor had he consented to meet with Marcus Head and the other investigators into Jennifer's death. It was very odd and disturbing. All of Jenn's family, even the boys, had given statements to the detectives. Bart absolutely refused to be questioned.

Narda and Max went to the funeral home to arrange for Jenn's service. But when Narda started to pick out a coffin, the funeral director told her that a coffin might not be needed. "Dr. Corbin has arranged to have Mrs. Corbin cremated," he said.

"No!" Narda gasped. "We don't want that. It's difficult enough to explain to her sons that she's gone forever. How on earth could we tell them that their mother is going to be burned up?"

"I'm sorry," the mortician told her, "but that isn't for you to decide. Legally, of course, Dr. Corbin is the next of kin, and he has already made arrangements. In fact, Mrs. Corbin is about to be cremated—in less than an hour."

"I haven't seen her," Narda said faintly. "I have to see her."

"But you do understand that the arrangements are up to Dr. Corbin?"

Narda Barber didn't understand anything. Bart hadn't come to them to share their common loss, he hadn't come to see his sons—how could he be the one to plan what was to be done with Jenn's body?

"I want to see her," Narda insisted, and finally, almost grudgingly, an attendant led her to a room where they wheeled out a gurney with her daughter's body.

"She was all wrapped in a plastic bag or something," Narda recalled. "I kissed her little face and her hands and her toes. It was my only chance to say goodbye to my sweet Jennifer. There was nothing else I could do."

The cremation Bart Corbin had ordered was carried out an hour later.

The Barbers were allowed to plan funeral services at the Sugar Hill Methodist Church, which would be followed by a private service at home, where, they hoped, Dalton and Dillon could participate and say goodbye to their mother. But they were told they could only "borrow" Jenn's remains for those ceremonies; Jenn's ashes belonged to Bart Corbin.

Jenn's funeral was scheduled for December 10, 2004.

*   *   *

NOT EVEN FORTY-EIGHT HOURS had passed when Narda answered the phone after midnight early on December 6. The caller was a woman named Lily Ann Holmes.* She explained that she had once worked with Jenn Corbin at the Sugar Hill Methodist Church, where Jenn taught preschoolers, although Lily Ann was now retired.

"I want you to sit down, Narda," Lily Ann said. "I have something to tell you that might be upsetting."

"I am sitting down," Narda said, wondering how anything could be more upsetting to her than losing Jenn.

Lily Ann Holmes explained that she had a relative—a

dentist—who had attended the dental school in Augusta at the same time Bart did. And her relative had known Bart. "Everyone kind of knew each other," she added.

"Did you know about his girlfriend in Augusta," she asked Narda now. "And about what happened to her?"

"What girlfriend?" Narda asked, feeling a chill in her bones. "We don't know much about Bart before Jenn met him."

Lily Ann said she was unsure of the name of the woman Bart had dated, but she thought it might have been "Dorothy" or "Dolly."

"She's dead," she continued. "She's been dead for fourteen years, Narda. She was shot in the head. That's all I know about it, but I thought you should know."

It was difficult for Narda and Max to grasp. How could it be that Bart had once had a girlfriend who died of a bullet in her head? Why hadn't he ever told them—or Jenn—about that?

When Heather heard about this mysterious woman who had once been a part of Bart's life, she was just as amazed as her parents had been. If Jenn had known that Bart had a girlfriend who died violently, Heather was sure her sister would have told her. She and Jenn didn't keep secrets from one another; they had shared almost everything since they were little girls.

Suddenly, Heather remembered the time when Jenn asked her if she ever wondered what Doug had done before they met. Now, Heather wondered if Jenn had had good reasons to be concerned about Bart's past.

At Narda's suggestion, Lily Ann Holmes called Marcus Head the next morning and told him about Bart's former girlfriend who had died in June 1990. The manner of death was said to be suicide. She was sure now of both the first and last names of the woman: it was Dolly Hearn.

For Head, too, this was electrifying news. Very few men lose even one woman in their lives to suicide by gunshot; the number who have lost two had to be infinitesimal. There were two ways to look at this grim coincidence—if it was a coincidence. If Bart had nothing to do with either shooting, losing two women he loved in such a horrible way might explain his refusal to cope with reality. Maybe he could not accept these double tragedies.

And then again, maybe his behavior had caused one or both of the women's deaths, and that would explain why he was stonewalling the police. He was in an extremely tenuous position.

Head made a phone call to the Richmond County Sheriff's Office in Augusta and spoke to a records clerk there. He asked her to check for any archived cases involving someone named Dolly Hearn. She reported back that she couldn't find any cases in the sheriff's files with the name "Hearn."

Head kept pushing. He called the Richmond County Vital Records Office. He got more information there. There was a death certificate on file for a Dorothy Carlisle Hearn who died on June 6, 1990.

The cause of death was listed as "Gunshot wound to the head with destruction of the brainstem, and secondary exsanguination [massive blood loss], apparently self-inflicted." This suggested suicide, but Dr. Sharon G. Daspit, the medical examiner who signed the autopsy report, had not fully committed to that. She listed the manner of Dolly Hearn's death as "Undetermined."

Marcus Head had the death certificate faxed to him, and the Gwinnett County detective found the name of the funeral home that had handled the arrangements for Dorothy Hearn's services. When he called the office in Washington, Georgia, he was given the phone number of Dr. Carlton Hearn, a dentist in Washington, who was listed as Dorothy Hearn's father.

Without immediate access to police files from 1990, Marcus Head had no way to learn further details of Dorothy Hearn's death. But her father would know. And, in the meantime, Head would determine which investigators in Augusta might have worked the Hearn case.

Head made the phone call that Carlton Hearn Sr. and his wife, Barbara, had been waiting for for fourteen and a half years. Dr. Hearn agreed to talk with Marcus Head as soon as possible. The detective headed east toward Augusta, a two-hour drive.

"I wanted to see," Head said, "if there were any similarities or likenesses in the two [crime] scenes and the victimology."

From his interview with the Hearns in the quaint and charming town of Washington, Head discovered so many common factors in the deaths of two young women that his investigation took on an almost fictional feel. The crime scenes, possible motivation, and the MOs were almost identical, and seemed more suited to a novel than to something that might have occurred in real life.

That didn't mean that a solution to either death would soon be forthcoming. Rather, it meant that the investigation would become more complex, and considerably more challenging to solve. If this were, for instance, a knitting project, it would be the difference between a simple square made of basic stitches and an argyle sweater with five different shades of yarn. It would take far more than a single detective to sort it all out.

There had to be other law enforcement departments involved, and hopefully more witnesses and evidence. Fourteen years! That was a very long time. People retire, die, move away, and tend to forget even the most shocking events.

Head hoped devoutly that there would be enough witnesses and possible evidence left from Dolly Hearn's death investigation to re-create everything that happened way back in 1990. Her parents and brothers had tried for all the years in between to discover the truth about what had happened to her. Like the Barbers, the Hearn family suspected Dr. Bart Corbin. For a while, they had managed to keep close track of him—but he had moved often, and by 2004, they heard of him only occasionally. But they had forgotten nothing. And they were anxious to see the probe into Dolly's death reopened.

CHAPTER ELEVEN

DECEMBER 10, 2004

DOLLY HEARN HAD DIED on June 6, 1990, and Marcus Head and the other investigators from the Gwinnett County Police Department and District Attorney Danny Porter's office knew very little about the circumstances of her death at the time Jenn Corbin's funeral took place on December 10, 2004, at the Sugar Hill Methodist Church.

This was the church where she had taught in the daycare facility. It was a disturbing day in so many ways. Just hours before Jenn's services began, Danny Porter filed an affidavit where he named her estranged husband as a suspect in her murder. Moreover, the current Richmond County district attorney, Danny Craig, had announced in Augusta that he and detectives in that jurisdiction were reopening the long-becalmed investigation into the death of Dolly Hearn.

The two prosecutors—the "two Dannies"—would work together, along with their investigators and county detectives, to unearth long-buried evidence—both circumstantial and physical. It would be necessary to form grand juries in each jurisdiction to see if there was enough cause to issue murder indictments. Very few people in Gwinnett County had any idea who Dolly Hearn was and what her connection to Bart Corbin might be.

The Hearns and the Barbers knew, and perhaps Bart Corbin's family knew. It was difficult to tell because they were no more enthusiastic about talking to the investigators or reporters than he was.

Both Dolly Hearn and Jenn Barber had apparently been in the process of moving out of Bart Corbin's life when they died. Investigators did not yet know the details of these estrangements. If anyone, other than Bart's family, remembered Shelly Mansfield—the first woman who had broken up with Bart—they didn't tell the detectives about it. And neither did Connie or Gene Corbin, nor did Bart's twin or his younger brother, Bobby.

Gossip simmered that Bart had also been involved with at least two other women while he was married to Jenn. All three major television networks' docudrama shows had crews circling Gwinnett County, eager for interviews. The *Atlanta Journal-Constitution* compared the Hearn-Corbin cases to the much publicized Laci and Scott Peterson case in Modesto, California. It was an expected evaluation: on November 12, three weeks before Jenn's death, Scott Peterson had been convicted of murdering his pregnant wife at Christmas 2002, and disposing of her body in San Francisco Bay. Even as Jenn died, the penalty phase of Peterson's trial was taking place in a Stanislaus County, California, courtroom. Like Corbin, Peterson had been involved in extramarital dalliances, and was reluctant to talk with investigators.

*   *   *

AS 3:30 APPROACHED ON THAT CHILL FRIDAY, no one expected to see Bart at Jenn's funeral. Surely he must be aware that he was emerging as a suspect in two alleged murders. Surely, he wouldn't subject himself to the stares and whispers of those attending Jenn's services. He had already complained indignantly about reporters who were staking out the parking lot of his dental office.

But there he was in the church, not far from the metallic casket with a huge spray of flowers on top of it. Narda Barber wondered why there was a coffin at all; Jenn wasn't in it. She had already been cremated. She assumed that Bart and his family must have ordered it from the funeral director.

Bart, Brad, and Bobby had gone to the Mall of Georgia and hurriedly ordered their "funeral suits," and now, dressed in his perfectly tailored dark suit, Bart strode past the cameras from Atlanta television stations and newspapers, and took his seat beside his mother in the front pew of the Sugar Hill church. Jenn's family sat across the aisle from the Corbin family. They were startled to see Bart there, and his presence made them jittery. He seemed not to grieve or weep as he sat quietly through the hour-and-a-half-long ceremony. The expression on his face was unreadable.

Heather Tierney gave her eulogy for her lost sister, her voice trembling as she spoke. She told those gathered there about the Jenn she knew, the Jenn who wakened with a smile every morning. With tears streaking her cheeks,

Heather spoke of Jenn's all-encompassing love for her little boys, and also for the fourteen children she had taught in this very church—up until only seven days before.

"I feel robbed that children are not going to be blessed by her every day, especially Dalton and Dillon. And I pray to God that they will remember how much she loved them."

Heather's voice almost broke as she praised Jenn and thanked the many friends and people who had done their best to comfort her family, and for their love. But she could not suppress her rage that Jenn's life had been taken so viciously.

"I am angry," Heather said. "I am so angry. But the one thing I know is that the heart is a million times stronger than anger. And today is about my beautiful sister."

Heather looked down upon the man she had accepted and loved as a brother for almost nine years. Bart did not raise his eyes to meet hers.

As they always are after a homicide, detectives were placed discreetly in the sanctuary during the funeral. It is not unusual for killers to attend the funerals and even the graveside services of their victims, and, now, the Gwinnett County investigators scanned the faces of those in the church. While they watched Bart, they also looked for some stranger, or even an acquaintance of Jenn's who might be acting in a way that indicated guilt. At this point, it was impossible to know how many suspects there might be.

If Jack Burnette, the supervisor of Danny Porter's investigators, Chief Assistant DA Tom Davis, and Investigator Manny Perez had hoped to talk to Bart, they were out of luck. As soon as the funeral was over, he moved rapidly toward a rear entrance, and, shielded by his family, slipped away.

Jenn's sons had drawn portraits of their mother and they were tacked up now, next to the guest book as the mourners left the church. There was a seven-year-old's depiction of a yellow-haired angel with a halo, her arms holding two small stick figures who were clearly Dalton and Dillon. It was almost more than those signing the guest book could bear. Many were tearful as they left the sanctuary, murmuring quietly.

And then, suddenly, their eyes were drawn upward. There was a magnificent rainbow tracing its colors brilliantly across the sky. A photographer from the *Atlanta Journal-Constitution* caught the image and it was featured on the front page of the paper the next day.

For the first time since Jenn's murder, Heather felt her heart lift. "I had been praying for some kind of a sign that Jenn was okay, and then to walk out of her funeral to see that rainbow spanning the sky from end to end. It was the most vibrant rainbow I have ever seen. I wanted to drop to my knees and say 'Thank you, God.' I really felt that rainbow was painted just for Jenn."

Still, for every moment like that, there would be thousands that reminded Jenn Barber Corbin's family that she was gone forever. At the church, both friends and strangers did their best to bond with them, many of them awkwardly slipping into the familiar, empty words everyone murmurs at funerals. "I know how you must be feeling," or "Jennifer's gone on to a better place in Heaven. We must try to understand God's will."

That was impossible for Jenn's family to do as they carried her ashes to their car. They would have their sad little private memorial ceremony at home, something Dalton and Dillon could participate in—even though they were too young to truly understand.

After the public services, the Barbers gathered at Heather's house. They placed roses, daisies, and Jenn's favorite flower—tulips—on a coffee table. There were pictures of Jenn with Dalton and Dillon there, and, in the center, the urn with Jenn's ashes. A white candle flickered atop it. The boys didn't understand that this was all that was left of their mother's earthly body, and that was as it should be. Narda knew they couldn't comprehend that, and she didn't want them to. They all joined hands and said a prayer.

Two days later, the funeral home representative called to say that Bart Corbin wanted Jenn's ashes back— immediately. That seemed to be a monstrous joke to Max and Narda Barber. This was all they had left of Jenn; shouldn't the cremains of their lost daughter belong to them?

Legally, Jenn's ashes did not. When Jenn died six days before, she was still married to Bart Corbin. Unless she had specifically spelled out her wishes in writing, Bart was heir to everything she left behind. But she had left no instructions; there had been no suicide note, nothing to indicate that Jenn knew she was about to die.

Actually, Jenn had believed she was about to start a new life. Although Bart hadn't known how carefully she was planning her future away from him, she had gone about it methodically. As the investigation progressed, it would become more and more evident that Jenn had wanted desperately to be free of him.

Heather recalled something else Jenn had asked her once. Jenn had had a forlorn look on her face when she said, "What if you find your one true love and you're already bound to someone else?"

At the time, it had seemed a rhetorical question.

*   *   *

AS PEOPLE WERE FILING OUT after the funeral service, a middle-aged couple had moved out of the crowd of mourners, and approached Heather. For a moment, she didn't know who they were, and then it hit her with a jolt. They were Dolly Hearn's parents—Dr. Carlton and Barbara Hearn—who had driven for hours from their home in Washington, Georgia. Perhaps more than anyone in the world, they understood exactly what the Barbers and their surviving daughters felt. They had come to express their condolences to Max and Narda. Heather led them into a quiet corner where they could talk without being overheard.

The Hearns had spoken empathetically, yet cautiously; Marcus Head had asked them not to compare notes with the Barbers. "He told us not to have a 'pow-wow' with the Barbers," Barbara Hearn recalled, "and we honored that."

That might have contaminated future witness testimony and statements. Carlton and Barbara Hearn had never believed that Dolly was a suicide, nor had they ever had a satisfactory conclusion to their search for answers, even though they had hired their own private investigators to look for evidence leading to the person who they believed had killed their daughter.

In all these nearly fifteen years, they had never been able to get law enforcement to focus on Bart Corbin enough so that arrest warrants and charges resulted; he had stalked Dolly when she tried to leave him.

Jenn Corbin's death and her funeral services had ripped away layers of healing for the Hearns, and thrust them back into the horrific moment when they first learned of Dolly's death.

PART THREE

Dorothy Carlisle Hearn

"DOLLY"

CHAPTER TWELVE

1956–1990

BARBARA HOGE WAS IN HIGH SCHOOL in Alexandria, Virginia, in 1956 when she agreed to go on a blind date with a first-year dental student at Georgetown University. His name was Carlton Hearn. She was a very pretty blond and he was a slender, somewhat serious young man. They liked each other immediately but didn't date exclusively; he had to finish dental school, and Barbara hadn't yet started college.

When Barbara graduated from high school, she enrolled in Randolph Macon Women's College in Ashland, Virginia, and explained to Carlton that she intended to finish. But he persuaded her to get married by promising her she could still graduate from college. They were married in Virginia in 1959, and then moved to Washington, D.C., where Barbara worked toward her degree at Georgetown

University. But Carlton had two years of public service ahead of him, and was assigned to Springfield, Missouri. Barbara Hearn finally finished college at Drury College in Springfield. And then they were transferred to Atlanta, Georgia.

Their first child, Dorothy Carlisle Hearn, was born at Emory University Hospital in Atlanta on July 6, 1962, a beautiful, dark-haired baby, the oldest cousin of her generation, and the only girl in that first phalanx of cousins. Her birth coincided with her parents' move to a big white Colonial house in Washington, Georgia, population 5,000.

Having a first baby brings about great changes in any young family, but Dolly's arrival during the week they were moving from an apartment into a new house demanded very complicated logistics. Barbara and Dolly remained in the hospital while Carlton Hearn and Barbara's mother managed somehow to move furniture, clothes, and everything else they owned into the home where they would put down deep roots.

"After that move, my mother said 'Never again!' Barbara recalled. "She said, 'I'll come if you have a baby, and I'll come if you move, but I won't come again if you do both at once!' "

There would be no more moves, but the Hearns did have two more babies. Carlton Jr. was born in 1965 and Gil in 1972. By the time Gil was born, Dolly was ten and considered herself a "second mother" to him.

*   *   *

THE HEARNS' HOUSE IN WASHINGTON, GEORGIA, was built in 1854, survived the Civil War, and remained a proud example of Southern architecture. There was a sense of history and permanency in the old house and the twenty acres that surrounded it. The huge oak tree in the front yard was decades old, its lower branches curving so close to the ground that children could easily climb up and perch there. There were countless towering pecan trees, the ground beneath them thick with so many nuts in the fall that the Hearns gave them away and, at times, even sold them. The magnolia tree that Barbara won as a door prize at her garden club when it was barely more than a twig, grew to be more than twenty feet tall. Dogwoods abounded. There was a Confederate rose bush alongside the driveway leading to the back of the property.

"Every year, I tended to think it wasn't going to bloom," Barbara recalled, "and then, in October, it was suddenly full of blossoms."

And so it bloomed, long promised and finally delivering just when everyone had given up. As other trees and bushes take on the hues of autumn, the Confederate rose is light pink, with layers of delicate, translucent silky petals.

Dolly and her little brothers once played under one of the tall pecan trees, just beyond a small wooden shack that surely dated back before the Civil War.

The Hearns' home was full of antiques, many of them handed down through generations of Hearns and Hoges. In the entry hall, there was a framed family tree that traced Barbara's roots back and back and back. And she treasured it. The house Dolly and her brothers grew up in was charming, but not in the least ostentatious. Built in the days before central heating, it had many fireplaces, vented through four white chimneys that rose from the roof.

The Hearns had both pets and farm animals, ducks and peacocks. Between the peacocks and the jaybirds, a cacophony of birdcalls sometimes demolished the silence of a sultry summer afternoon. Carlton and Barbara started collecting objects with a peacock motif many years ago.

"I was so glad," Barbara Hearn said, "when my parents moved to Washington and lived close to us. Their names were Gilmer and Dorothy Hoge, but Dolly nicknamed them 'Mama Buns' and 'GoGo Pop.' "

Carlton established his own dental practice in Washington, the youngest dentist in town then, and he could walk or drive home for lunch along the narrow streets that radiated from the quaint town square. Barbara's father and her husband went fishing together, and the old man taught his son-in-law how to garden—especially tomatoes.

Theirs was as close to an idyllic life as any family could have, and Barbara and Carlton appreciated it. When she was in college, one of her friends had told Barbara that Washington, Georgia, was a safe place to live. When they moved there, the Hearns felt the same way.

*   *   *

DOLLY, CARLTON JR., AND GIL slept upstairs in the big white house. They got along with one another, although, like most siblings, they sometimes had fights. They went to grade school and then to Wilkes Academy for high school. Dolly might have been the only girl among all the boy cousins, but she gave no ground.

During her elementary school years, Dolly demonstrated that she was an exceptional swimmer, and she was remarkably agile, twirling her baton as a small majorette. She won the Golden Eagle Award for school spirit in her high school years. Despite her slender, almost delicate appearance, she was a high jumper and a shot-putter on the

Wilkes track team. Anyone who has ever "put" the shot knows that those iron spheres are extremely heavy. Most girls can't even lift them, much less throw them for any distance.

Dolly was also a tap dancer. She appeared in little theater productions like *South Pacific,* played the piano, and sang alto in choirs. And somewhere along the way, the little girl in braces became heartbreakingly beautiful. If she hadn't been so nice to everyone and so unassuming, Dolly would have been the kind of teenager who made other girls jealous. But they weren't, even when she was chosen as captain of the cheerleading squad at Wilkes Academy.

Dolly was too much fun to inspire envy, and, like her father, she loved to laugh. She pulled pranks on friends, whether it was to stake out a flock of pink plastic flamingos on somebody's lawn, or pack friends' rooms and cars full of balloons on their birthdays. Holidays were made for her; one Halloween she dressed up as a tree that had been "TP'ed"—draping herself with toilet paper.

Christmas was Dolly's favorite holiday, though, and she planned for weeks ahead to find gifts for her family and friends.

Besides holidays, Dolly was enthusiastic about cats, all kinds of cats. Wherever she lived, there were pictures of cats, cat pillows, ceramic cats, and real live cats.

Her signature flower was a red rose. Dolly made many of the banners that the Wilkes Academy football players tore through as they raced onto the field just before a game, and her most memorable banner was made of red roses. She also composed several cheers for her squad. Three decades later, her "Hello!" cheer remained a favorite of cheerleaders young enough to be her daughters.

With exquisite features, beautiful eyes, and thick

black hair that cascaded over her shoulders, Dolly Hearn looked like no one so much as Snow White—surrounded by red roses. Although she dated occasionally, and a lot of boys in Washington wanted to ask her out, she was more likely to be a pal and a friend to them. She wasn't anxious to fall in love; she figured she had all the time in the world for that. She wanted a marriage like her parents had, and she admired them tremendously.

From the time Dolly was a little girl, Barbara Hearn taught her to sew, and to embroider and cross-stitch, although she couldn't know how precious the pillows and tapestries Dolly made would become. Dolly had a special bond with her dad, and one Father's Day she gave him a gift she had spent painstaking hours on. After finding the perfect poem for a man who loved to fish, she embroidered the lines:

> I pray that I may
> Live to fish
> Until my dying day
> And when it comes
> To my last cast,
> I then most humbly pray,
> When in the Lord's
> Great hanging net
> And peacefully asleep
> That in His mercy
> I be judged—
> BIG ENOUGH TO KEEP!

Chapter Thirteen

1980–1987

WHEN SHE GRADUATED from Wilkes Academy, Dolly had no particular career in mind, other than a desire to work in some kind of helping field. In the fall of 1980, she enrolled first in North Georgia College, which is located in Dahlonega about two hours' drive from home. She considered careers as a pharmacist, an optometrist, or a physical therapist, and earned average to excellent grades in her undergraduate years, although she attended three colleges: North Georgia, Augusta College, and Mercer in Macon, Georgia. Her grade point average was just under 3.0 (B average) when Dolly realized that the best career for her had been right in front of her all along. She had helped her father as an assistant during her summer and Christmas vacations, and, working beside him, realized what an artist he was. Indeed, one of Carlton's fellow

dentists—who was a professor at a dental school—
worked on one of Hearn's former patients and was
amazed at how precise Carlton's work was.

"He wrote to Carlton," Barbara Hearn recalled, "and
said the dental work was so good that he was using it to
teach his dental students."

Although he had never pushed her in that direction,
Dr. Hearn was proud in the winter of 1986, when Dolly
applied to the dental school at the Medical College of
Georgia in Augusta.

In the distinctive handwriting that all her friends recognized, full of graceful loops, Dolly wrote:

"[I] have decided that a career within the field of med-
icine would bring the most satisfaction, especially realizing
that I could use my knowledge and skills to ease the suffering of individuals afflicted with various illnesses and dis-
comforts."

On May 28, 1987, Dolly was disappointed to receive
a letter from MCG saying that the dental classes were all
filled up. Her application for admission could be moved to
a list of alternates, and if any students dropped out, there
was a chance she could still start dental school in the fall,
or she could wait and apply the next year. Fingers crossed,
Dolly chose the alternate list.

She was delighted when, a few weeks later, she was
notified that a place in the class of 1991 had opened up.
And so Dolly Hearn entered dental school in Augusta. She
would be in the class a year behind Bart Corbin's.

Dolly found an apartment at 3077 Parrish Road in
Augusta. It was one of several townhouse-type rentals
common to the area. The Wintergreen section was a newer
building built of dun-colored bricks, set in deep shade for
most of the daylight hours because of the tall pine trees

that surrounded it. She moved in, posted a "Roommate Wanted" notice on the bulletin board at MCG, and registered with the student housing office.

Although they were strangers when they met through the roommate finders' service, Dolly and Angela Garnto soon became close friends. Angela was three years younger than Dolly, and studying to be a doctor's assistant. She moved in with Dolly in October 1988. They would live together in their pleasant apartment on Parrish Road for almost two years.

Angela always spoke of Dolly's bright smile and friendliness, remembering how she could walk into a room and light it up, and how friendly Dolly was to everyone.

They both loved the apartment with its two bedrooms and a bath upstairs, a kitchen, living room, and half-bath on the ground floor. There was a little fenced-in patio area off the kitchen that could be reached through sliding glass doors.

Dolly soon put her stamp on the apartment, although nothing she chose to furnish it with was very expensive. She had a plaid couch and a small television set in the living room, and twin bookcases made of thin veneer that she had assembled herself—mostly filled with textbooks. Her décor was sentimental: candles, some artificial roses, heart-shaped picture frames, sheaves of straw bound with red bows, family photos, cat images, and a scratching post for the cat she had adopted from the Humane Society: Tabitha.

It wasn't long before Dolly Hearn was familiar to many of the students at MCG. She said "Hi!" to everyone, and her ebullience cheered people up. And, of course, Dolly was beautiful. Although she scarcely needed makeup to enhance her natural glamour, she was rarely without it. She applied it dramatically, framing her eyes with carefully smudged black liner, and brushing her thick lashes with several coats of mascara. Her high cheekbones were always dusted with blush, and her full lips painted scarlet. On anyone but Dolly, it probably would have been too much. But somehow, on her, it worked.

Dr. Fred Rueggeberg, a professor at MCG, found her dynamic and vivacious, and said she brought excitement and life to a boring dental school.

Dolly's landlord, Dennis Stanfield, who soon became a close friend, described her in a curious oxymoron: "Dolly was flamboyant in a very conservative way."

Like everyone else, Stanfield felt she uplifted the spirits of people she met because she was so positive, and so vibrant.

As a dental student, Dolly took required courses with daunting titles like "Applied Head and Neck Anatomy," "Dental Systemic Histology," "Biochemistry," and "Oral Diagnosis."

But despite the grind of her studies, she always looked like a movie star. There was nothing vaguely conventional about Dolly, and her new friends both respected her and delighted in her company.

In between her heavy schedule of classes, Dolly relaxed by watching midday soap operas on her small television set. A lot of college students were doing that in the 1980s, sitting in dorm lounges and keeping track of the daily television Sturm und Drang during their lunch breaks. The actors always had astounding personal relationships, tragedies and near-tragedies, and erotic sexual problems. Dolly sometimes laughed and said she was addicted to her soap operas. She figured out where the characters got their names: "The writers pick them from nature," she explained to her family. "See—'Thorn,' 'Brook,' and 'Lake'?"

Her mother said that Dolly's fascination with the soap operas soon got her whole family watching them, too.

Dolly was also a loyal fan of Steve Martin during the days when he and fellow comedian Dan Ackroyd were in their "wild and crazy guy" phase. She giggled out loud at Martin's silly gags. Her delight in ridiculous fictional situations, pranks, and jokes was contagious. It was probably inevitable when she met Bart Corbin that she would find his quick wit captivating, even though his humor tended to be much darker and somewhat meaner than her own.

Still, she liked him a lot when she first met him. It was something more than the fact that he was handsome and funny, but his dead-on humor initially drew Dolly's attention. She knew a lot of handsome men, and many of them would have been pleased to date her. But she chose Bart.

Some of her friends at that time felt that Bart was the love of her life. Others weren't so sure. Both Shelly Mansfield, Bart's former lover in college, and Dolly Hearn were lovely, and each had long dark hair and dark eyes. Both were confident young women. The small percentage of Bart's acquaintances who knew both women must have suspected that he was replacing Shelly with Dolly. And they were concerned.

There is no indication that Dolly ever knew about Bart's failed romance with Shelly. She believed she knew him very well and that they had few secrets from one another. But there were facets of Bart's personality that he kept completely hidden from her—at least in the beginning.

CHAPTER FOURTEEN

FALL 1988–FALL 1989

IN 1982, WHEN BART CORBIN and Shelly Mansfield first shared a class at the University of Georgia in Athens, Jenni Barber was only twelve years old and in the seventh grade. When Dolly Hearn and Bart Corbin began dating in the fall of 1988, Jenn was still eight years away from meeting him. Jenn was in her senior year in Central Gwinnett High School, and Bart was infatuated with twenty-six-year-old Dolly Hearn.

Jenn Barber hadn't been very lucky in love. She dated a boy named Ted all through the ninth and tenth grade, and then her friends told her he'd been cheating on her, and she broke up with him. Jenn continued to believe in love, but after that she was a little less trusting.

There was every chance that Bart and Jenn would never meet, but in time the smallest veering off changes whole lives—sometimes for the better and sometimes for the worse. If Shelly and Bart had gotten married after their long romance in Athens, Bart wouldn't have become obsessed with Dolly Hearn, either. Once some lives intersect, however, there is no going back.

*   *   *

BART WAS ENTRANCED with Dolly from the moment he met her. They began to date, and were soon seeing each other exclusively, something Bart insisted on. He rapidly became so besotted with Dolly that his friends were worrying about him. Fellow dental student Eric Rader, one of Bart's closest friends, urged Bart to slow down. It was clear that Bart was becoming much too involved emotionally. Rader warned him that he might be headed for a broken heart.

Those who knew Bart Corbin best in dental school at MCG realized that the confidence he evinced was fragile. Combined with that vulnerability, they suspected that he may have promised himself he would never again allow a woman to walk away from him. He hadn't dealt well with losing Shelly, and now he had plunged into a deep relationship with Dolly. No matter how cogent his friends' arguments, Bart wouldn't listen.

He thought he and Dolly went together perfectly. He could dress dramatically, too, and they sometimes chose to wear black outfits as they walked on campus. By now, he had his ears pierced and wore earrings. He was a chameleon, alternating from plump to cadaverous as he gained and lost weight.

Although Dolly was attracted to him both physically and emotionally at first, she wasn't nearly as interested in a locked-in relationship as Bart was. It was hard enough for the dental students to combine their studies with a social life; their time was so filled with classes, projects, and studying. Maintaining a romance and an acceptable GPA at the same time was almost impossible. Bart at least had a solid year at dental school behind him, but Dolly was just beginning to build a firm foundation at MCG, and she was adamant that she could not have her study time interrupted. She wanted to become an oral surgeon, and that would require that she have top grades. She knew it was a long shot, and, if she had to, she would adapt to a less lofty goal. But she was going to give it a try.

One of Dolly's closest friends on campus was Travis Hampton; they would become "office partners" at the dental school where each of them had a tiny cubicle where they kept their patient records, projects, and other items vital to their studies. Travis's brother, Derrick, was a good friend of Bart Corbin's, and Travis himself became one of Dolly's closest confidants soon after she arrived at the school. Theirs was a purely platonic relationship; Travis was about to be married to someone else. He observed Dolly as she dated a number of men, but she didn't appear to be in love with any of them—not until she met Bart Corbin.

Travis watched Dolly's romance with Bart from its onset. It was his impression that Bart was the first man Dolly had been intimate with, and he believed that for more than a year Dolly considered Bart "her one true love," although she still wasn't ready to commit totally to any relationship. They seemed to be happy together, and Dolly once confided to Hampton that she had never felt about anyone the way she felt about Bart Corbin. As someone a year behind Bart in dental school, Travis admired Bart at first.

Of all of Dolly's friends, the two who probably knew the most about her romance with Bart were Travis and her roommate, Angela Garnto.

Dolly didn't take Bart home to meet her family for quite some time, perhaps sensing that he wasn't going to go over with a bang in Washington, Georgia. She worried that he was too sarcastic, and not quite genteel enough, considering his profanity and his outspoken views on a lot of things. Still, she wanted her brothers and her parents to meet him, hoping that maybe she was wrong about how Bart would appear to her parents.

Barbara invited Bart to dinner, and it turned out to be a rather awkward evening. Barbara and Carlton sat in the small parlor that was just off the first-floor room that had become Dolly's bedroom, and talked with Bart about his interests. Since their guest was well on his way to becoming a dentist, Carlton naturally brought up the subject, thinking it would be an area where he and Bart would have a lot in common.

"I can hardly wait to graduate," Bart said with arrogance, "so I can stick it to people."

He expected to get rich off his dental patients. He had not wavered from his undergraduate days in Athens. He was in it for the money. Dolly's father and mother stared at him, wondering if they had heard him correctly.

Carlton Hearn was disturbed and "nauseated" to hear why Bart had chosen dentistry as his life's work.

While Bart was expansive and clever in his conversation, Barbara and Carlton Hearn weren't at all impressed with him. They found him somewhat crude and lacking the sensitivity necessary for someone about to go into the healing arts.

*   *   *

IT WAS DIFFICULT to say when things began to go wrong between Bart Corbin and Dolly Hearn. It wasn't anything her parents said; they were smart enough to keep their opinions about him to themselves. Dolly was her own woman. She and Bart had dated exclusively—with short periods of breaking up—for almost two years. Although Dolly had mentioned getting married to Bart one day and having children, Travis Hampton noticed sometime in 1989 that she had begun to back away from Bart. She was still attracted to him, but their goals were dissimilar. Dolly wanted to help people, and Bart wanted to make money.

Dolly could be an unconscious flirt; she didn't mean anything by it when she smiled or winked at a man. And she was so beautiful that people were naturally drawn to her. Bart resented that, and became even more controlling and sulked jealously.

Dolly began to feel trapped.

Shelly had never seen Bart angry, and their years together had been fairly serene. But Dolly and Bart's relationship was often tumultuous, and sometimes they quarreled—mostly because he clung to her so tightly, smothering her as he tried to own her. And she struggled to get free. It wasn't that he was ever physically violent with Dolly. Bart never struck her, but their arguments were verbally fierce.

Dolly and Bart broke up often, only to resume their relationship when he promised to give her more breathing space. But Bart inevitably slipped back into his old patterns. In mid-1989, they walked away from each other yet another time, only to reconcile in early fall. Bart Corbin was an accomplished actor who could put on a convincing mask. Even though Dolly had heard the same pleas from him before, he managed to persuade her that he had finally changed. He would place no strings on her, and he wouldn't be jealous. She could have male friends and he would believe her when she said they were strictly platonic.

That didn't last. By October, it finally seemed to be over between them. After much agonizing, Dolly found the courage to break up with Bart for good, and she did that knowing full well now that it wasn't going to be a gentle parting. Part of her still hoped for a clean break, but she didn't expect it to happen. Dolly's and Bart's friends were relieved when the couple agreed to go on with their lives without the huge upheaval everyone had expected.

But despite his calm mask, Bart Corbin was seething. Once again the woman in his life wanted her freedom. He had grown up believing that men were always in charge. More than ever, Bart saw himself as a man betrayed by love. He could not bear to see Dolly out with other men, even though she was dating only casually.

So when Bart met a girl named Sally Fox* on Halloween night, 1989, he asked her out, although in retrospect she would realize that he was dating her just to make Dolly jealous.

Dolly probably had some lingering feelings for Bart, even though she knew their relationship had no real future. When she encountered Bart and Sally at a party in late 1989, she was a little shaken. Dolly wore her favorite outfit that night—a black tuxedo jacket cut to fit her snugly, with a cummerbund. Sally noticed the brunette in the tux because she was very pretty and quite dramatic-looking, and because Sally saw Bart exchanging glances with her.

Bart didn't introduce the two women, and Sally had no idea that Dolly was his ex-girlfriend.

Sally was intimate with Bart a few times, staying over at his house, but she soon caught on that Bart was only using her to attend dental school functions where they would be seen together, and he could be sure that word got back to Dolly. Sally realized that she was always the last-minute date. Sometimes he didn't show up at all. She refused to go out with him again.

The days were growing shorter as the fall of 1989 progressed. Dolly concentrated on studying, and for a few weeks she had more peace of mind than she had known for two years. While she missed Bart—or, rather, missed the way she had felt about him in the beginning, and the hopes she had once held for their relationship—she was intensely relieved to be away from his dominance. She truly wished the best for Bart, and had encouraged him to talk to a counselor. He had said he would, but instead he began to call his friends in Augusta—a couple he had met at the Halloween party, and his fellow dental student friends Derrick Hampton, Eric Rader, Tony Gacita, and Vicky Martin. He phoned them at all hours of the day and night, frequently breaking into sobs when he talked about Dolly.

Dolly wasn't truly frightened of Bart—not yet. But her demeanor changed subtly. She had trouble concentrating in class, and she startled easily. Dolly, however, was resolute that she would not allow herself to be stalked or terrorized by Bart. She believed she knew him, and that she could reason with him. As much as she knew they could never go back to those first good days, she wasn't afraid.

*   *   *

AND THEN, DOLLY'S WORLD changed radically. Even places where she had always felt safe—her apartment, the dental college, the campus—seemed dangerous. Dolly had always moved with a lilt in her step, her shoulders squared and her head up. As the holiday season approached in 1989, however, everyone who knew her found her to be either distracted or frightened of something. The concept of Dolly Hearn as a woman afraid was shocking; she wasn't the type.

It had to be about Bart. He was the one person who could cast a shadow on her life. He had begun to behave irrationally, alternately crying and saying horrible things about Dolly.

Bart was stalking Dolly. Even when she didn't see him, she sensed that he was always close by. Too late, she realized that she didn't know him at all. Dolly still lived in her off-campus apartment with her roommate, Angela Garnto, but suddenly she was afraid to stay alone whenever Angela was away.

Angela had lived with Dolly for all of the "Bart years," and she had seen him be charming and attentive as well as sulking and suspicious. Dolly was convinced that Bart was behind a series of disturbing incidents in November and December of 1989, although neither Dolly nor Angela actually saw Bart do anything, nor were there any other witnesses. Taken singly, they wouldn't have seemed so alarming. But viewed in a pattern, they were ominous.

If anyone knew what mattered most to Dolly Hearn, it was Bart Corbin. He knew how much she loved Tabitha her cat. She had rescued Tabitha from the pound, and wherever Dolly went, Tabitha went, too—even to dental school. Tabitha was long-haired and fluffy, with tiger markings and a white nose, vest, and paws. Tabitha was an "inside cat"; Dolly worried that she might be hit by a car or come to some other harm if she got out. At least partly because of their concern for Tabitha, both Dolly and Angela were very careful to shut and lock their doors behind them.

On November 14, 1989, the two roommates were very worried when they came home one night and saw that the sliding glass doors were slightly open. Nothing was missing, but they couldn't find Tabitha anywhere, and their hearts sank when they agreed that the door was open just enough for a cat to slide through. The weather had turned cold, and Dolly agonized that Tabitha couldn't survive very long outside.

Dolly had a strong sense that Bart had been in her apartment several times when she wasn't home. At first it was difficult to say what had been moved or disarranged, but it was discomfiting to realize how easily someone could get in, and now Tabitha had gotten out.

Dolly reported her suspicions to the Augusta police the next day. Then there was no question that someone had been prowling around. The patrol officers felt that someone had forcibly lifted one of the apartment's heavy glass sliding doors off its track after opening the unlocked screen door.

She had no way to prove who the intruder was. Following the officers' advice, Dolly inserted a thick wood dowel into the sliding door tracks so that they couldn't be opened again.

When Bart heard that Tabitha was missing and saw how upset Dolly was, he was very considerate, and seemed to go out of his way to help her find her lost cat. Even though he and Dolly were estranged, he came over and helped her look for Tabitha in the neighborhood along Parrish Road. But they found no sign of Tabitha, and Dolly grew more and more frantic about her cat's fate as days passed. And then it was a week.

After Tabitha had been gone for two weeks, Dolly almost gave up hope. Between the traffic that rumbled close to her apartment and the icy weather, Dolly began to fear that Tabitha was dead. And she was heartbroken.

Her life was growing increasingly stressful. On November 21, a maintenance man at the dental school found some of Dolly's patient charts in a garbage can in the oral surgery section. Someone had taken them from her little lab office. She was meticulous about filing her charts, and protecting the privacy of the patients she treated in her lab. The next day, more of her records disappeared. She also discovered that a set of wax rings and casts of one patient's teeth were gone. In this lab course, Dolly's entire grade was determined by the dentures she would make from the casts. Only she and Travis Hampton had keys to the office space they shared, and she knew Travis wouldn't have allowed a stranger in there, or lost track of his keys.

Thanksgiving fell on November 23 in 1989, and both troubled and terribly sad about the loss of Tabitha, Dolly drove home to Washington.

Travis Hampton didn't know who might have taken Dolly's charts and wax casts. But he had his suspicions about what had happened to Tabitha, and so did Bart's friend, Eric Rader. It would be November 29 before the dental students actually confronted Bart and asked him some serious questions about Dolly's missing cat.

Dolly's weeks in a kind of twilight zone had only just begun. According to Lee Reardon, her brother Corey

Reardon, and several other male dental students, Bart had concocted a weird *Gaslight* plan to frighten Dolly Hearn.

Corey said that Bart was trying to make Dolly look paranoid. In reality, he felt it was Bart who was acting bizarrely.

Indeed, he was. He spent a lot of time calling his friends—and sometimes Dolly's friends—asking for advice about how to get her back. He would alternately cry and laugh when he talked about Dolly. She had broken off with him, but he thought his dating other women would bring her back. He had reason to regret it. He'd wanted to teach her a lesson and he was stunned to find Dolly wasn't in the least interested in their getting back together. In fact, she had seemed relieved that he was interested in someone else.

On November 27, Dolly showed up at the dental school with her eyes watering and bloodshot. She was nearsighted and usually wore contact lenses. She told Travis Hampton that her eyes had begun to burn as soon as she inserted the lenses.

Here," she said, holding out the small plastic bottle of lens solution. "Does this smell funny to you?"

Hampton sniffed it and said, "It smells like hair spray."

"That's what I thought," she said. "No wonder my eyes hurt."

This wasn't a joke; Dolly's eyes could have been permanently damaged. Moreover, Angela Garnto's contact lens solution had also been tampered with—also with hair spray. Her eyes were burning, too. Someone had been in the women's apartment while they were gone, doctoring up their lens solution.

That person would have needed a key. The wood

dowel was still in the sliding glass door track, and the windows were securely locked. At the same time, Dolly discovered that her gas tank cap was missing. Now, she looked on her key ring. She was a woman who liked things to line up neatly, and she had arranged the keys on her ring so that they all pointed in the same direction. Looking closely, Dolly saw that her apartment key must have been removed at some point, and then replaced; it was facing in the wrong direction, and was in a different spot on the ring than it had been.

Dolly went to her landlord, Dennis Stanfield. He had become a good friend, and, within twenty minutes, Stanfield had changed the locks on Dolly and Angela's apartment doors.

*   *   *

DOLLY HAD KNOWN BART was depressed and that he wanted to reconcile with her once again. She expected his phone calls, and wasn't surprised when he often began to sob, but she had never believed that he could be a physical danger to her. Now, there were times when she was actually afraid of him. The idea that he had been able to copy her keys and come and go at will in her apartment was creepy. On November 29, Dolly made a formal complaint to the MCG Campus Security Office about the incidents in her apartment and the damage to her car.

Later that day, Travis Hampton questioned Bart closely about Dolly's still-missing cat. Travis warned Bart that if he ever wanted Dolly to come back to him, he had better not have done anything to Tabitha.

"I don't know if you're responsible for Tabitha being

missing or not," he said, "but if Dolly doesn't find that cat, she's going to hate you forever."

"Yes," Bart said inscrutably. "I need to call her."

Ten minutes later, Dolly called Travis to say she had news about Tabitha. She had heard from Eric Rader, who put Bart on the line and ordered him to admit to tormenting her by destroying her property. Moreover, she told Travis, "Bart's going to take me someplace to look for my cat."

When Bart and Eric called her, Dolly had flat-out accused Bart of taking Tabitha, and he had begun to cry.

"What did you do to her?" Dolly demanded.

Finally, he admitted that he had taken Tabitha, and he said he would take Dolly to where he'd last seen her cat. He drove Dolly across the city, almost to the far side of Augusta, and parked near a low-income housing project behind the Augusta Mall.

Dolly jumped out of his car and started knocking on doors, asking the residents in the tiny houses if they had seen a fluffy, striped cat. Finally, one woman said, "I do believe I've seen a cat that looked like that around here sometime back—haven't seen it lately, though."

There was so much traffic here, and Dolly was afraid that Tabitha wouldn't have been able to find any food; she was a pampered pet who wasn't used to catching mice or digging through garbage. But then Dolly spotted a cat rolling in the sunshine on a cement walkway.

"That looks like Tabitha!" she shouted to Bart. "It really does."

When she called Tabitha's name, the cat came running and Dolly swooped her up and hugged her. She was thin and scruffy-looking, and the pads on her feet were all torn up, but she was alive and purring. At that instant, Dolly knew that Tabitha had survived with no thanks to Bart. What he had done was the meanest thing he could do to Dolly, but Bart couldn't comprehend that. He had always told her a cat was only a cat, and that he didn't care much for animals, anyway.

"We found her!" Dolly told Travis Hampton. "Bart knew where he dropped her off!"

Bart admitted that he had contaminated Dolly's and Angela's contact lens solutions with hair spray, and he apologized to Angela for putting it in hers, saying, "I didn't know whose solution was which—and I had to put it in both to cover my tracks."

There was more. Bart admitted that he'd been in their apartment two days earlier, and taken Dolly's black tux outfit—which was her favorite—and other clothing. She hadn't discovered that theft yet.

The locks were changed again, Bart seemed to be truly contrite, and Tabitha was home safe at last. Quite probably, she had used up one of her nine lives.

*   *   *

WITH CHRISTMAS FAST APPROACHING, Dolly made it clear to Bart that their relationship was over. On December 9, she went to a party, and the next morning, as she headed for class she saw that her car had been vandalized during the night. One tire was flat—its sidewall slashed with a sharp object. Two fog lights were broken, and there were broken slivers from a tequila bottle on the ground near the broken lights. Someone had deliberately used a key or some other sharp object to leave ugly scratch marks in the paint on both sides of her car. Dolly reported this to the Richmond County Sheriff's Office.

The stalking had begun again, and this time she was sure it was Bart Corbin who was following her.

The very next day, Dolly discovered that her mailbox had been broken into. She had ordered two hundred business cards and she was expecting a package from the printer, but it hadn't arrived. She checked with her post office and talked with the letter carrier on her route who recalled delivering that package on December 10.

She reported each incident to the police. After the mailbox theft, she told the Augusta police officers that she suspected Barton Corbin, her ex-boyfriend, emphasizing that he was a "person of real concern" to her.

Dolly told her friends not to send her any Christmas mail, warning them that it would probably be stolen from her mailbox.

*   *   *

DOLLY HEADED HOME to Washington to celebrate Christmas with her family. They were relieved to hear that she was through with Bart Corbin for good. She seemed to mean it. But while her car was parked at her parents' home, paint—or something like it—was dumped into the gas tank, contaminating the fuel. Her father had it analyzed to be sure.

Carlton Hearn had recently replaced Dolly's old Volkswagen Bug with a good used black Pontiac Grand Am with a sunroof, and having someone systematically trying to destroy it was just one more stress for her.

As the new year began, Dolly started making the dentures that would count for her entire grade in the spring of 1990. She was working with a soft-spoken old lady, who came into Dolly's tiny office many times as Dolly measured and adjusted the false teeth. They were coming along extremely well, and Dolly was elated. She was fond of her patient, and always walked the woman out of the building to be sure she met her ride or got on her bus without any trouble.

But troubling things continued to haunt Dolly. In January and February, Dolly made serious allegations to the Medical College of Georgia Police. She had lost dental supplies. First, she lost $1,495 worth of dental tools. Next, she had a more serious loss in terms of her time and artistry. Someone had taken the full set of dentures she had worked on for class credit. The material in the dentures had been worth only about $110, but her time was invaluable and she had fashioned them so meticulously. The single dental instrument that had been stolen this time was worth about $275. That instrument, a prosthodontic articulator, was discovered on the third floor of the dental school a day later, but the dentures had completely vanished.

Dolly would have to begin again because the false teeth were part of her graduation requirements. A dean in the dental school, Connie Drisko, said that every student had to have a certain number of finished dentures to graduate, stressing that they required a great deal of work, and took weeks—even months—to make.

Dolly had no way to prove that she had virtually finished this project. All she could do was start over. She knew in her heart that Bart had taken them. Hoping to find proof of what she suspected, she slipped a microcassette recorder into the pocket of her white lab coat one day, and then she asked Bart if he had taken her denture project. In that tape, Bart asked her repeatedly if she was taping him, trying to get evidence against him. Although the voices were garbled, there was enough there to suggest that he didn't believe she would really record him. At the end, he told her that she would never find the dentures, so she might as well stop looking for them.

When Dolly spoke to fellow students at school about what she had lost and Bart's harassment, he hinted again to people that Dolly was getting "a little paranoid" and imagining things.

When she took him before the Student Honor Board, he was furious. The Honor Board's investigative process was fairly simple. When an accusation was made, a committee consisting of a faculty member and a dental student investigated the circumstances, and then reported back to a subcommittee of the Student Affairs Committee. The latter considered the evidence that has been gathered and decided whether there was enough there to bring to a hearing. If not, the matter was dropped. Thereafter, all documents pertaining to the probe were destroyed.

Frustratingly, many of the things that had happened to Dolly were circumstantial and it seemed unlikely that Bart Corbin could be linked absolutely to her complaints, although a final decision would come later.

Bart had been before the Honor Board before when he was accused of treating a patient without a professor being present. "He talked his way out of that," another dental student recalled.

Not ready to accept defeat, Dolly applied for an externship in oral surgery, although, as Travis Hampton would later recall, "Dolly didn't have a chance in hell of making it. Her grades just weren't good enough."

He wasn't being mean; he was being realistic. Events over the previous months had sidetracked Dolly from her studies. Anyone would have a hard time concentrating when she was the target of a stalker—even though she knew her stalker.

Dolly still didn't believe that Bart was capable of violence, but he had put hair spray in her contact lens solution; kidnapped her cat; stolen her patient files, the almost-finished dentures she had worked on so carefully, and her expensive dental tools; slashed her tires; and snuck into her house. Even someone as steadfastly positive as Dolly Hearn was devastated. And frightened.

As 1990 began, Dolly dated other students casually, and often went home on weekends. At home in Washington, Georgia, she had long since abandoned her childhood bedroom, and moved downstairs. The bedroom off the parlor was hers. It had a separate door to the outside, a fireplace, and an adjoining bathroom. It was a charming room with a four-poster bed and a rocking chair. Of course, the décor featured cats and roses and bows. She often wore big bows to catch up her hair, and she kept the bows pinned in a vertical display near her front door. Her childhood home was a safe place for Dolly.

In February 1990, Dolly began to date another student occasionally. It wasn't serious—at least on her part—although Jon Everett* was very happy to be with her. On February 23, Dolly planned to cook dinner for Everett in her apartment, but at five that evening Everett happened to be driving past Bart Corbin's house, and spotted Dolly and Bart on the porch. He couldn't hear what they were saying, but it was obvious they were having a very heated argument. At seven, Dolly called Jon Everett and asked if they could change their plans; she didn't say why, but she thought it would be better if she came to his place. When she arrived half an hour later, he could see that she was distraught. She told him Bart was so jealous that it might be better if they went out to eat instead. They ate at a local restaurant—Chi-Chi's—and then rented a movie from Blockbuster: *Her Alibi*.

At midnight, they heard a wild pounding on the door. It was Bart. He called through the door that he "just wanted to speak to Dolly."

Neither Dolly nor Jon answered, but he could see that she was terrified. She began to tremble and weep while pleading with Jon not to let Bart inside.

Bart kept knocking, and Dolly dialed 911. But by the time the police arrived, Bart was gone. He came back at 4 A.M., and began pounding on the door again, demanding to talk to Dolly. She was even more upset; she wasn't having a romantic tryst with Jon Everett—she was just afraid to go home. They called the police once more, and this time the patrol officers arrived and warned Bart that he would be arrested if he didn't leave the premises, which he did.

Dolly told Jon that Bart would not leave her alone. Jon tried to protect her, and they spent the next day studying together, but they both realized that dating was impossible for her. Bart wouldn't allow it.

Dolly's complaints to the college security office had made little impression; there were even some employees there who thought she was making it up to get attention and wanted her to take a lie-detector test at the Richmond County Sheriff's Office. Anyone who knew Dolly would have found that ludicrous. But the whispering campaign that Bart had started, stressing her "paranoid tendencies," was circulating as he had planned.

Dr. Carlton Hearn had had the contents of Dolly's gas tank tested at the Wilkes County Sheriff's Office. Many weeks after the incident had taken place during Dolly's Christmas 1989 trip, the gas, which had turned the milky pink color of Pepto-Bismol, was found to have been adultered by paint.

Dolly's father was a quiet man, but he had had enough. He drove to Augusta and confronted Bart Corbin. He warned him to stay away from Dolly and stop harassing her, but it seemed to make little impression on Bart, although he said later that he was afraid that Dr. Hearn might harm him.

Dolly borrowed a handgun from Travis Hampton for protection, just until she could get her own. Her father bought her a .38-caliber automatic revolver, a Smith & Wesson. Then he and her brother Carlton Jr. took her to a firing range where they taught her gun safety and how to shoot.

She kept the revolver in a shoebox under her bed in her upstairs bedroom, although it gave her only a modicum of reassurance. She and Angela were very careful about locking up their apartment, and they watched for strangers lurking outside in the the shadows of the tall pines in their yard.

In February 1990, the dental school's Honor Board dropped Dolly's complaint against Bart.

CHAPTER FIFTEEN

SPRING 1990

IN MAY 1990, after all the chaos of the past year, the long bad time seemed to be over. Knowing that Bart would be out of her life soon and headed toward his first dental job, Dolly reasoned that it might be safe to spend a little time with him—on a "friends only" basis." Despite all she had been through with Bart, something within Dolly was still attracted to him. He seemed to accept the rules she laid out, and she was happy that they didn't have to part angry. She had loved him once, and she still sometimes longed for the old days when they were together and he behaved like a different person.

The incidents that had frightened her and Angela had stopped completely. Dolly almost forgot about the gun under her bed. Sometimes Bart dropped by her apartment on Parrish Road in the middle of the day, and occasionally she visited at his house. As always, when Bart was nice to her, he was very nice. They still had their disagreements and she was impatient with him when he wanted her to come to his house one evening even when he knew she had to study for an exam the next day. But he finally convinced her that he would let her study if she just came over. Of course he didn't, and Dolly stomped out.

Even so, Dolly's grades on her final exams were the highest she had ever earned at MCG. She had managed to redo enough of her work to be taken off of academic probation, and she had every chance of being "a rising senior," the last stage before being a full-fledged dentist the following year. Best of all, despite those who doubted her, she had won an externship in oral surgery! During that late spring of 1990, her world brightened a great deal.

Dolly looked forward to going home to her brother Gil's graduation from Wilkes Academy. Gil was the valedictorian of his class, and she was so proud of him.

Dolly wore a black lace dress with a short skirt and high-heeled black pumps for the occasion, and her hair and makeup were flawless as always. She looked wonderful as she posed for pictures and videotapes with her family.

She told her grandmother gleefully, "Next year, you can call me Dr. Dolly!"

The spring semester was over, and Dolly would have two weeks off. In a few days she would join her family on their annual trip to one of the little islands in South Carolina, close by Beaufort and St. Helena Sound. They would enjoy the Atlantic Coast on Hunting or Fripp Island there. Her parents wanted her to stay the whole two weeks, but she told them she loved her apartment in Augusta, and she wanted to spend some time there without the pressures of dental school. She planned to stay with her parents and brother several days, and she promised to bring her usual pumpkin muffins and spaghetti sauce.

Dolly was happy and serene on her visit to her hometown on the first weekend in June 1990. Although she didn't mention it to her family, she was going to see Bart during her vacation. She knew her parents wouldn't approve. Whether she hoped that she and Bart could erase the past and start over, only Dolly knew. More likely, she realized that they were not meant to be together beyond these last sunny days in Augusta, and she was ready to start life fresh without him. Her senior year would be demanding, and so would her externship in oral surgery. None of Dolly's future plans appear to have involved Bart, but she had always strived for happy endings. She thought she could manage one last week with him—a week that would let them part without any bad memories.

Dolly hugged her family, and waved cheerfully as she left Washington to return to Augusta.

Her vacation wasn't going to be that relaxing. She was going to do the spreadsheets in her landlord Dennis Stanfield's business ledgers. Stanfield liked her neat but dramatic handwriting, and Dolly welcomed the extra income.

On Wednesday, June 6, Dolly set out the ingredients for the pumpkin muffins, and removed a package of hamburger from her freezer so it could thaw for her spaghetti sauce.

While she waited, she watched her soap operas and worked on Stanfield's ledger. She wore dark shorts and a black-and-white-patterned, short-sleeved blouse. She was barefoot as she sat cross-legged on her plaid couch.

PART FOUR

The Investigation

AUGUSTA

wrote could not even begin to describe the shock, horror, and grief that would be felt in the apartment Dolly and Angela had shared for almost two years.

When Angela had arrived home shortly after five that afternoon, she unlocked the two locks on their front door, and stepped into the living room. The blinds were closed, which was unusual; Dolly rarely lowered the blinds. The room was dim, lit only by the flickering of the small television screen and a single small lamp beside the couch. Angela saw Dolly at the end of the couch, her head tilted to the left so that it extended over the pillows near the sofa's arm. Except for the fact that her legs were crossed, almost in the lotus position used in yoga, Dolly looked as though she had fallen asleep. Angela laughingly asked her, "What kind of joke is this?"

Dolly neither answered nor moved, and Angela felt a terrible prickling at the back of her neck. She walked slowly over to Dolly and saw that her roommate's entire face was stained scarlet. It was long-dried blood. Dolly had lost a great deal of blood. It had cascaded from a wound somewhere around her right ear, down the left side of her light blouse, and then made horizontal striations on her left thigh.

Dennis Stanfield's ledger was open on the table in front of her, also spattered with her blood.

Tentatively, Angela touched Dolly, trying to find a pulse, but there was none.

There was no doubt in Angela's mind that Dolly was dead, and that she probably had been dead for several hours, but Angela was in such profound shock that it was difficult for her to make any sense of it. Her fingers trembled so badly that she couldn't dial their phone, so she ran next door and asked the young women who lived in the

CHAPTER SIXTEEN

JUNE 6, 1990

AT 5:24 IN THE AFTERNOON of June 6, Richmond County Deputy Sheriff Paul Johnson responded to a radio call directing him to 3077 Parrish Road, Apartment C. An apparent suicide had taken place at that address, and the complainant listed on his "Miscellaneous Incident Report" was a young woman named Angela Garnto.

"Complainant stated when she returned home, she found her roommate, Hearn, Dorothy Carlisle, W/F, on the couch in the living room with a gunshot wound to the right side of the head. A .38 caliber revolver found in the lap of the victim. Coroner Sims and Investigator Ron Peebles, Car 708, were called to the scene. Subject was pronounced dead by Coroner Le Roy Sims."

The short form was written, as all police documents are, in terse, unemotional phrases. What Deputy Johnson apartment there to call the police and the EMTs from the fire department.

Next, she ran toward a nearby apartment where a young doctor lived; he was serving his internship in the emergency room of a nearby hospital. Angela was afraid to go back into the apartment she shared with Dolly, and she waited outside while he checked to see if Dolly had any signs of life.

She did not.

No more than ten minutes had passed since Angela had come home when Deputy Paul Johnson walked into the scene. He saw the loaded revolver in the dead woman's lap, and, worried about the safety of bystanders and the EMTs, he decided to remove it. Using a pen, he lifted it away from the body and placed it on a rattan stool.

He had no camera, so he couldn't photograph the scene before he moved the weapon. Without a photo, there would be no way to absolutely reestablish the position of Dolly Hearn's hands or the gun itself. That would prove to be a significant loss in this early investigation.

Investigator Ron Peebles was notified at home and hurried to the scene. He was having a busy week. His son, Scott, was graduating from high school; Scott was the same age as Dolly's brother, Gil, and he hoped one day to go into law enforcement.

Peebles took a few dozen photographs of the scene as he found it, and he and Johnson were in agreement about their first impression that Dolly Hearn, twenty-seven, had committed suicide. There were no signs that she had been involved in a struggle—her position was too relaxed for that. Johnson told Ron Peebles that the revolver had been between her hands, with her left hand on top of it.

Angela told the crime scene investigators that Dolly

Hearn was not the kind of person who would commit suicide. "When she had a problem," she said, "Dolly would just get a little more quiet than usual."

Asked about any relationships Dolly might have had with men, Angela mentioned Bart Corbin. She had last seen him at Dolly's only the day before. "They were talking. I didn't hear what their conversation was about, but Dolly didn't mention any argument to me, and I talked to Bart afterward and he was very pleasant."

It had been months since the upsetting incidents when Dolly's dad had bought her the gun she kept under her bed. Yes, Angela felt the gun in Dolly's lap looked like that gun—but she hadn't seen it for a long time.

Coroner Sims officially pronounced Dolly dead at 6 P.M. Paper bags were taped over her hands so that tests for gunshot residue would not be contaminated, and her body was taken to the University Hospital Emergency Room to await autopsy.

Peebles and Johnson, along with Sergeant Billy Hambrick, Captain Gene Johnson, and Lieutenant John Gray checked the rest of the small apartment. The sliding glass doors to the kitchen were locked. The patio area beyond the door had an intact lock on the outside of the privacy fence that surrounded it. There were no forced entry marks or gouges around the front door, which Angela Garnto thought had been locked.

Dolly's answering machine was blinking, indicating new messages. They rewound it and listened for any messages. One was from Bart Corbin. He was telling Dolly that he wouldn't be able to take her to a party that night, but suggested maybe they could hook up later. As far as Angela knew, Dolly had had no plans to go to a party with

Bart that evening. Why would he have called to break a date that never existed?

It was eleven P.M. when Dolly's parents were notified of her death. When they heard the word *suicide,* they shook their heads. Dr. Carlton Hearn suggested that the investigators talk to Bart Corbin, explaining that Corbin had caused his daughter a great deal of trouble over the prior nine months. "It would be wise to check him out," he said.

Both Gray and Peebles knew of Dolly's problems with Corbin. They recalled her reports to their department the previous fall. But Dolly Hearn herself had come down to their department's Criminal Investigation Division to tell detectives that she had decided not to prosecute him.

Carlton Hearn listened to a description of the gun found in Dolly's lap, and he said it sounded like the .38 revolver he had given her to protect herself.

When the Hearns were asked if Dolly had any history of depression or emotional problems, they were astounded by the question. They certainly had never seen any evidence indicating that. The Dolly they knew was cheerful, competent, and enjoying her life—particularly in recent weeks.

Only three days before, she had been as happy as they had ever seen her—perhaps happier. It was almost impossible for them to believe that she was dead. She had had so many plans for her future.

The Hearns were stunned by sorrow and loss. Instead of planning a vacation, they would now plan a funeral. Instead of watching Dolly become a dentist and join Carlton in his practice, they would bury her a few blocks from the big white house where she grew up.

It was much too much to take, in an evening or a week or, quite possibly, in a lifetime. She had been the most vital person her family and her friends had ever known, and now she was gone.

*   *   *

BART CORBIN HAD A NUMBER of supportive friends on the MCG campus or nearby. Eric Rader had been Bart's office partner at the dental school for two years, and they were close. Eric was married, and there were several other couples, most working toward a dental degree, who had befriended Bart. They had listened to his concerns about his on-and-off relationship with Dolly, and worried that he was often so depressed that he broke into tears. Many of them believed that Dolly really was the "bitch" that Bart often described. He had once mentioned that she had the "cheerleaders' syndrome," explaining that she expected to get every thing she wanted. And even upon hearing about her externship, he had scoffed at the idea that she could hope ever to be an oral surgeon.

Dr. Tony Gacita and his fiancée, Dr. Vicky Martin, were inclined to believe him. They had met Bart in October 1989 and felt Dolly was tormenting him, flirting with him when she had no serious interest in him. Vicky thought Dolly's makeup was excessive and wondered why she wore it when she was already very attractive. She also disapproved of Dolly's clothes, remarking that they were too flamboyant and sexy.

Vicky felt sorry for Bart because he loved Dolly so much. One Sunday shortly after they met him, Tony and Vicky joined Bart for breakfast. He was all dressed up and said he had been to church. He told them that he hadn't been to church in years but just felt like going. He went home with them after breakfast and began to talk, crying and upset over Dolly. "I have guns at home," he said somewhat ominously, and that worried them.

Fearing he might kill himself, the couple persuaded Bart to give them his guns. They tended to believe everything Bart said about Dolly, and her indecision about making a commitment to him. And, worse, he said that Dolly was trying to ruin his career by reporting him to the Honor Board at MCG after the alleged incidents at her apartment and the damage to her car.

Word of Dolly's death had flashed around the dental school, and many people knew of it even before her parents had been notified. Late in the evening, Bart showed up at the Gacita-Martins' asking to have his guns back. Neither Tony nor Vicky knew about Dolly yet, and Tony brought the weapons out and gave them to Bart. Then Tony's mother called and he had talked to her while Bart waited in the living room—checking out his guns.

Another call came in, this one informing Tony that Dolly Hearn was dead—an apparent suicide. He and his fiancée panicked about what Bart might do when he found out, and even wondered if he had already been told and that was why he came for his guns. The couple huddled together, speaking softly, as they tried to decide the best way to tell Bart what had happened. He would surely be very distraught when he heard the news.

They decided to take him to Eric Rader's house. He was usually the best one to handle Bart when he veered off track. Vicky told Bart she needed a ride to Eric's and managed to maintain a calm tone when she told him "just to leave the guns behind."

Once they got to the Raders' home, they led Bart to a

couch and Vicky told him that Dolly was dead. He looked shocked and seemed consumed with grief. Eric took Bart for a drive where they could talk alone. As much as he liked Bart Corbin, Rader believed—as Tony Gacita and Vicky Martin did—that he was very unstable, and they kept a close eye on him. Eric knew about Bart's thefts of Dolly's dental projects, her charts, and her instruments, because Bart had confessed privately to taking them when Eric accused him. But that was all in the past; if Dolly had forgiven Bart, Eric certainly could.

But now, after an initial show of grief, Bart calmed down and acted almost normal. Nevertheless, his friends refused to give his guns back to him. They called Gene Corbin, Bart's father, and explained their concern. To their surprise, his father didn't feel that there was anything really wrong with Bart. He thought his friends were probably overreacting.

* * *

THE NEXT MORNING, on June 7, 1990, Dr. Sharon Daspit, a medical examiner for the Georgia Bureau of Investigation, performed a postmortem examination of Dolly Hearn's body. Dolly was five feet seven inches tall, and weighed 110 pounds. Every organ, every system in her body had been healthy, normal, and working well until the moment a gun barrel was placed against her skin just in front of her right ear, the "pre-auricular area." The wound was a contact wound, its edges blackened with gunpowder and barrel debris. As the bullet entered there, just below the ridged petrous bone on the right, it had traveled through the brain in an almost-straight line, severing and macerating her brainstem, and ending just below the petrous ridge on the left side of her head.

She had died instantly.

There was no indication that she had been raped or beaten, nor had she any defense wounds that might suggest that she had fought back against an attacker. She had no alcohol or drugs in her blood.

Daspit estimated the time of Dolly's death as probably between 1 P.M. and 3 P.M. on June 6. The "CAUSE OF DEATH" written on Dolly Hearn's autopsy report read: "Gunshot wound to the head with destruction of the brainstem and secondary exsanguination, apparently self-inflicted."

And then Daspit had added: "Undetermined." There was something about Dolly Hearn's manner of death that disturbed her, and she herself still had questions.

To Dolly's friends and family, any presumption of suicide seemed a monstrous mistake. But the investigation was in its early days. Perhaps evidence or eyewitnesses, or even a confession from a killer would erase those words.

CHAPTER SEVENTEEN

JUNE 7–10, 1990

BECAUSE SO MANY PEOPLE had mentioned Bart Corbin immediately after Dolly Hearn's death was discovered, he was, of course, the first person the Richmond County investigators wanted to talk to in depth. Whatever their relationship was on the day Dolly died, he had been some part of her life for the past few years. Her postmortem examination was still under way when Bart arrived in the Criminal Investigation Division offices at five minutes to eleven on June 7. Lieutenant John Gray conducted the interview, and Chief Bruce Powers of the Medical College of Georgia's security force observed.

The taped interview would later prove to be highly significant.

* * *

BART GAVE HIS birthdate, phone number, and his address on Parnell Street in Augusta. His occupation? "Full-time student, School of Dentistry, Medical College of Georgia."

He said he had lived in Augusta for four years, and that his home was in Snellville.

John Gray began.

Gray: You're getting ready to graduate, I understand. What are your plans after that—or general idea of what you're going to do?

Corbin: Go back to Snellville for a month and hopefully find work within that month and go hopefully out of state.

Gray: Okay. Yesterday evening—of course, I know you're aware of it and what happened. It was 5:00 or so, they found the body of a Dolly Hearn. Are you familiar with this person?

Corbin: Yes I am—she was my ex-girlfriend.

Gray: When was the last time you saw Dolly?

Corbin: The previous day at about 2:00 in the afternoon.

Gray: Was anybody there with her?

Corbin: Her roommate, Angela Garnto.

Gray: How long did you stay . . . Or what did y'all—

Corbin: Thirty minutes. Forty-five minutes. I stopped by to see how she was doing. She had been sick recently.

Gray: The gist of the conversation—I'm not being totally personal, but—

Corbin: Small talk—nothing important.

Gray: Did y'all have any type of argument or disagreement while you were there?

Corbin: No sir.

Gray: When you left, did you call her later that evening or were y'all supposed to see her later that evening?

Corbin: The evening of the sixth or the evening of the fifth when I saw her last?

Gray: I guess it would be. Were you supposed to see her later that night?

Corbin: No.

Gray: When was the next time you were supposed to see her?

Corbin: There was no next time. I was hoping we could have dinner one more time before graduation because she was going on vacation Friday for about a week or so, and I would be taking Boards when she got back, and I would be leaving after.

Gray: All right, let's go to Wednesday morning—June 6th. Let's just kind of start your day off. What time did you get up?

Corbin: About nine. I was late getting up so I just slapped on some clothes and went to school so I could practice for my Boards. I stayed at school until about noon.

Gray: Did you talk to anyone from 9:00 to noon?

Bart could not be sure, he said, whom he had talked to yesterday morning. He mentioned a few names, "perhaps Eric Rader, or maybe the office maid." No, he wasn't required to sign in when he went to his office—the one he shared with Eric.

Gray: Was he there?

Corbin: He was in and out. He had patients. I'm through with my patients.

Gray: So he was in and out, and saw you there. Some of the names you gave us are actually students?

Corbin: Yeah, all the ones I mentioned are students in my class.

Gray: You stayed until about noon and what did you do then?

Corbin: I left with John Harpers to go down to Atlanta Dental to pick up some denture teeth that I needed for my state Boards. After that, I went home, got my car, drove to Rally's, got some lunch, and I went back to school—left probably at 12:35 and got back about a quarter to one, I reckon.

Gray: So you ran and quickly got a hamburger and ate it between the car and the school?

Corbin: Well, I got home and ate it.

Gray wondered how Bart Corbin could have accomplished all those errands in forty-five minutes, but he didn't comment on it.

Bart said that he had a lot of things to do at the dental school. He was sorting through things he didn't need anymore and throwing them out, and he was sterilizing and organizing his instruments to prepare for Boards.

Gray: So you stayed finishing up a few loose ends until about when?

Corbin: 2:00—then I walked home and took a shower and made a couple of phone calls, and then came back to school.

Gray: Who did you call when you got home?

Corbin: I called Dolly. Do you want to know what we talked about?

Gray: Yeah.

Corbin: We just discussed that I could not make the party that she wanted me to go to with her that night and that I would try to communicate with her later that night.

Gray: Did she answer the phone?

Corbin: No, she didn't. I talked to the answering machine. There was a party but we did not have a date with each other.

Gray: Was it the kind of situation where both of y'all were simply invited or what?

Corbin: Yeah, that's what it was.

Bart said he couldn't remember the name of the person who was giving the party. "Teddy . . . something." But he obviously wanted John Gray to know that this phone message had to have been left for Dolly between 2:00 and 2:30 P.M. His memory for the afternoon Dolly died was remarkably precise. He had called another girl to see if she was coming to his graduation, and then returned a phone call to a male friend who had said he couldn't make their weight-lifting session at 3:30 P.M. He figured he'd made this call at 3:30—or closer to 4:00.

Since his weight-lifting partner couldn't come to the gym until five, Bart said he'd decided to get a haircut, and he called his hair stylist and made an appointment.

Corbin: It was at Accent on Hair with Wanda Wood. It was at 3:15—I had to rush to make it.

Gray: And you went and got your hair done and came back. Is that right?

Corbin: Right. It was about four. I went to my house. I don't have a parking permit so I park at my house and walk to school. I basically hung around and talked to some people there and bulled, and just didn't really do anything and then left about ten to 5:00 to go stretch out before we worked out at 5:00.

Gray: And who did you work out with?

Corbin: Scott Silliman—he's a senior dental student. We worked out until 5:40–5:45.

Gray: What did y'all do then?

Corbin: Drove to my house where I called a young lady I was supposed to be seeing that night to see if she was gonna want to go to the party. She was not at home, so I decided to go on to the party with Scott. He had already left so I drove over to his house as soon as I could grab a towel. I got to his house about ten to 6:00.

John Gray switched gears. Although some of his estimates overlapped, Bart Corbin had just accounted for virtually every minute of his time from noon to 6 P.M. Dolly Hearn had likely died during those six hours.

Gray: Basically you and Dolly had been dating about how long?

Corbin: About a year and a half.

Gray: What was the context of your relationship. I mean was it real serious, or was it—

Corbin: It was real serious.

Gray: Had y'all discussed marriage?

Corbin: Yes, sir. It was my idea.

Gray: In the last few weeks, how has the relationship been?

Corbin: It's been off. I'm graduating and I can't stay around for just a girlfriend. I told her that.

Gray: And what was her reaction?

Corbin: It depended on the day. Sometimes it upset

her, and sometimes she understood. Her moods would change from day to day. I mean she always projected the same mood [publicly], but in private, she varied.

Gray: How had her mood been within the last week, as far as personality and everything?

Bart Corbin seemed relaxed, and appeared to almost enjoy discussing Dolly's state of mind. He became more voluble, now.

Corbin: [She was] less upbeat that she has been. Instead of talking about what was possible, she talked about things in terms of dreaming. She said what she was going to try to accomplish was probably just dreams, anyway. She told me a few days ago. It was about general practice residencies or oral surgery residencies. And for her to be realistic is for her to be down.

John Gray asked Bart to go over the prior day again. Bart continued to insist he had not seen Dolly for two days—and particularly not on "the day of the incident." He hadn't stopped by yesterday to see her. He was sure of that.

"What kind of car do you drive?" Gray asked.

"A silver Monte Carlo, 1988, with a black T-top, license plate KD 982 and a black 'bra' on the front of it."

* * *

THE INTERVIEW continued.

Gray: What were you wearing yesterday?

Corbin: At school, I was wearing a royal blue knit shirt, beige shorts, and Docksiders. When I got my hair cut, I was wearing my weight-lifting clothes that I changed into after my shower.

Gray: Do you own a gun?

Corbin: I don't think it's in my name or not. I have like a .25 caliber my father gave me.

Gray: Have you ever seen Dolly's gun before?

Corbin: No, I have not. I didn't know she had one. She never mentioned it to me.

Gray: In other words, you have never seen or never touched that gun, have you?

Corbin: I've never been near any kind of weapon. I didn't think she carried one.

Bart was growing nervous again.

Gray: Do you have some keys to her house?

Corbin. No, I do not. She has keys to my house. I do not have a key to her apartment. When we originally broke up, I'd given her key back. She just never had another one [key to her apartment] made up to give [back] to me.

Gray: She had her locks changed, didn't she?

Corbin: That's what I understand.

Gray: To keep you out?

Corbin: That's what I understand.

John Gray asked to see the keys on Bart's key ring, and Bart painstakingly explained what each one was—from his mailbox key to his car keys, to the key to his father's apartment, to his dental school keys. Even though he had admitted to Dolly and Angela that he was the one who stalked them, he would not admit it now; instead he replied noncommittally. He stressed that he had given

Dolly the chance to marry him, and she had chosen not to—and that had been the end for them. He had loved her, but he was moving on.

"Well, I mean," Bart said, "that there comes a time in a relationship you've got to decide where you're going to go. Either it's going to go further, or you ain't gonna go with it at all. And it was not going at all, so it was time for me to go. I was burnt out on trying."

If he and Dolly managed to see each other to say good-bye in the three days they had had left, it would have been nice—but he insisted they had made no plans to do that. After Boards he would be pulling out of Augusta.

Asked to recall the night before when he heard that Dolly was dead, Bart said all of his close friends had gathered at Eric Rader's house so they would be there for him when he found out. And then Vicky Martin told him Dolly was dead.

"I didn't believe it," Bart told his interviewers. "I don't think she would be making a joke about anything like that, but I didn't believe it. Even if I did believe it, I didn't know how Dolly could have done it. I still don't."

Bart guessed that Dolly must have been very depressed because she was "down in her grades," and she had had such high aspirations to be an oral surgeon. "She's always been tops at this and tops at that. She just used to think that she could get things done without having, necessarily, the grades, and maybe she just realized the bottom line was you had to have them. I don't know."

* * *

THE INTERVIEW ENDED, and after Bart left, John Gray and Bruce Powers sat there silently for a few minutes. Corbin had seemed remarkably in control of his emotions for a man whose longtime love had died violently less than twenty-four hours earlier. A skeptic might even have sensed a glint of "I told her so" in his eyes as he talked about Dolly's alleged failure in dental school—a "failure" that would prove to be totally untrue. She had not only made up her fall quarter's deficit, but she had sailed through the spring quarter. She had been on her way.

Could anyone—anyone—recall his entire day in fifteen-minute segments as Bart Corbin had just done?

Or was he, perhaps, hiding something?

* * *

BART CORBIN WAS BACK in the Richmond County CID offices the next evening. This time Detective Ron Peebles joined Lieutenant John Gray. Gray explained that he needed to ask a few more questions that would help him better understand Corbin's relationship with Dolly Hearn.

Bart nodded.

Once more, Gray asked Bart if he was absolutely sure he hadn't seen Dolly on June 6, the day she died. And this time Bart admitted that he *had* gone by to see her.

Corbin: Yes, sir, I did. I went by—close to one o'clock.

Gray: What was the purpose or occasion to stop by her apartment?

Corbin: Same as it had been on previous occasions, to see how she was doing, to see if we could possibly have dinner that night like we tried to do before she got sick.

Gray: Okay. What did you do? Did you go up there and knock on the door and she responded to that?

Corbin: Yes, sir.

Gray: Okay. When she came to the door, what was she wearing?

Corbin: Black shorts, I think—and a gray and white striped shirt.

Gray: So she let you in the apartment and you came in? What happened then?

Corbin: We just sat down and talked and she was watching her soap operas. We were sitting on the sofa.

Gray: What was basically the conversation?

Corbin: Small talk. We talked about that party that she had mentioned that she was considering going to, this party [inaudible] that I had been talking about earlier, sending her an invitation and me an invitation.

Gray: Okay. Now, you stayed for how long?

Corbin: Thirty minutes.

Gray: Did anyone come over?

Corbin: Yes, some girl from the office where she's working at came by.

Gray: Did she see you?

Corbin: I don't think so. I heard her come up when I was heading toward the bathroom at that time, and I went to the restroom. By the time I got out, she was leaving.

Gray: Did you go anywhere else before you came up to Dolly's house—when you pulled up to her house?

Corbin: I knocked on the end door of the apartment [units]. When you're facing the door, the farthest door on the left.

Gray: Why?

Corbin: Because—um—our state Boards, we need certain patients for certain lesions, and she, Dolly, knew these people, and I was trying to get people in to screen them, which means we take a couple of X-rays and see if they, you know, got any lesions. It doesn't cost them anything, 'cause we're sort of desperate for patients, that we have to have to get our license.

Bart couldn't recall if he had knocked on the neighbors' door before or after he visited with Dolly because he had been to their door twice before during the week, and found no one home. They hadn't been home on June 6, either. He didn't know if Dolly knew them or not, but she knew several people in the complex, although probably not those at this apartment. "She didn't hardly associate with those people."

After seven years of college, Bart Corbin occasionally slipped into "country" grammar, and it sounded odd coming from his mouth. But that wasn't what fascinated John Gray and Ron Peebles. Each of them had been surprised by the changes in Corbin's recollections. Thirty hours earlier, he had given a very different description of his movements on June 6. Had he perhaps realized that someone had seen him at the apartments on Parrish Road, and felt the need to revise his recall? Or had he been so shocked and saddened by Dolly's death that he hadn't been able to remember his movements accurately yesterday? Gray and Peebles asked him about Dolly's mood on the afternoon she died.

Corbin: [She was] sort of . . . um . . . non—I don't want to say nonchalant, I mean, I don't know. I mean just sort of normal, I guess I would say. (Inaudible.) She was busy, and she was still complaining about the guy she was working for on the last few days, because he'd been jerking her around about getting the hours she needed to work that he had promised her.

Gray: Was that the apartment manager?

Corbin: Yeah.

Gray: Did she need money?

Corbin: She said she needed money.

Gray: Did you know if she was in any type of financial debt?

Corbin: I don't think so, because her daddy gives her most anything and pays for everything. I didn't know her to be hurting for anything.

Gray: Okay. What was your mood when you went by to see her that day?

Corbin: Ah, say, I guess sort of busy, fairly upbeat, I remember.

Gray: Okay. All right. Did you have a lot to do that day?

Corbin: Yeah, I've got a lot to do for several days.

Gray: So you just went by there to just, generally talk to her. Right?

Corbin: Right. 'Cause, I mean, I had found out that morning that a patient of mine—one of the patients I was gonna use—this is sort of hard to explain without you being a dentist or something, you know. I mean the lesion they had wasn't gonna work out the way I had planned it, and so I was sorta desperate for patients. I had been to Dolly's before and the last couple of days I came to knock on doors and see if these people would come by just for me to take a look at then, and, 'cause—um—it—you know, it was almost like going up to a stranger, and she knew them at least, and that was the main reason I was coming up.

The two detectives noted that Corbin was nervous, stuttering and stammering, and still failed to show any sadness that the woman he had hoped to marry had been shot to death two days before. He was laboring over why he had been at her apartment, alternating between reasons. He denied going upstairs while he was there, and said he hadn't taken a shower there.

Gray: You're positive?

Corbin: I'm positive.

Gray: So did y'all come to some kind of agreement whether that y'all were gonna go out together?

Corbin: That night?

Gray: Yeah.

Corbin: No. She didn't know if she wanted to go to that one party and I didn't remember until later that I'd forgotten we had that dean's [Dean Wallace Edwards] party to go to.

Gray: Did anybody call while you were there?

Corbin: I can't remember if somebody called or not. It's possible that maybe one person called—I can't remember.

Gray: Do you remember what you were wearing?

Corbin: I don't remember. I thought it was jeans and a T-shirt that time.

He had described two different outfits during his interview the day before. Still, Bart was doing a fairly good job of weaving this new version—where he admitted to being at Dolly's apartment in the early afternoon—into his perambulations around the campus of MCG and Augusta. The message on Dolly's answering machine supported his contention that they had talked about going to a party, although Bart continued to be very vague about whose party it was.

Corbin: I called Dolly because after we talked about that party, I remembered that I was supposed to be taking this other girl out to this other thing. And I called her [Dolly] back up to tell her I didn't think we were gonna be able to hop over to this other party, but that I'd try to catch up with her later that night.

John Gray reminded Bart that he had phoned someone else on the afternoon that Dolly was shot, but he said he didn't remember who that was.

Gray: Let me kind of refresh your memory. Did you call the hairdresser—to get your hair cut?

Corbin: Yeah, when I was at the school. I thought you meant when I went back to school.

Gray: All right. And you decided to get your hair cut?

Corbin: Right. She said she could fit me in, probably around 3:15 so I left at, like, three o'clock.

Gray: I need to ask you this. You were already up there where you were supposed to be to get your hair cut. Why did you drive all the way back and then decide to get your hair cut?

Corbin: Because I originally didn't have an appointment at that time. I didn't think I had time to get my hair cut because—or even—as I was driving back there, I was supposed to be working out at 3:30 with Scott. And—um—when I got, like I said, back to the house and took a shower to come back to the school, there was a message on my phone saying "I can't make the appointment." Because I had a patient show up the next day, so I had to take care of her. She was long distance. So I decided to call and see if maybe I could just get my hair appointment moved to that day. If she had space because she originally told me that she could fit me in like 1:15 or something like that, and at that time I didn't think there was any way I was gonna be able to make it, because I was running over on some work.

The rest of Bart's story about the time between 4 and 10 P.M. was the same as he recalled in his first interview. He had worked out, gone to Dean Edwards' party, and then gone to Vicky and Tony's house.

Corbin: They live over by the Sweetheart Cup factory. I went to pick up some things they were keeping for me, and while I was sitting there, Tony was having a conversation with his momma, so I was hanging around just to see how it would come out. Vicky wanted me to go up to Eric Rader's house.

Bart avoided telling Gray that he had gone to Vicky and Tony's house to pick up his guns. Gray skipped over that and the moment Bart learned that Dolly had been shot to death. Instead, he asked if Bart had ever been to counseling—and, if he had, why? Bart acknowledged that he had, explaining that it was because he was stressed, both because of his studies, and about his relationship with Dolly.

Gray was puzzled. Corbin had clearly been intensely fixated on Dolly Hearn, but now his affect was flat—almost unconcerned—as he spoke of the last days of their being together.

Gray: I'm gonna ask you again, and we brought it up and I know it's a long night, and I'm not trying to continue—we're gonna cut it off very shortly. The situation with you and Dolly was, if I understand correctly—it was gonna come to an end?

Corbin: Yes, sir.

Gray: And when was that?

Corbin: When was the end gonna be?

Gray: Yeah.

Corbin: We didn't ever set a date as far as I was concerned. It—the ending, I mean—if you're talking in any kind of permanent sense. It was over. It had been over, really, for a while. It was just sort of a hanging on kind of thing. But, I mean, it was over for a few weeks. By this time, we had broke up off and on, off and on, so much [that] it was sort of nonchalant this time around.

Detective Ron Peebles cut in, saying to John Gray, "I know you interviewed him earlier, and he mentioned he had not been around the apartments up there [on Parrish Road]. For the record, I'd like to hear him state why he lied or failed to tell the truth the first time with you, John."

Bart had a quick answer for that.

Corbin: I failed to tell the truth because, back in January, Dolly's father was under the impression that I had done certain things to her, which she had told him, and he made, in so many words, verbal threats to me back in—it was probably the second week in January, which I cannot prove because I was the only person there, and I was alone that day. And I did not want to be connected in any form with any kind of thing that might have went on or had any influence on it because of fear for myself.

It was a truly rambling explanation. This tall, healthy, and muscular young man appeared to be terrified of Dr. Carlton Hearn, a slender man thirty years his senior, or so he wanted to imply. Dolly's father had, they understood, warned Corbin not to hurt his daughter, but he hardly seemed to be a man who would act violently toward anyone.

Gray continued his questioning implacably.

Gray: Would it also be fair to say that this part of the story was not completed for reasons that you were possibly fearful that the authorities would be looking at the circumstances in a suspicious manner?

Corbin: I guess, subconsciously, but that wasn't my main concern.

Gray: Your concern about the whole thing was the fact that you thought her daddy would hold you responsible. Is that correct?

Corbin: And I still do.

The interview was coming to an end, but when John Gray asked Bart if he had anything to add, he said he wanted to mention other men that might have been dangerous to Dolly.

Corbin: You asked me earlier if I knew if she was seeing anyone else. I don't know if she was, but I know this boy—this Jeff kid—he's some high school boy and he went out with her, but he's just little bitty old thing. He's a waiter over at the Steak & Ale, 'cause that's where they used to work together. She told me about that. That's been about a week or so.

Gray [incredulously]: Did they date?

Corbin: They did before I ever started dating her.

Gray: How old is he—how old is Jeff?

Corbin: He's probably eighteen or something now.

Gray paused. That made no sense at all to him. According to Bart's reckoning, he had been with Dolly for two years, and if "Jeff" was eighteen now, he would have been fifteen or sixteen when Dolly first dated him! Gray suspected Corbin was trying to plant a red herring into this investigation.

Gray asked Corbin when Dolly had seen this "Jeff" last.

Corbin: She didn't see him. She hasn't seen him in years. She told me about the note the guy had left one night when she went to bed early. He knocked on the door, and she didn't answer. Because she doesn't answer the door late at night when she's home alone. And, ahhh—she didn't see him that night, either. That's what she told me. I don't know. I wasn't there.

*　　*　　*

THE NEXT DAY, Dr. Bart Corbin graduated from dental school at the Medical College of Georgia. He was grinning broadly as he received his diploma. Those who had known and loved Dolly Hearn were stunned to see how carefree he appeared; it was almost as if he had never known her, never loved her. On June 10, he attended the wedding of Drs. Tony Gacita and Vicky Martin, seeming to enjoy himself at the ceremony and reception.

Bart was on his way to a career as a dentist. There would never be a "Dr. Dolly" now, but already he appeared to have moved on, without so much as a backward glance.

Detectives Gray and Peebles read over the transcripts

of Bart Corbin's two conflicting interviews. On the day that Dolly died, he had been a very busy man indeed. He had traveled back and forth to the dental college, sterilized and packed instruments and unneeded items in his office, gone out to lunch, picked up denture teeth at a dental supply company, taken a shower, stopped by Dolly's apartment, knocked on doors to find dental subjects for his state Boards, made numerous phone calls, left messages, changed clothes three times, gotten a haircut, worked out at a gym, attended the dean's party, attempted to pick up his guns at Vicky and Tony's house, and then learned that his longtime girlfriend had died suddenly of a gunshot wound.

And he remembered every minute of that day.

And Dolly? Had her actions been those of a woman about to commit suicide? She was packing for a trip to the beach with her family, preparing to make muffins and spaghetti sauce, working on her landlord's business ledgers, watching her favorite soap operas, and designing invitations for a party that she planned to celebrate her own birthday in a month, on July 6. Angela had shown the investigators a number of different invitations, all of them written in Dolly's distinctive, almost joyous, swoops and swirls of ink.

According to close friends, Dolly had not broken up with Bart Corbin but was looking forward to spending time with him during her two-week vacation between semesters.

No one could talk to Dolly about her recall of June 6, of course, so detectives would have to reconstruct her day and attempt to find physical evidence that would support their suspicions about Bart Corbin. They could hardly cite probable cause to obtain an arrest warrant just because his demeanor appeared oddly cheerful rather then grief-stricken or at least saddened.

— Barbara and Carlton Hearn Sr., and Dolly's brothers—Gil and Carlton Jr.—fully expected that Dolly's cause of death would be changed to "malice murder" (according to Georgia statute definition) as the probe went on, and that Bart Corbin would be charged with the crime.

That, however, was not to be. The Richmond County Sheriff's Office had no blood spatter experts in 1990. The gun used to shoot Dolly had been moved before any photos were taken, making it almost impossible to reconstruct her shooting. And Dolly's case was officially closed, leaving "Suicide" as the method of her death espoused by the Richmond County Sheriff's Office, and "Undetermined" by Medical Examiner Dr. Sharon Daspit.

Dolly's parents nevertheless hired a private investigator, Sarah Mims, to continue the investigation into her death. And Mims located a number of people who had heard Bart Corbin talk about killing Dolly. She talked to Dolly's neighbors and to Dennis Stanfield's secretary—who had seen Dolly twice on June 6. In the end, the information that Mims gleaned would prove invaluable.

The Hearns buried Dolly in an historic cemetery in Washington, Georgia. She would rest forever just a few minutes' drive from home. Her beloved grandparents, GoGo Pop and Mama Buns, would soon lie in the graves next to her. They were very old when they died, but Dolly's life had only just begun.

Chapter Eighteen

1990–1997

THERE HAS NEVER BEEN any indication that Jenn Barber Corbin ever heard Dolly Hearn's name, or knew anything at all about her. Eight years of separation at their ages might as well have been twenty or thirty for women as young as they were. Nonetheless, Dolly Hearn and Jenn Barber had many things in common. Like Dolly, Jenn was interested in sports in high school, and she loved animals, too. Jenn was always as concerned as Dolly that other people were happy. Each came from loving, stable families with traditional values. They both prepared for careers that would benefit others. On the day she died, Dolly was one year away from becoming a dentist; Jenn planned at one time to be a nurse, and she was working as a teacher when she was killed. Perhaps they would have liked each other if they had ever met.

*   *   *

SHORTLY AFTER HIS GRADUATION Bart packed up his belongings in Augusta and returned to Gwinnett County. Although he had told the Richmond County detectives that he hoped to practice dentistry in another state, he remained in Georgia. He substituted for vacationing dentists for a while, and then worked for Dr. Huey's dental clinic until he could afford to open his own practice.

During the early 1990s Bart was briefly involved with a number of women, but none of those relationships matched the intensity of his obsessions, first with Shelly, and then with Dolly. It was as if Bart Corbin had grown a shell that gradually became harder and harder until he was impervious to hurt from others.

Bart did meet one woman who would remain in his life for over a decade, even after he married Jenn. Dara Prentice* worked records and billing in a nearby medical clinic, and occasionally did temp work in the practice where Bart worked. Dara was married, and the mother of two small children whom she adored. Even so, when Bart employed his considerable charm, Dara succumbed to it. She believed that he really cared for her, and, as the years passed, that it was only their mutual concern for their children that kept them apart. "Someday," he told her, "we can be together."

Dara was a very attractive woman, somewhat buxom, with short wavy bright red hair. She resembled neither Shelly nor Dolly. Having married young, and caught in a marriage with a much older man who was sometimes cold and dismissive, Dara was a vulnerable target for Bart Corbin. It was ironic, of course, because in some ways, Bart wasn't all that different from her husband. They both occasionally put her down, and rarely, if ever, apologized for their actions toward her.

Dara did whatever Bart asked of her, accepting the small niche he allowed her to fill in his life. She had heard about how he treated the women who worked in dental offices with him, first when he was little more than an intern, and later when he had his own practice. Sometimes, when she worked for him as a temp at tax time or to bring his billing up to date, she observed how quickly his temper could erupt, seemingly out of nowhere. He shouted and swore and even threw things at the women who worked for him. Even as he became more successful in his career, expanding his patient roster, and able to afford larger homes and newer cars, he seemed to take little satisfaction in it. His rages meant he couldn't keep his employees for long; once they became the objects of his wrath, most quit and moved on.

Perhaps Dara continued to work for Bart because she wasn't usually a target for his anger. And, of course, they were having a physical affair; she believed that they were in love, and that she was special to him and someone he turned to when he had problems.

When Bart started to date Jenn Barber, Dara accepted that she was in no position to be jealous; after all, she wasn't free and she couldn't ask Bart not to see single women. Jenn would never know that Bart had discussed her first pregnancy with Dara, that he had betrayed her in talking about her most personal issues with his mistress. She didn't know then that he had a lover, or that Bart and Dara had actually debated whether he should break up with Jenn, urge her to have an abortion, or marry her. Bart told Dara in 1996 that he was very angry when Jenn became pregnant, and that he wanted her to abort the baby.

"I told him that I thought he should marry Jenn," Dara would remember ten years later. "It seemed to me that that was the honorable thing for him to do. And I guess he loved her, too, but I admit that I felt really bad when he got married. I think I expected more."

*   *   *

INEXPLICABLY DARA PRENTICE liked Jenn, and didn't consider her a rival. As the years went by, she often socialized with Bart and Jenn, going to get-togethers on their houseboat and at ball games, or to family gatherings at their homes. Still, Dara often felt guilty, although she was usually able to rationalize her affair with Bart by telling herself that she wasn't really hurting his marriage. Jenn was his wife—and she wasn't. Jenn had him in her bed, on vacation, for holidays, and it was Jenn who bore his children. Dara was the woman outside looking in.

There was at least one other woman that rumor suggested Bart knew perhaps too well, although no one could be sure how intimate their connection was. Her name was Harriet Gray, and she was employed in one of the dental offices where Bart worked part-time to supplement his income. She was a good deal older than Bart, fifty to his thirty, but she was still a very handsome woman.

Harriet was recently divorced, and her relatives noticed that she was striving to change her middle-aged image. None of them knew whether that was because "makeovers" are often a natural response to midlife divorces, because Harriet had a lover, or simply because she wanted to be fit and look her best.

"She bleached her hair very blond, and she got a different haircut," an ex–sister-in-law recalled. "She dieted, and then she took up yoga. She lost weight and she looked terrific."

But then Harriet Gray vanished suddenly, a week after Labor Day, 1996. That was the weekend after Bart and Jenn were married. One day Harriet was there, and the next she was gone. Months went by with no word of her, and her daughters and extended family were worried sick about her.

*　　*　　*

JENN WAS A LITTLE OVER two months pregnant when she married Bart. But for her, theirs was anything but a shotgun wedding. She loved him then and would have married him anyway, and she was thrilled to be expecting their child. In 1996, it wasn't uncommon for couples to live together before they got married, and there were no whispers at all about her premarital pregnancy. Their friends were just happy for Jenn and Bart. The only odd note was their wedding rings, which didn't match. Bart spent a lot more on his ring than he did on Jenn's—his ring had a large diamond in it. But, when asked, he had an easy explanation for that; he pointed out that it was important for his career that he look affluent.

It was a large wedding, and most of their friends were there. Even Dara Prentice attended the wedding and reception. "It tore my heart out," she admitted. "Not surprisingly, I drank too much at the reception. I was dancing with a lot of Bart's friends, and he asked one of my girlfriends to make sure I made it home okay and that I didn't do 'anything stupid.' "

Bart and Jenn didn't have a real honeymoon; they spent the rest of the weekend on the Barbers' houseboat on

Lake Lanier. It didn't matter. The weather was perfect and the lake was like glass.

*　　*　　*

NARDA AND MAX BARBER stayed closely connected to the young Corbins. Jenn's parents and her sisters and brothers-in-law liked Bart a lot at the beginning, and for a while they loved him. He and Max got along and participated in a lot of activities together. Most weekends, the young Corbins visited Max and Narda.

Bart didn't have many close male friends beyond his brothers, Bobby and Brad. One of his few friends was a man whose nickname was "Iron"—he worked out in the same gym with Bart. Another was Richard Wilson, a man about his age who lived in a small town in Alabama. Wilson had worked for Gene Corbin's business at the same time Bart did. Although Wilson's home in Alabama was a good distance away from Gwinnett County—a three-hour car trip—he and his wife, Janice, usually came to Georgia for the Corbins' Fourth of July celebration.

Initially, of course, Bart and Jenn couldn't afford their own houseboat; Bart hadn't hit his financial stride yet, and for him, of all people, that was frustrating. He had never hidden the fact that he was in dentistry to make a lot of money—or, as he once said to Dolly Hearn's parents—to "stick it to his patients." He had expected his practice to take off far sooner than it did.

Eventually, Bart and Jenn were able to buy their own houseboat. It wasn't new, but it had a living room/kitchen combination, two bedrooms and a bathroom, and was surrounded by a large deck with equipment for barbecuing. They would have lots of parties there, and on Narda and Max's houseboat, moored at the next dock.

Jenn was blissfully happy in the first months of her marriage, thrilled about her pregnancy, in love with her husband. And Bart seemed to look forward to their baby, too. Even so, there were some things about the Corbins' early marriage that were jarring to her family.

Jenn had a beloved pet dog when she started dating Bart—she'd had him for years—and of course she took him with her when she got married. Sebastian was a big old yellow Lab who, true to the breed, liked everybody he met. Except for one person—and that was Bart. One night at about seven or eight, Narda got a frantic call from Jenn. "Mom," she said urgently, "you have to take Sebastian! He keeps trying to bite Bart, and Bart's going to kill him unless I get him out of here!"

Jenn wasn't exaggerating; Bart hated Sebastian as much as the dog hated him.

Max and Narda adopted Sebastian, incredulous that of all people Jenn's dog would snarl at, it was their new son-in-law. "Jenn missed her dog a lot," Narda recalled, "but she couldn't take Sebastian back to her house."

That was a minor problem, compared to the way Bart began to treat Jenn within a few months of their wedding. He had professed his love for her before they were married, but oddly now, he set about chipping away at her ego—at first only when they were alone.

"For some reason," Narda said, "he tried to make Jenn feel inferior—and often over such minor things. He made her stop wearing nail polish! Jenn always kept her fingernails and toenails polished, but Bart told her he hated the pearl-pink polish she was using. Finally, she just stopped painting her toenails because Bart asked her not to do that anymore. It wasn't worth an argument to her to object."

Despite some of the bumps in the Corbins' early marriage, Narda and Max, Rajel and Heather, and the rest of the extended Barber family welcomed Bart. "He was brilliant," Narda remembered. "He belonged to Mensa, and he could make us laugh, too."

Bart and Jenn settled down in a small bungalow in Atlanta. It was a funky little house on the edge of a parking lot, and Bart's first dental office was next door to a convenience store and gas station. They had very little money. Bart planned to eventually remodel their house into a real dental clinic. One of the reasons they had no honeymoon was that they had been in Italy so recently, but Bart was also saving his money for his practice. Jenn was glad to economize toward that end.

Bart graciously offered free dental care to Jenn's family, and they appreciated that. For a man who husbanded his assets so carefully, that was a generous gesture.

Bart and Max often went fishing together, and, in time, of course, the Barbers and Corbins docked their houseboats side by side on Lake Lanier. In a crowd, Bart was usually fun to be around. He and Jenn came to all the family functions, and Jenn's family made a big event of everyone's birthday or anniversary, not to mention holidays. The family often ate out, crowding twenty-five or thirty adults and children around tables that were pushed together.

*   *   *

DALTON WAS BORN IN MARCH 1997, less than seven months after Jenn and Bart were married. Both his parents appeared to be overjoyed with their new baby. Jenn was a serene stay-at-home mom, and Bart usually seemed fine with that, although he sometimes told Jenn that he felt ignored. He resented it if Jenn cleaned house when he was home because that meant she wasn't giving her full attention to him. He wanted their house to be immaculate, but he didn't want her doing housework and "neglecting" him when he was home.

* * *

BOTH BART AND JENN kept journals, and he wrote in his that, "Jenn spent an hour cleaning the kitchen when she could have been spending that time with me . . ."

To those who had known him in college, Bart's behavior would not have seemed unusual. He was a man who had to be first in his female partner's life, and he had an almost insatiable need for power and control. While he had managed to keep that hunger banked when he first dated a woman, it had always surfaced in time. Sometimes Jenn wondered if he was one of those men who made perfect boyfriends and fiancées, but as husbands shed their disguises like a cicada sheds its skin.

She had reason to be concerned. Now, he rarely complimented her on her accomplishments or her appearance, and he was quick to criticize her—as if diminishing her would somehow make him stronger. That was in private, of course. When they were out with her parents or with other couples, Bart seemed as devoted to Jenn as he always had been.

And there were good times. Their family scrapbooks were soon full of snapshots of Bart and Jenn and, later, with their little boys, enjoying vacations and trips. In these pictures, they appeared to be having a wonderful time.

Baby Dalton was much loved by all of his relatives, and Jenn—who had once been focused on a career—proved to be a natural mother.

During the first years of Jenn's marriage to Bart, her sister Heather was in college at the University of Georgia, studying to become an attorney. Heather often visited Bart and Jenn's little house, and happily became Dalton's main babysitter. On the nights she looked after Dalton, Heather stayed over, sleeping on their living room couch. Whether she wanted to or not, Heather was privy to Bart's "put-downs" of Jenn, as he explained her inadequacies to her and outlined how he expected their marriage to proceed. Jenn rarely argued, but simply waited out his tirades. It wasn't as if she hadn't known that Bart considered women in general far less important than men, so his picking at her was no surprise. Like so many brides, Jenn believed that, in time, he would change.

Heather liked Bart well enough, but she found him odd. She usually woke up to hear Bart muttering angrily to himself. He was the grumpiest person in the morning she had ever encountered. Getting ready for work, he moved between the kitchen and bathroom—unconcerned that he might wake Dalton or that Heather could hear him. It was almost as if he was having a conversation with someone, but he was talking to himself, and he was always mad about something. He threw things around in the kitchen, and slammed cabinet doors.

It was the same way in the evening. Everything was always Jenn's fault—even if it was only that he couldn't find a wine cork.

"He didn't care if I was listening or not," Heather remembered. "She would just sigh and say 'Whatever,

Bart . . . ' and roll her eyes at me. Bart could be hilarious, but he could also be mean and thoughtless."

Narda Barber was more distressed by his behavior. Jenn eventually admitted to her mother that Bart had told her before they were married that he was willing to marry her—as long as Jenn remembered that he was a *doctor*, and would always be the person in charge. She was to do what he told her, and he had given her her job description. Jenn was to be the perfect helpmate, housekeeper, and social partner. Bart had even told Jenn that she was only "the bimbo," and that she could never be of his caliber, never be equal to him.

Once, Narda actually heard Bart say that to Jenn, and it almost broke Narda's heart. But Jenn had a light way of handling things, and later just shrugged and said she understood how Bart was, and that he really didn't mean it when he said such things. "He just wants to be 'The King,' Mom," Jenn said. "Don't worry about it, please."

It certainly wasn't the kind of marriage that Narda and Max had, but Jenn seemed to be okay with it. And Bart did have his very likeable side. He was so funny, a lot more than Jenn was; he still made everybody laugh. When he behaved badly in public, Jenn made excuses for him, saying, "That's just Bart. If I leave him alone, he'll be fine in a while."

Narda noticed that her new son-in-law reacted to "small, dumb little things" more than big things, such as a $10 charge he hadn't authorized. Jenn never bought anything major without checking with him. In the beginning he had her on a very low budget, which had to cover groceries and everything else. In time, it increased. But Bart would still be enraged by some little thing Jenn did.

Half-laughing, Jenn once told her mother, "I could

wreck the car and run over three kids, and I'd get no reaction from Bart—but if I bought something he didn't think we needed, that would set him off."

"It was always the same. He laid the line down," Narda sighed. "In some ways, Bart could be very generous and very kind. Sometimes things were very good. We had some very sweet times."

Jenn never thought of ending her marriage—not in the beginning. The good times more than made up for Bart's sometimes autocratic ways.

He continued to work in his little office, or helping out more affluent dentists, saving and planning for the day when he would have his own perfectly appointed dental clinic.

It wasn't too long after she got married that Jenn began to have an uneasy feeling about Dara Prentice, but she didn't know if they had had a liaison that existed before she and Bart were engaged. And she soon realized that Bart had "secret" meetings with Dara. Ashamed, Jenn didn't talk about it. She didn't want to acknowledge it. She was so in love.

Jenn finally confided her fears about Dara to Heather. "We were having lunch in Applebee's and Dara came in," Heather recalled. "Jenn said, 'I think Bart's having an affair with her.' I didn't believe that at the time and I thought 'No way!' But as it turned out, Jenn was right."

Bart always seemed to be on the telephone with Dara, although he had an explanation as to why. He said they had to talk about "situations at the office."

He was fixated on his business finances. "He would be on the phone, ranting and raving and throwing things—it wasn't natural," Narda said. "I saw it more when we moved our houseboats together. One time, Dara told him that some cash had been deposited improperly and he was just tyrannical. People on the dock heard it. He was just furious."

As for Dara, she tried to break away from Bart—not once, but several times. "Sometimes I threatened to tell Jenn," she admitted. "But he knew I wouldn't. I didn't want to hurt her—or him, for that matter. I was just angry sometimes. When I called it off, he became unbearable to work with. I gave him my notice several times, but he just tore it up and told me I wasn't going to quit my job. He would always, jokingly, say that he knew where I lived, and that he could always 'get me back,' but he smiled when he said it. He was a charmer."

Dara Prentice knew a little more about Bart's past relationships than Jenn did. He told Dara about a former college girlfriend who had come from New York—that would be Shelly. He also mentioned to Dara that a woman he'd dated "occasionally" in dental school had committed suicide. It never occurred to Dara that it might be dangerous to break off her relationship with Bart completely. It was a moot point, anyway. In the end, Bart was always able to get Dara to stay in their affair.

Jenn still didn't know that Dolly had even existed. Bart never mentioned her, and Jenn had no idea that Bart had been questioned about her "suicide." His dental student friends in Augusta had done their best to cushion the shock of Dolly's sudden death for him, but he left them behind when he drove out of Augusta and headed back to Snellville in June 1990. For Bart Corbin, it was if his years with Dolly had never happened—as if her mysterious death never happened.

Apparently, Bart had simply erased Dolly from his memory.

CHAPTER NINETEEN

1998

JENN FOUND OUT she was pregnant again in the late spring of 1998, and she told Heather before she told Bart.

"She was terrified to tell him," her sister recalled. "And I said, 'Jenn, you're married! Why are you so upset?'

"So she bought a baby rattle or baby socks or something like that and wrapped it up in a box, and gave it to Bart. He was so mad that he threw the box."

Nevertheless, Dillon Corbin was born in January 1999, just before his mother's twenty-eighth birthday. He was a mellow baby, and Jenn handled two children as easily as she had managed one. Bart posed for pictures with his new son, and no one would have suspected that he wasn't pleased to have another child.

Bart had been all smiles and "normal-acting," according to Heather, when Dalton was a baby. But that changed when Dalton was about two. They had Dillon by then, and Bart was impatient with Dalton. Annoyed, he would turn to Jenn, and say, "Jenn, deal with him."

Bart elected to have a vasectomy after Dillon's birth, telling a friend that as far as he was concerned, both his children were "accidents."

When their boys were small, Bart didn't appear to resent Jenn's devotion to them. But there was no question that he was jealous when she spent time with someone outside their immediate family. He often remarked that he wouldn't share her with anyone but his sons. That caused some friction because Jenn was a woman who had always had time to listen to people's problems, and Bart thought that was ridiculous.

*   *   *

THE BARBER GIRLS WERE all settling down. Heather was soon engaged to Doug Tierney, and theirs was a case of love at first sight. They had met in early 2000 through his work as a computer support technician.

Doug fit into the Barber family easily. He was very welcome the first time he met them, especially since it was in the middle of a crisis. Heather had received a call that Jenn and Bart's houseboat was sinking at its slip. Doug and Heather arrived at Lake Lanier just in time to help bail out the boat. From then on, the younger couple were with the Corbins almost every weekend, playing croquet, volleyball, and board games.

Doug Tierney grew up in Baltimore, in a strict Catholic family. His family never had emotional scenes, and Doug was an easygoing man, so he was shocked at some of Bart's behavior, especially when he was rough with his little boys.

"He had outbursts and got irritated with Jenn and the kids and he would just march off. He was a very short-tempered person. I'd seen it in other people—but not in someone so close to me."

On December 30, 2000, after they had dated for nine months, Doug and Heather got married. They bought a home in Jenn and Bart's neighborhood. Now that the two couples spent even more time together, Doug realized that Bart had virtually no friends, other than his brothers. The people the Corbins socialized with were all Jenn's friends, or someone they met through Heather and Doug.

"I asked Bart once to invite some of his friends to go fishing with us," Doug said. But he had no friends from college or anything. It was strange. He had no background, it seemed, no one from his past that he still saw."

Doug was a genius when it came to computers, and he and Heather started a business together, troubleshooting for corporations. Doug was quite different from Bart, and very supportive of Heather. Even so, despite his new brother-in-law's hair-trigger temper, Doug liked Bart well enough.

If Jenn talked to anyone, it was to Heather, and the few years between them didn't matter much now that they were both married. Soon Heather and Doug had two children—Max and Sylvia—who were a few years younger than Dalton and Dillon. Rajel's children were quite a bit older, and she had lived away from Georgia for several years.

Much more than most families, the Barbers were often together, a loving and solid unit—perhaps because Max's jobs as a sales manager had meant frequent moves, including six states in six years. They felt like perennial newcomers during that time and relied on each other. Even though they had lived in their house in Lawrenceville for many years and were fond of their neighbors, their family links were the most important to them.

As mothers of small children, Heather and Jenn made a pact. If anything should happen to either one of them, they vowed that the surviving sister would adopt the other's children. Of course, they were both young and healthy, with no likelihood of trouble ahead, but they both felt more secure.

Heather knew of Jenn's disappointments and frustrations in her marriage, but the word *divorce* hadn't come up. Theirs was not a family where divorce was the easy answer. Jenn still believed that Bart would change—if only she could find what it took to make him happy.

*   *   *

WHEN HIS SONS WERE TODDLERS, Bart showed little interest in them, but as they grew just old enough to participate in peewee league athletics, he stepped in to be sure they would reflect well up on him. He and Jenn had entirely different parenting styles. He thought she was too easy on their boys, and she felt he demanded far too much of them. As young as they were, he wanted them to be stars and he shouted angrily at them when he felt they weren't trying hard enough in school or Little League games. Jenn taught them they could do anything they wanted, and she gathered them to her with hugs and kisses while Bart glowered at her.

When Dalton was up to bat at a game, he couldn't

concentrate because every time he swung, Bart would yell, "Dalton get your hands up! Get your legs apart!"

Jenn stopped sitting with Bart at Dalton's games.

Heather tended now to agree with Jenn's suspicions that Bart was cheating on her. He *did* spend a lot of time talking to Dara on the phone, but he always said they were talking about things important to his dental clinic.

Dara kept turning up at the kids' ball games, but there was an explanation for that, too. Her own boys played ball, although they were much older than Dalton and Dillon. It wasn't that Bart was blatant about his interest in Dara or any other woman.

As time passed, Jenn couldn't erase her uneasy feeling about Dara. If nothing else, it was the fact that Dara kept agreeing to come back and work for Bart from time to time when most of his other female employees couldn't wait to quit.

Dara Prentice made no move to leave her husband, recalling that it was not a viable option for her. "And Bart never asked me to leave," she said. "He seemed perfectly content with the way things were, so I guess I thought that maybe someday the time would be right."

And Dara knew that if her husband found out, he would leave her. Bart wouldn't want any scandal that might hurt his business, so he would undoubtedly refuse to hire her on a full-time basis. She would need a job to support her sons. Bart seemed to enjoy having two women in love with him, and so Dara continued to drift along with him, hoping for a future commitment.

There were occasional long periods when Jenn believed Bart had broken it off completely with the woman she sometimes called his "office wife."

Jenn kept trying to be the perfect wife for him, the perfect mother for his children, and even tried to convince herself that Bart loved her more than any other woman because she was the one he had married. She believed him when he told her that he had stopped seeing any other woman.

Jenn had never known about Harriet Gray, who had been missing for a long time after vanishing in 1996 on the weekend after she and Bart got married. Or about Shelly Mansfield, and especially not about Dolly Hearn.

Harriet Gray never came home. As it turned out, she couldn't. Eighteen months after she disappeared, a scuba diver discovered the hulk of a car at the bottom of Lake Tuscaloosa in Alabama. The car's registration came back listed to Harriet Gray. Her body was floating inside the car, her hands duct-taped to the steering wheel. That obliterated even the slightest chance that she had committed suicide.

Harriet's murder is still unsolved today.

*   *   *

JENN'S OCCASIONAL MUSING to Heather about how much a wife should know about her husband's background was an indication that she sensed some darkness in Bart's past. "He won't look me in the eye," Jenn told her sister. Still, she never tried to probe back through the years before she knew him; she had enough trouble trying to figure out the combination to the emotions that he kept locked away from her.

When Dillon was old enough to go to preschool, Jenn went back to work, teaching the classes at Sugar Hill Methodist Church. She enjoyed it, made a little money of her own, and she was able to keep up her chores at home and do things for Bart without any extra effort. Although they had hoped that things might get better, Jenn's mother, sisters, and her father had to accept that her marriage was not happy. Almost from the beginning, Bart had seemed determined to destroy his wife's self-confidence.

That hadn't been easy to do because Jenn Barber Corbin had gone into her marriage as a woman who knew who she was: strong, popular, and talented. If she had a vulnerable area, it was about men. When her longtime teenage boyfriend had betrayed her, it came at a vulnerable stage in her life and left a lasting impression.

"Bart was still trying to make Jenn feel inferior," Narda said. "He shouted at her, and called her names. She didn't let on how much it hurt her, but we could tell it did. Heather knew more than I did—but she didn't tell us. I think she was trying to protect Max and me."

The Barbers invited Bart's family for holidays, outings, and celebrations, and occasionally they accepted. But Bart's father never came, not since Jenn's wedding. By 1997, he had a whole new life with his younger woman and the son who wasn't much older than Dalton and Dillon.

Connie Corbin and Bart's brothers did join Jenn's family from time to time, but the visits were a little strained. Narda and Connie had virtually no shared interests. They had nothing at all in common, except that their children were married to each other. Narda felt an invisible wall between herself and Bart's mother, some transparent blockade that Connie hid her real feelings behind. Probably Connie felt the same way.

Brad Corbin, Bart's twin, was quite removed, too—either shy or out of his element. But their younger brother, Bobby, was friendly. "Bobby seemed to have a good heart," Narda said. "It was hard to read the others in Bart's family."

Many families—probably the majority—fail to mesh completely when their children marry. And Bart's and Jenn's families were no different. Jenn was always the one who tried to bring them together, and went out of her way to visit Bart's relatives. Jenn loved to throw parties and oversee family celebrations, and she did that with Bart's family as well as with her own. She and Bart appeared smiling and united at Bobby's wedding to Suzanne. And Jenn loved Bobby's children—Zachary and Riley—who were Dalton and Dillon's first cousins and almost the same age. Jenn got along fine with her mother-in-law and with both Brad and Bobby and their wives.

Max Barber made it a point to attend Dalton's and Dillon's ball games as often as he could. Everyone had noted that Bart was "different, somehow" after the little boys were born. He seemed to love his sons, but he had such impossibly high expectations for children so young. It got worse as the boys grew older. On one occasion, Max was a witness when Dalton struck out in a Little League baseball game, and Bart was furious. As he often did, he screamed at Dalton, who was then only about six, calling him a "loser" and "an idiot."

Max was disturbed enough by Bart's behavior that he stepped between Bart and Dalton in an attempt to stop the tirade against his grandson. He knew he was stretching a grandfather's duties, but he couldn't stand seeing Dalton's shoulders slump as he fought back tears. Yet Max also excused Bart. He thought that this was the way Bart and his brothers had been raised. Maybe Bart just didn't know any better. For Bart, winning was the most important goal in sports—and in life.

Bart demanded as much of himself. The once-overweight teenager worked out to hone his body to top condition. He rode and raced mountain bikes. Fishing was about the only leisure activity Bart was involved in that didn't require a lot of physical effort. He was a desultory golfer, although he recognized that that was a sport almost required of a young dentist on his way up. So he played golf and pretended to enjoy it.

Bart urged Dalton to ride bikes with him, but his oldest son didn't match up to Bart's expectations there, either, and he whined when his father insisted he go.

*   *   *

A SEA CHANGE was coming over Jenn. She had been able to cope with Bart when he picked at her and criticized her. But she would not allow him to undercut the boys' confidence. At six, Dalton had begun to beg not to go places with his father. Would Dillon be far behind?

By Christmas 2003, Jenn and Bart were still making stabs at saving their marriage, but she couldn't hide the sadness she felt. She had long since accepted that she had not married her "soulmate." She and Bart had had such a romantic trip to Italy once. Now, he treated her and their sons to a Caribbean cruise and Max and Narda joined them. But Jenn was only acting, pretending to be having a good time. All the smiling photographs they took served only to mock her. The expensive trip didn't make up for the isolation she felt in her marriage. Worse, she knew the cruise was something he could brag about to prove how successful he was.

Bart's practice had grown slowly, but he got into financial trouble. He tried gimmicks to draw patients in, even giving away coupons that offered "Elite Care, without an Elite Price!" And, after moving his practice to Hamilton Mill, Bart made sure locals knew he had long been an active supporter of youth athletic teams. Although he was disappointed with what he considered his own sons' lack of dedication to sports, he sponsored the 2002 Dacula Falcons' twelve-year-olds' football team. The next year, he was the assistant coach of the Indians' T-ball team, and sponsored the Dacula/Mill Creek eleven-year-olds' football team. In 2004 he sponsored the T-ball "Reds" team at Bogan Park and the Mill Creek eighth-grade football team. Bart liked baseball, and it was good for business, too.

But Bart had stretched himself and his finances a little too thin when he moved his practice to Hamilton Mill. He wasn't attracting anywhere near the number of new patients he had expected. He had two civil suits in State Court, filed against him because he had defaulted on payments for expensive dental equipment.

He had more coupons offering his "elite dental techniques" printed up. Even though Bart was very intelligent, he apparently wasn't a particularly effective dentist. Technically, he was okay, but from the start of his private practice, many patients complained to their families and friends that he lacked empathy and concern, and was brusque with them. He didn't recognize that many people are fearful about going to a dentist—any dentist—and that a little compassion and patience would have taken him a long way.

The mother of a teenage girl recalled that her daughter had left his examining room after her initial visit visibly upset. "She said she never wanted to go back to that dentist again," the woman said. "Of course I thought that he might have touched her inappropriately—but she said it wasn't that at all. He just scared her, and she couldn't explain why. We never went back."

One woman never forgot her nightmarish experience in Bart's office. She had sought a dentist who was skilled at fitting multiple crowns on front teeth, and Bart assured he was "very good" at that. But in two sessions that lasted twice as long as he'd promised, she was stunned by his unprofessional manner: he shouted at his chairside assistant, mumbled obscenities, and hyperventilated. Dr. Corbin not only seemed out of control emotionally, but he finally admitted he had virtually no experience with the procedure she needed.

She regretted that she had already paid in full—more than two thousand dollars—especially when she began to hemorrhage severely, and Bart held his head in his hands and told her he didn't know how to stop the blood that threatened to choke her.

After blurting out that she would never sit in his dental chair again, she ran out of his office in a panic, still bleeding, with tissues pressed against her gums, to seek competent medical attention. She never got the crowns for her teeth from Bart, and she filed a complaint with the Georgia Board of Dentistry, asking for a refund of the entire amount she had paid.

When Bart was questioned by the board, he offered to refund $1,452 of the $2,272 she had paid. She refused. Almost two years later, she received word from the board that the entire amount would be forthcoming.

"The Board, however, has expressed its very serious concern to Dr. Corbin about the circumstances which led to the complaint being filed," the letter said. Although Bart was never officially censured, he was forced to write a check for the entire amount, and word of his incompetence circulated among his peers.

On occasion now, Bart's hands shook so badly that his patients wondered if he had some kind of palsy. He drank—but not excessively—and no one ever suggested that he used drugs. Perhaps it was only his agitation over the state of his marriage, which had begun to have dark places. As he and Jenn struggled with a marriage that was not working, his insensitivity in his clinic grew more apparent, reflecting the agitation he felt. Women had walked away from Bart before, and each abandonment had cut him more deeply. He was incapable of treating a woman as an equal partner; he needed to possess her absolutely. For more than seven years, he had felt secure that Jenn would follow his directives and show him the respect he deserved. Now he realized that she was slipping away from his control.

His financial status was shaky, too. He could no longer afford to employ full-time chairside assistants. Only Dara Prentice remained loyal to him.

Another dentist in the area was surprised to receive a scrawled note from Bart asking him to lunch to discuss the possibility of Bart's working part-time in his office.

"He was willing to work for me more than two days a week," the other dentist recalled. "That would make it impossible for any doctor to keep up his own practice."

*   *   *

THINGS WERE FALLING APART in Bart's life. The Corbins' house on Bogan Gates Drive was impressive, but it had a sterile air about it. Jenn didn't argue with him, but she no longer believed that Bart was going to change. Everything

was all about him, what he wanted, how she could enhance his image. They were intimate only when he wanted
to have sex. And he was perfunctory about even that,
heedless of her needs. She no longer had any hope that it
would ever be any better. She didn't ask herself if she still
loved him; she knew she didn't.

They kept up a semblance of a social life. Bart and
Jenn Corbin liked their neighbors, but now they tended to
visit them individually, rather than as a couple. They still
spent time on their houseboat, and they went to all the
family gatherings. They had birthday parties, visited Janice and Richard Wilson—their friends in Alabama—and
stayed close with Jenn's best friend, Juliet Styles, and her
husband, Darren. The two couples vacationed together at
least once a year. Except for the Wilsons, the Styles were
like most of their friends—introduced into their social circle by Jenn. Bart and Darren Styles often played golf
together.

"Our kids were best friends," Juliet said. "I was Jennifer's best friend, and Darren and Bart were pretty close,
at playing golf—whatever, however men are close."

But by 2003, Bart probably spent more time with his
brothers than he had before, often going out for drinks
with Brad and Bobby, and "Iron," his friend from the gym.
Bart was the only one of Gene Corbin's sons who had kept
in touch with him after Gene and Connie split up. Now,
even though they lived close to one another, Bart and his
father rarely saw each other.

Brad's first marriage had ended in divorce, and he
moved in with his mother in Snellville. He was a medical
transcriber, and he worked from home, which he much
preferred to the business world where he felt uncomfort-

able. In 2003, Brad married Edwina Tims, and they established their own home.

*   *   *

JENN AND BART often watched Court TV's coverage of Scott Peterson's trial while they had coffee with Heather and Doug. Like much of America, they were both horrified and transfixed by the seeming smugness of Peterson during his trial for the murder of his pregnant wife, Laci, and their unborn child,

"We all talked about it," Heather said, "at whoever's house we were at. I was watching with Bart once and I said something about Scott Peterson, and how awful it was. And Bart replied, 'Scott Peterson only got caught because he didn't keep his mouth shut.' "

"And I said, 'Well, God, Bart—I hope I'm never gonna be your enemy.' That conversation stuck with me for a long time."

Although Heather had learned to accept Bart's control over Jenn as an inherent part of his personality that her sister had long since learned to deal with, Jenn sometimes surprised her.

"Don't you ever wish that sometimes you could just make cold cereal for your kids for breakfast?" Jenn once asked Heather.

"I told her I did give them cereal if I felt like it. But she said she couldn't because Bart wouldn't allow it. He told her, 'If you won't cook for my children, I'll marry someone who will!'

"I think she lived like a Stepford Wife. Bart gave her money, but she always had to explain what it was for. She had to keep receipts for things like toilet paper and bubble gum. She didn't have her own money until she started working at the preschool. And, even then, she made such a piddling amount. But one time she donated two months' pay to a lady who'd been injured in a motorcycle accident."

Jenn worried about people who were barely making it, and she did what she could to help. Once, she and Heather were in a Publix Super Market in Buford. Jenn nodded to a man who was clearly homeless, ragged—but clean. As she shopped, she picked out a whole roasted chicken, mashed potatoes, vegetables, and a large bottle of Coca-Cola. When the two sisters went through the checkout line, Heather noticed that Jenn had left one shopping bag behind, and pointed it out to her.

Jenn shook her head slightly, and said, "I'll explain outside."

"She'd bought dinner for the homeless guy," Heather recalled. "She didn't want to embarrass him by giving it directly to him, but she told the checker to hand it to him. I found out she did that quite often—she was afraid he might be hungry."

Jenn did most of the chores around her home, even those that husbands usually performed. She mowed the lawn and planted the trees. She was extremely strong, usually pitching in to help any of her family in their moves. Once, she helped her brother-in-law Doug carry a heavy pool table up from their basement. She never seemed to get tired.

* * *

JENN HAD SUFFERED a disturbing loss in the spring of 2004, one that troubled her a lot. It was her close connection to a case that wasn't so different from the Peterson case, and she was extremely troubled by the disappearance of a woman she had considered a close friend for almost a decade. Ever since the romantic trip she and Bart had taken to Italy in 1996, Jenn had treasured her friendship with Mary Lands. She kept a photograph of herself and Bart laughing with Mary and her husband, Gary, in Italy framed on a wall of her home, a reminder of a happier times.

Mary and Gary eventually divorced, and Mary moved north to Marshall, Michigan, a small town about ten miles from Battle Creek in the southwest portion of the state. In 2004, Mary was working as a surgical nurse, and living in a townhouse with her fiancé.

Jenn was horrified to learn that Mary had apparently gone out for a walk alone at 10:30 P.M. on Friday, March 12, after she and her fiancé had argued. She'd last been seen wearing her surgical scrubs and a leather jacket as she walked out of the golden circle of light from a pole in the complex where she lived, and disappeared into the darkness beyond.

She was never seen again, although the Michigan State Police and the FBI assisted the Marshall police in an intense investigation.

"She's dead," Jenn insisted. "I know she's been murdered."

And Jenn was probably right. Mary's car and cell phone were left behind, and she left no paper trail at all—her bank account was not accessed, nor any of her credit cards. She walked out into the chilly Michigan night and vanished completely.

While Jenn's own life was in upheaval in September 2004, she prayed for Mary Lands when her family and friends marked the six-month anniversary of Mary's disappearance with a candlelight ceremony many states away from Georgia.

It was impossible not to note the irony in the two young women's long friendship. Only three months later, there would be a candlelight ceremony on Bogan Gates Drive memorializing Jenn herself.

CHAPTER TWENTY

2003–2004

ALL LIVES, NO MATTER HOW PROSAIC, have their secrets, and we never know what is actually going on in even our closest friends' worlds. Jennifer Corbin was no different. Her involvement with someone outside her marriage began quite innocently. Narda Barber and her girls had always played old-fashioned games together. Over Christmas, in 2003, Narda heard about a Sony PlayStation game called EverQuest. She didn't realize when she purchased it that it might require an Internet hookup. She didn't have one, but intrigued by the "G-rated" game, she decided to invest in everything she needed to play.

"I suppose I spent about $100 to get set up," she recalled. "It was something like *Dungeons and Dragons,* and it sounded like fun."

EverQuest encompasses numerous games of fantasy

using rich animation and 3-D effects on a television; the player selects characters in which to lose himself. As an artist, Narda was intrigued with the quality of the graphics that virtually invite players to enter another world. While they are there, they can choose to be anyone they want: knights, maidens, assassins, sorcerers, kings, queens, villains, and heroes, all anonymously. One game, for instance, suggests, "Create a noble human paladin, a vicious dark elf or necromancer, a greedy dwarven rogue—or any of the more than one hundred character combinations."

The game offers players a way to step out of their own lives for a time. Narda found EverQuest relaxing and entertaining, and she mentioned it to Jenn. When Jenn seemed interested, Narda bought her the software so that they could play together. They had a lot of fun, dueling with one another, talking on the phone, and sometimes laughing until their cheeks hurt.

The game is completely interactive, and the graphics are very real. The characters can gesture to one another, and even flirt. There are "guilds," which are akin to families. While Heather thought EverQuest was ridiculous, she knew it was an escape for her sister. Jenn even taught Dalton and Dillon how to play a simpler form of the game, and showed them how to beat "the bad guys."

Because the game is played over the Internet, there is always the opportunity to meet others involved. Writing under her game name "wizwiz148," Jenn exchanged messages with basically nameless participants, including someone named "sirtank1223." Jenn's Wizard character on EverQuest soon became entranced with his inventive postings. Sir Tank may have sought Jenn out, or it might have been the other way around—but they definitely thought on the same wavelength. Soon they decided to exchange emails outside the confines of the game. Jenn learned that sirtank1223 was a man named "Christopher," who was also thirty-three.

Jenn didn't have a lot of time to spend on the Internet, she was so busy teaching preschool, taking care of her boys, and keeping house. She also worked for Narda a few afternoons a week at the Lake Arts studio, where they filled orders for artists' canvases to ship all over the world.

Even when she wasn't actually playing, Jenn could usually find messages waiting for her from Christopher, and she looked forward to that.

When she met Christopher online, Jenn Corbin had come to a place where she had precious little joy in her life. There seemed to be no harm in exchanging her thoughts and philosophies with a man who lived seven hundred miles away. They were separated geographically; he lived far from Georgia—in St. Louis. More and more, they slipped away from the game of EverQuest to exchange private emails on the Internet.

Many of their emails have been lost, but it was probably sometime in the early summer of 2004 when Jenn and Christopher began to write more often. She never expected to meet him, and that made it easier for her to talk about the things that mattered to her and, eventually, about problems in her life. As their emails flew through the Internet, Jenn found herself attracted to Christopher. She didn't feel unfaithful to Bart; this was no more intimate, really, than playing EverQuest. But she felt less lonely—as if there might be someone out there who could truly love her if she were ever free of her suffocating relationship with Bart.

She was a young woman who had expected love in her life, but she realized too late that Bart didn't want her for anything more than to enhance his own image, and to pick on and belittle. Now there was a man out there who offered a shoulder, a listening ear, and who seemed to understand her.

What harm could there be in having a modern-day pen pal?

Both Jenn and Christopher still logged on to EverQuest to play out their fantasy games there, and they wrote to other correspondents in their online community. Several of them shared their feelings and their concerns for one another. It was a little like being on a plane or a train, talking to a stranger in the adjoining seat, knowing that at the end of the journey, they would all go off in their own directions to pick up their real lives.

Jenn enjoyed "talking" to Christopher, but they made no plans to meet. He wrote that he was divorced, and worked in a restaurant. He lived with his mother, and he was raising his sister's two children. He seemed somewhat in awe of Jenn's standard of living and education. She was, after all, married to a professional man who appeared to be quite wealthy, at least compared to what Christopher did. The way Jenn described her house apparently made Christopher feel inadequate. Still, a small affair of the heart was happening, and Jenn treasured Christopher's emails. They were soon in the habit of writing to each other in the early mornings before Christopher went to work and Jenn left for her mile run, and then again late in the evening if Bart wasn't home.

*　　*　　*

THE EXTENDED BARBER family and their in-laws led a fairly serene existence throughout most of 2004. Narda not only ran her Lake Arts business, she sold her own paintings, too. Max was working for a Ford dealer close to home in Lawrenceville. Rajel was home from California, and Heather and Doug Tierney were about to move into their new house in Dawsonville. It was a wonderful house, with a five-hundred-square-foot master bedroom, soaring ceilings, and a huge backyard. While Heather and Jenn would no longer be close neighbors, they vowed to see each other as often as before. Not to do so would be a loss for the sisters who were used to having coffee together every morning while their children—the four cousins—played together. Still, they both worried that it wouldn't be possible.

Perhaps that problem made Jenn feel lucky to have Christopher, someone who seemed to understand her completely. Christopher's emails revealed him to be a man who was both kind and responsible, as well as secure in his masculinity. Jenn didn't know his last name at first, but she formed a clear picture in her head about what Christopher looked like. She hadn't heard his voice or seen a picture of him—but she felt that she knew him better than most people she had ever known in real life. When she asked him what he looked like, he said "a little like the Marlboro man."

She didn't know if he was joking but complained to him teasingly, "There are lots of Marlboro men, and most of them wear hats so you can't see their faces anyway!"

It was the perfect opportunity for him to attach his picture to an email, but he didn't send one. And still Jenn accepted Christopher on faith because it didn't really seem to matter what he looked like. By the end of the summer, the two strangers' correspondence revealed that they had begun to think that one day they might actually have a future together.

In September 2004, Christopher confessed that he was falling in love with Jenn, and expressed some anxiety that Jenn might just be "putting him on." She quickly wrote to reassure him that she was as serious as he was.

"Christopher, you don't need to apologize to me again," she wrote. "I'm just sorry you felt like I could maybe play you. It's o.k. to be scared, Christopher. I'm scared. We are both gonna have to make big changes in our life if we want to be together, and that is never easy. I love how you make me feel. I love that there are no walls with you. I love that I feel I can tell you just what I feel at that moment . . . I know with you that my whole life is going to change, that our love is going to be so powerful that it's going to be overwhelming.

"I don't know why it is we feel like we do. How did I meet a man so far away from me that can affect me the way you do—a man I've never laid eyes on—I've never seen smile or heard laugh. A man that I can confess every thought I have or bad moment I have ever had, and I'm comfortable doing just that. I want you to feel comfortable doing just that."

*   *   *

SOME MIGHT SAY that Jenn Corbin was an accident getting ready to happen. She was caught in a loveless marriage, starved for affection. Like most women in their mid-thirties, Jenn was at her sexual peak, but she had no outlet for her feelings. She confided in Kelly Comeau that she had not experienced an orgasm in years. She told her sister she had *never* had an orgasm with her husband.

Jenn had stayed on the computer all summer long. She told Kelly at the end of July that she had met some really interesting people on the computer, but she didn't seem seriously interested in anyone. Still, things were different that summer, and Kelly couldn't ignore that. She and Steve had always enjoyed going to the houseboat with Jenn and the Corbins, but that didn't happen in the summer of 2004.

Worried, Kelly once asked Jenn if she was in love with the person she had met online.

"I haven't even met this person online!" Jenn said, avoiding a direct answer.

Kelly knew that Jenn had never cheated on Bart. "We had a girls' night out once," Kelly recalled, "and some guy really, really wanted her, but Jenn wasn't interested."

By 2004, it was painfully obvious to Jenn that Bart didn't love her, even though he expected her to be available to him whenever he wanted sex. And yet she was torn about Chris. Was she being fair to Dalton and Dillon? As hopeless as she felt about the likelihood that her marriage was salvageable, she wasn't willing to deprive her sons of a two-parent home, or to yank them out of the elementary school they loved, not to mention away from their friends.

If she did leave Bart, could they make it on their own? Jenn scribbled out budgets, and they only showed her that it would be very difficult for her to earn enough money for herself and the boys. She had no savings of her own, and Bart was parsimonious enough when they were living together. She doubted that he would agree to pay her child support or alimony without a huge court battle. He would consider it as paying for a dead horse.

When Jenn finally told Heather about Christopher in the late summer of 2004, Heather was surprised and concerned.

"Jenn," she said with exasperation, "you have no idea

who this guy is! He could be anybody, and you can't simply believe what he tells you. He might be married, for all you know—"

"Well, I'm married," Jenn cut in, "and I know he's divorced."

"How do you know?" Heather said. "He may be some weirdo pervert who's sneaking around on his wife. He may be sixty years old. Or an ex-convict. You don't even know for sure where he lives. For all you know, he's one of those Nigerian con men! You're taking everything on faith, and that isn't safe. Especially on the Internet!"

But Jenn would not be swayed. She was sure she knew who Christopher was through the emails he sent her every day now.

And now, several times a day.

Jenn made little pretense about how lonely she was in her marriage. And the gentleness and respect in Christopher's emails made her more aware that Bart made an effort to be nice to her only when he wanted something. She had put on a brave and cheerful face for too long. She talked to her co-worker Jennifer Rupured at the Sugar Hill Church preschool about how empty her marriage was, how abusive Bart was emotionally, and how much she wanted to be free of him, if only she could figure a way out that wouldn't hurt her boys. Her best friend, Juliet, knew too, as well as Kelly, and, of course, Heather. They were all pulling for Jenn to find happiness.

Sometimes, Jenn talked to her mother as well, although Narda was more likely to discourage her from making any sudden changes. She feared for Jenn if she stepped away from her marriage. It wouldn't be easy for a woman in her mid-thirties with two small boys.

On the afternoons Jenn wasn't teaching, she was usually in Lawrenceville, helping Narda with canvas orders at Lake Arts. Working for her mom, Jenn knew she could always be done in time to pick up Dalton and Dillon from school. And she liked being with Narda. But she still didn't make nearly enough money to support a family. Sometimes Narda paid her a salary, and often she bought things for Jenn or the boys—things that Bart wouldn't give her money for.

*　*　*

IT WAS PROBABLY INEVITABLE that the tone of the emails between Jenn and Christopher became a little more intimate each week until it was sometimes downright steamy. But they had never seen each other—not even a photograph, although Jenn continued to ask Christopher to send one. Finally, she sent him a picture of herself playing her guitar in a cowgirl costume she once wore in college, and a picture of Dalton and Dillon. She had gained some weight after Dillon's birth, but with running and dieting, her figure was now as slender as it was when she was in college. Christopher kept making excuses about why he hadn't gotten around to sending a photo of himself.

Couldn't they at least talk on the phone, Jenn asked? He promised that they would—soon. Anxious for Christopher to be more real to her than merely someone who sent emails, Jenn tried sending him some semi-emergency messages so he would phone her. He didn't call. And Jenn still didn't even know Christopher's last name. If he should ever disappear from her email inbox, she would probably lose him forever; she didn't know exactly where he lived, or his phone number. In a way, the fact that their relationship was so ephemeral made it more exciting, but it also kept Jenn off balance, fearful that it could all vanish in an instant.

On occasion, they had misunderstandings and one or the other would apologize. Once, on October 15, when Christopher felt he had been too demanding about a commitment from Jenn, he wrote regretfully, "Jennifer, nothing I can say will excuse my behavior last night. I am sorry and I promise I will let you go whenever you need to. I don't ever want to make you feel anything but good. I do know you love me and I know I am blessed for that."

Jenn wrote on October 18: "I love that you take your job seriously. I love that they [your bosses] scare you. I love that you were strong enough to run when you needed to, then moved them [his extended family] when you were strong enough to get them on their feet again. I love that you can go a little crazy with me but yet stay strong enough for both of us. I love that you always question me, making me think through for the truth in my answers. The bottom line is, Christopher, I am in love with everything about you. I would love to be yours to keep, and one day I will be. I understand it can't be now, but it's so hard when you want it so much. So we will both have our strong moments and some weak ones, too . . ."

Every day, Christopher asked Jenn to tell him what she was wearing; it would make her seem closer to him. So she dutifully described her outfits every day, even though they were mostly bland, serviceable clothes suitable for teaching preschoolers or cleaning her own house. Once, she told him about her short green nightgown, but more often she described jeans and sweaters.

On November 11, they exchanged numerous emails from morning to late at night. Christopher often sounded a bit like a character in a Harlequin novel as he declared his passion for Jenn, a man most women long to find—but suspect is not within the realm of possibility.

"Good morning, Sexy," he began. "Jennifer, have I told you I can't wait to make love to you? Damn, with every passing day, the growing sexual tension for you elevates to new levels I have never dreamed possible. You, my darling Jennifer, are a very amazing woman. I love you."

She answered in kind. "Christopher, I am madly in love with you, and you have changed me forever. You have taught me more in these past months than I have experienced in my lifetime. I want a lifetime exploring these new places with you."

Late in the afternoon, Jenn wrote to Chris that she was cleaning out closets, thinking of when she could walk out her front door, and be with him. It was understood that her sons would come with her, and Christopher often said he admired her for that.

Bart still wasn't home by 7:21 P.M. It would have been a time when she and Chris could have talked on the phone, but Christopher kept finding excuses why they couldn't do that. And he was still insisting that he wasn't good enough for her.

"Chris," Jenn wrote, "I hate that I can't just talk to you. I want to hear your voice, Chris. I'm sorry to be saying what I said I wouldn't do, [but] it just doesn't change the fact that I want it every day. Damn, I sometimes don't understand you. You have said a few times that you don't deserve me or something to that effect. Why Chris? What makes you so bad or me so good? For me, I would love to be attracted to you, but looks aren't everything. I want you to be attracted to me, but maybe you won't be. I think I look a lot different than anyone you have dated before. I'm not someone you would have seen and said, 'Damn! She's hot!' I'm not smart—not in the book sense, anyway. I struggled to get through high school. I did well in art school, but I didn't graduate. I didn't do so good in nursing school. By then, I had other things on my mind and I was tired of being in school. So, like you, I fell into the food service world. I loved my job—had lots of fun doing it. Not sure I want to go back into it though because of the long hours. And I'm selfish and want to be home with my children at night. I have decent street smarts, and a good sense of direction. I have lots of love in my heart, but so do you. So where is it that we are so different? I'm in love with you, Chris. And I already know who you are. Jenn."

But did she know? Really?

*   *   *

HEATHER CONTINUED TO WORRY. She knew that Jenn was naïve, much less savvy about the world than she was, even though Jenn was the older sister. Heather was the realist who thought the whole EverQuest game idea was silly and perhaps dangerous.

Bart sensed that their marriage was deteriorating— that their relationship had grown flat and perfunctory. Where Jenn had always tried cheer him up or calm him down when he was in a rage, she no longer even attempted to placate him, much less please him. And she would not sleep with him. That distressed Bart the most; he had always prided himself on being a good lover.

As the Corbins become more estranged, they often confided in their neighbors. Sometimes it would be Jenn who came over to the Comeaus for coffee or a drink, but more often it was Bart. He seemed to Kelly to be in the most pain, extremely anxious over the possibility that his marriage might be headed for divorce.

He seemed very lost. Kelly had always respected Bart, and she called him "Dr. Bart," rather than just plain "Bart."

"He was trying to save his marriage," she said. "It seemed as though he would do whatever it took to make it work."

Bart cried as he asked Kelly's advice, begging her to tell him what he should do "to make Jenn love me again."

*   *   *

HE WAS BESIDE HIMSELF. He went to his in-laws for backing, first approaching Heather, even though he knew that she would probably stick with Jenn. Then Bart appealed to Doug Tierney on a man-to-man basis. Doug was embarrassed, but he liked Bart well enough to feel sorry for him, and he tried to be available to at least talk to his brother-in-law. Still, they had never been close friends, and like many men, Doug wasn't comfortable listening to intimate details about someone else's marriage. He nonetheless saw that both Jenn and Bart were, in his estimation, "acting weird." They had both lost a lot of weight, particularly Bart. He said he'd lost sixty pounds, and it sure looked as if he had. Bart's clothes hung on him, and the fullness had vanished from his face, leaving him with the gaunt look of a man suffering from some fatal disease.

Beginning in August or September of 2004, Bart had avoided spending time with Jenn's family, and Doug found him quite distant.

Bart pulled out all the stops. He went to Narda, seeking her advice. He proposed taking Jenn on a trip in the hope that would help them reconcile, and find the love they'd once had. Narda agreed that might be a good idea, and suggested that Bart talk to Jenn about it.

"But she won't have sex with me," he complained. "I'm not going to take her on a trip if she won't sleep with me. Why would I waste my time and money? If I take her on vacation, she is going to have to have sex with me."

Narda was not a judgmental woman, nor was she a prude. She could understand that Bart missed having a sex life with her daughter, and at his urging she promised to talk to Jenn. She did—the next time she and Jenn were working in her studio.

Choosing her words carefully, Narda said she felt Bart was basically a good man, and that maybe it was Jenn's duty to stay with him. She had already told Bart he was putting too much pressure on Jenn, and asked him to lighten up, believing he would take her advice. Narda would regret her words later, but, at the time, she didn't know how sad her daughter really was. She just didn't want to see Jenn throw away the eight years she had invested in her marriage, especially when they had two wonderful little boys together. Narda asked Jenn if it was possible for her to work things out with Bart.

At this point, Narda knew that Jenn wrote regularly to Christopher, but she had no idea that their online relationship had progressed far beyond friendship. She gathered that Jenn was enjoying it a lot, but Jenn didn't talk about Christopher much to her mother because every time she did, Narda would caution her about starting even a pen-pal correspondence with someone she didn't know anything about.

"What is that guy's name, again?" Narda asked her once.

"Mom—don't worry about it," Jenn said.

"His name's Chris—that's it, isn't it?"

"You're not gonna contact him, are you?" Jenn asked suspiciously.

"Just leave it alone, Mom," Jenn said. "Don't worry about it."

*　*　*

NARDA DID WORRY ABOUT IT, and she felt Jenn would be a lot better off if she could just work things out with Bart. It was mid-November 2004, and the holidays were fast approaching when Narda tried once more to reason with Jenn about Bart. She urged her to at least try to work on her marriage. Bart might be a miser with his money, but she pointed out that he had increased Jenn's household allowance by quite a bit over the years. He was, after all, the boys' father. And even though he could be tough on them, Narda felt he loved them, and that he loved Jenn, too. Jenn acknowledged that part of her would always love Bart to some degree, because he was the father of her little boys. He had given her that much, "the most precious gifts of my life."

"He really loves you," Narda said, not totally believing her own words. "I think Bart really loves you."

But when Narda looked in her daughter's eyes, she saw no wavering there.

"He doesn't love me, Mom. You have to understand," Jenn said forcefully. "I just don't want to be married—to be there anymore. He disgusts me. He gives me the creeps.

He makes my skin crawl. I cannot bear to have a sexual relationship with him. I have tried so hard—but I cannot do it. I cannot bear to have him touch me at all. I just can't stand it."

And Narda recognized that her daughter's marriage was crumbling into so many pieces that it could never be mended.

"I don't know what to say—or what to do," Jenn told her. "You're just going to have to understand the fact that I'm leaving Bart."

It was obvious that Jenn was in the grip of major anxiety, and it wasn't about making the decision to leave her marriage. She was far beyond that. But she didn't know how she was going to make her life work with no financial support from Bart.

She wasn't giving up, Jenn said. But she was determined that she could do it without him.

"I have one credit card that he doesn't know about, but it has a pretty low limit. I know he won't let me stay in the house, but the boys need to stay in their school. I can get a small place, and I've already begun to buy a few things that we'll need."

Jenn said she had managed to save enough to put $2,000 in her private checking account; that was meant for first and last month's rent on an apartment. She knew she couldn't afford to rent a whole house.

And Narda knew that Bart still monitored Jenn's expenses. They still sat down every week and she had to explain how she had spent the money, so it hadn't been easy for her build a nest egg.

No longer the self-assured husband who had spent nine years cheating on her with other women, Bart was now clinging tightly to Jenn. He was a desperate man, a

Heather (left) and Jennifer Barber, ages five and nine. Close as kids, they would grow even closer as adults, with a solemn pledge that if either should die prematurely, the survivor would raise her sister's children.

The Barber family in the early 1980s. Thanksgiving was a favorite holiday—but their last Thanksgiving in 2004 was the precursor of tragedy. Left to right: Rajel, Heather, Max, Narda, and Jennifer.

1

Jennifer Barber, four, with the whole world ahead of her.

2

The Barber sisters, Christmas 1975: Rajel, Heather, and Jennifer. They grew up in a safe and friendly neighborhood in Lawrenceville, Georgia.

Jenn Barber, thirteen. She was in junior high in Lawrenceville while her future husband, Bart Corbin, twenty, was attending the University of Georgia in Athens.

Bart Corbin, twenty, in his prized yellow and white Chevy pickup at UGA. He was in love for the first time—with Shelly Mansfield.

Bart and Shelly Mansfield at Niagara Falls, New York, in 1984, as they boarded *The Maid of Mist*. They were visiting Shelly's parents, who found Bart a good choice for her, although Shelly herself had doubts.

Shelly Mansfield. She cared for Bart, her "sweet boy," but she had dreams of a career in journalism, and didn't want to be a dentist's wife. Bart was devastated when they broke up.

Dolly Hearn, five, in Washington, Georgia. She loved her family, pets, and holidays.

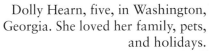

Dolly and her little brother, Carlton Jr., in the early 1970s in their yard in Washington.

Dolly and her father, Dr. Carlton Hearn Sr., at homecoming at Wilkes Academy. Later, she went to dental school so she could join her dad's practice in Washington.

Bart Corbin, twenty-five,
in 1988, at the Medical College
of Georgia Dental School in
Augusta, where he and Dolly
Hearn began to date.

Dolly Hearn, twenty-six, was popular, beautiful, kind, and much beloved
at the dental school. She and Bart Corbin had a tempestuous on-and-off
romance for years.

14

15

Dolly sits in the huge tree in the Hearns' yard. She often came home from college to be with her family.

Dolly leans against a pillar on her folks' front porch, sometime in the late 1980s.

16

Dolly's room in the Hearns' historic 150-year-old home.

The pine trees outside Dolly's apartment complex kept her front door in shadows even during the day. A stranger knocked on all four doors in this section in June 1990, perhaps checking to see who was home.

Dolly's beloved cat, Tabitha, age nineteen, who mysteriously disappeared from her apartment. Dolly was worried sick.

Dolly Hearn, 1990. A beautiful, young woman, happy
with her life, she was nonetheless often afraid of some
unseen presence in the dark outside her apartment
or beyond the lights on campus.

Dolly returned to Washington for her brother Gil's graduation from the Wilkes Academy, June 3, 1990. It was a happy occasion; Gil was valedictorian and their whole family planned a vacation at the ocean later that week. Left to Right: Carlton Jr., Dolly, Gil, Barbara, and Dr. Carlton Hearn Sr.

21

Her roommate came back to their apartment on June 6 and saw Dolly sitting silently on this couch. She thought Dolly was pulling one of her practical jokes—but, sadly, she wasn't. She was dead.

22

A female visitor earlier that day glimpsed a man hiding in the guest bathroom beneath these stairs. Later, she wondered if Dolly knew he was there.

23

A deputy moved this .38 revolver from where he first found it, making it impossible to reconstruct the crime scene exactly. It was Dolly's gun, given to her by her dad for protection.

Jenn Barber plays a bass guitar about the time she met Bart Corbin. She was tall, and lovely. He was handsome, witty, and fun to be with, and she fell in love with him.

Jenn and Bart's wedding
on September 1, 1996,
was everything she wished
for. With her mother, sisters,
grandmother, and niece.

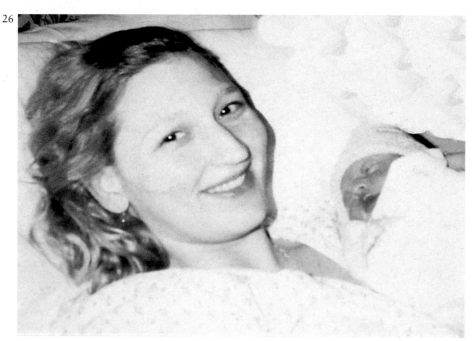

Jenn shortly after Dalton's birth. She was ecstatic when she gave birth
to Dalton. Two years later, she and Bart became parents of Dillon.

Bart pats Jenn's pregnant belly four months before she gave birth to Dillon.

March 1999. Heather holds Dalton (left) and Jenn holds Dillon
as they stand in Lake Arts, Narda's gallery.

Jenn with her two boys, whom she loved more than anything in the world. She didn't like this picture because she had put on weight, but she soon lost it.

Heather and Jenn just before Heather married Doug Tierney on December 30, 2000. They lived close to each other, and had coffee together most mornings.

Max, Narda, Bart, and Jenn raise a glass to toast the Barbers' anniversary.

32

Jenn and Bart with their two boys, about 2002, on a trip to the Atlantic Ocean.

33

Heather and Doug Tierney. Jenn's sister had a very happy marriage. Jenn was always welcome in their home.

Jenn and Bart enjoyed their lovely home on Bogan Gates Drive in Buford, Georgia, but Bart's practice wasn't doing as well financially as he had hoped.

Dr. Bart Corbin relaxes at home. Despite his calm demeanor, he could explode with anger in an instant. Jenn had grown used to it, but she worried for her boys.

Jenn (at center in Mrs. Claus's apron) oversees parents and children at the Sugar Hill Methodist Church preschool as they make Christmas angels.

Dalton Corbin tried to call 911 from the phone in his mother's bedroom, but the phone was dead—as was the phone in the dining room—so he ran across the street for help from his neighbors.

On December 4, 2004, the Gwinnett County patrol officers walked past the dining room and a half-decorated Christmas tree in the Corbins' foyer, and hoped that seven-year-old Dalton had only had a bad dream.

They continued down the hall where Jenn had kept a pictorial record of Dalton and Dillon from the time they were born.

Gwinnett County detectives stepped into the master bedroom, and observed the still form of Jenn Corbin, who lay across this four-poster bed. This room became the principal crime scene.

Gwinnett County Police homicide detective Marcus Head was in charge of the investigation of an apparent suicide in the house on Bogan Gates Drive. He had many unanswered questions about what had happened.

Experienced homicide detectives wondered how the old .38-caliber Smith & Wesson revolver could have ended up tucked under the comforter on the Corbins' bed. It did not jibe with the local newspapers' reports of suicide.

Sergeant Scott Peebles, left, and CSI blood pattern expert DeWayne Piper reopened the investigation into Dolly Hearn's death fourteen and a half years after her case was closed without answers. With modern forensic science and old-fashioned deductive reasoning, they finally solved Dolly's case.

Chief Deputy Richmond County DA Parks White and DA Danny Craig. They drew up an arrest warrant for Bart Corbin on December 22, 2004, on Corbin's forty-second birthday, charging him with the murder of Dolly Hearn.

DA Danny Porter (center) called for a grand jury investigation on the day of Jenn Corbin's funeral. He and his brilliant staff of attorneys and investigators, using high-tech methods, were determined to find the killer. From left: Senior Deputy DA Chuck Ross, Porter, and Investigator Russ Halcome.

Jack Burnette, center, the supervisor of twenty-three Gwinnett County DA's investigators, flanked by Jeff Lamphier and Mike Pearson. After almost two years of trying, they found a way to trace the deadly gun, which led to a shocking climax.

On December 23, 2004, Dr. Bart Corbin is led into the Richmond County Jail in shackles by Detective Don Bryant, charged with murder.

On December 16, 2005, Bruce Harvey, one of Bart Corbin's two top criminal defense attorneys, argues to Judge Carl C. Brown in an Augusta courtroom that charges against Bart in the death of Dolly Hearn should be dropped since "nothing had changed" in the fourteen-year-old case.

49

After almost a year in jail awaiting trial, Bart Corbin and his attorney David Wolfe listen intently to Judge Carl C. Brown in an Augusta courtroom on December 16, 2005.

50

Richmond County court officers lead Bart Corbin from a courtroom during a preliminary hearing.

Although there had still not been a trial in the death of their mother, Jenn Corbin's sons Dillon (left) and Dalton (right) hang a wreath in her honor in December 2005, in the atrium outside District Attorney Danny Porter's office.

Jenn's family on Wreath Day in December 2005. Doug and Heather were now raising Jenn's sons. Left to right, back row: Doug and Heather Tierney, Max and Narda Barber, Rajel Caldwell. Front row, left to right: Max and Sylvia Tierney, Dalton and Dillon Corbin.

53

Bart Corbin, gaunt and angry, stands alone in Judge Michael C.
Clark's courtroom in September 2006, as he waits for his trial
to begin at last.

54

Gwinnett County Superior Court Judge Michael C. Clark and attorney
Greg Lundy look over motions in the murder charges against Bart Corbin.
They expected almost anything—except what happened on September 15.

Bart Corbin stands at the defense table in Judge Michael C. Clark's Gwinnett County courtroom between his two defense attorneys: Bruce Harvey (left) and David Wolf. They were about to shock the gallery behind them.

Left to right: Max Barber (out of focus), Rajel Caldwell, and Heather Tierney fight tears as they sit in Judge Michael C. Clark's Gwinnett County courtroom. They had expected to attend Bart Corbin's trial in the murder of Jenn Corbin, their daughter and sister, for more than a month. And then, everything changed.

Left to right: Rajel Caldwell, Heather Tierney, and Max Barber (with Doug Tierney in right rear) stride from the Gwinnett County Justice Center on September 15, 2006.

Dolly's spirit, and the wonderful way she embraced life,
lives on. The scholarship in her name has helped dozens of
students become dentists. Members of her dental class
lobbied the Medical College of Georgia to award her a
degree posthumously. In June 2007, Dolly will become
Dr. Dolly.

Jenn Corbin, on a Caribbean cruise almost exactly one year before her murder, died on the verge of the new life she longed for. She will always be remembered smiling.

60

Barbara Hearn in October 2006.
She had the "GUILTY!" headlines
laminated and placed them on
Dolly's grave. Strangers covered
the grave with red roses,
both real and ceramic. Dolly
rests near her grandparents'
graves. And in the Hearns'
yard nearby, the Confederate
roses burst into bloom.

Dorothy Carlisle Hearn's grave.
She waited sixteen years, three
months, and nine days for justice.

61

dog in a manger with his paw clamped tightly over her—financially and emotionally, although not yet physically at least. He had never struck Jenn; he only demeaned her with words.

When Jenn tentatively brought up the subject of divorce, he seemed to have expected it. But he begged Jenn to stay in their house over Christmas. Couldn't they have one more Christmas as a family—something they all could remember? He argued that there was no rush about leaving, not after all the years they had been together. After New Year's, they could decide what they would do.

For the very first time in their relationship Bart apologized to Jenn and said he was sorry if he had hurt her. She stared back at him, shocked to hear him say he regretted the way he had treated her.

"You haven't been a very loving husband, Bart," Jenn said. She had nothing more to tell him. It was too late to change how she felt. If only he had apologized to her and promised to try harder years ago.

Now, Jenn agreed to stay with him over the holidays. It would give them both a short reprieve—two more months. She didn't know herself how she was going to manage, where she would go, how much money she would need, or if she could even get a full-time job.

*   *   *

THE LEAVES ON THE YOUNG TREES Jenn had planted changed to yellow and apricot, fell to the ground, and blew away, leaving the yard on Bogan Gates Drive looking forlorn. Jenn's garden turned fallow. She wondered where she would be in the spring when all her bulbs and flowers and trees bloomed again.

Only one thing kept a warm place in her heart, and a little bit of joy in her mind. She had Christopher. And it was possible that she and Christopher would find a way to be together, and that she might even find love again.

Christopher wrote that his mother was in the hospital and he didn't know when he could email her, much less make plans to fly to Atlanta for a meeting.

"When my mother ends up in the hospital, she is usually there for a week. To be able to be with her in the hospital is one of the reasons I quit my job. Jennifer, know that I love you and think of you all the time."

Christopher said he wouldn't be online, and he admitted something to Jenn; he had a girlfriend, but be quickly explained he was in the process of breaking up with her. Jenn felt guilty that she had put him in that position when she still didn't feel strong enough to walk away from Bart.

"It truly breaks my heart," Jenn wrote, "that I'm doing you more damage than good. I'm only trying to do what is right for my kids. It doesn't help that everyone here keeps telling me I have to work this out, that my life is going to be so hard if I go. My mom's scared that I'm gonna end up in a trailer. I'm just scared that I'm going to fail. I'm just trying to do what is right. I know that I will never be happy if I stay . . ."

And all the while Jenn was writing to Christopher, she was living her other life—making a cake for the Fall Festival Cake Walk at Harmony Elementary School, arranging for Dalton's bike rodeo in his Boy Scout troop, driving with her friend Juliet to take their boys to the north Georgia mountains to see the leaves change and to hike in the woods, making pies and casseroles and keeping her house immaculate. On Halloween, Jenn had taken her boys to a parade for the trick-or-treaters, and promised to help Heather move yet again.

In early November, Bart confronted Jenn and told her they needed to see a marriage counselor—something he had always resisted before. He also accused her of being addicted to EverQuest.

"He pretty much told me last night that we were done—again," she wrote to Christopher. "That we need to cut our losses, that he can't live with me and look at me every day if I don't love him. And what did I do—but give him a little small hope that maybe we can work this out. Why did I do this? It's not because I want to save my marriage, but more because of the kids, and I'm scared and want to wait until the school year is over."

As the days passed, Jenn was confused and torn apart by her conflicting emotions. How could she be fair to her sons, herself—and, yes, even to the husband who was suddenly begging her to stay with him after so many years of ignoring her? It was almost Thanksgiving, now. She had promised Bart she would stay until after New Year's Day. Maybe, for the boys, she should stay longer.

Increasingly she depended on Chris for emotional support, secure that he would be there for her. But then, on November 17, Chris virtually vanished from Jenn's Internet mail. She wondered if his mother's illness had become critical, or if he had been in an accident. If that happened, how would she know? Was there anyone in St. Louis who knew about her, who would call her?

In between cutting out pilgrim hats for her preschoolers' Thanksgiving play, she emailed Chris a dozen times, but he didn't answer. When Jenn clicked on, there were no new messages and no answers to her questions.

Jenn breathed a sigh of relief when Christopher's

email address finally turned up on her computer. But something was different. He seemed somehow removed, and responded to her only briefly, sidestepping her queries.

Jenn wasn't sure what she had done wrong, and she ended up in tears several times. The next day was worse. Chris was inexplicably drawing away from her. Without the Internet, their connection would be severed. And she couldn't bear it if that happened.

It was almost five on Thursday afternoon, and it was dark outside—one week to Thanksgiving—when Jenn wrote to Chris for the fourteenth time that day. "I keep hitting that brick wall. I feel you have come to know me better than anyone in my life—that I can tell you all my thoughts and secrets and I'm safe with you. I feel so safe when I'm with you, and yet I've never even laid eyes on you. Oh, Chris, don't you know how much we need to be able to see into each other's eyes, to hold that moment, and just look into each other's souls?"

There was no answer.

But sometime between 6 P.M. on Thursday, November 18, and 5 A.M. on Friday morning, Jenn Corbin learned why Chris had backed away from their correspondence and her insistence that they had to at least meet, or talk on the phone, or that he should send a photograph of himself. Jenn finally learned the truth about Christopher and she was shocked beyond belief.

Christopher wasn't married . . . or a convicted felon . . . or physically unattractive. He wasn't sixty years old. He wasn't an "Iranian ball-scratcher" as Heather had suggested, teasing Jenn. He wasn't anything at all.

There was no Christopher. There never had been. "Chris" was only a phony name used by someone who had good reason to be secretive. Jenn was absolutely stunned to discover that for months she had been writing to a woman. Not a man at all. Her last name was Hearn, a name that meant nothing to Jenn, because she had never known about Dolly Hearn.

And "Chris's" real first name was Anita. Anita Hearn. She was a bisexual who did live in Missouri and who apparently did take care of her sister's children—if, indeed, there were any children. The rest of the things she had told Jenn were partly true and partly false. Jenn found that out in a single email—one that she erased in her humiliation. An email that "Christopher/Anita" also destroyed.

At first Jenn was furious. It was a safer emotion than grief at her loss.

"GDI [God Damn It!]" Jenn wrote. "All I asked for was no lies, no games, and tell me your secrets. How could you? OMG [Oh My God] HOW COULD YOU? What is your name—and tell me the truth, or is this just another lie? Is this just another test 'cause I honestly don't know what to believe. Chris, Crystal, Christine—whoever. Don't you know how many times I have searched for your face in the crowd? How I stare at men's bodies to try to visualize what yours looks like? How many times I have heard you say my name, and how many times I have felt you pressed against my body? Damn you. I can't live this lie. It's killing me. I haven't slept yet. I can barely keep myself from breaking down in front of my kids.

"I even fell in love with the name Chris. I can't take it—I fell in love with Anita [instead]. I just don't know how you could do this to me. I trusted you with everything in me. How many times did I call you a man—or my shy boy? You have absolutely ripped my heart out."

Reading back over the emails on her computer, Jenn could see that "Chris" never spoke of possessing any male genitalia; the word *penis* or the slang *cock* could not be found in her emails. When their emails slid into sexual fantasies, "Chris" had never once responded to any discussion of male/female sexual intercourse, deftly avoiding that topic. Only now, in retrospect, Jenn realized that she had never noted this omission before.

Losing "Chris" was a crushing blow for Jenn Corbin. For months, she had been living in a fantasy—in love with someone she had always visualized to be a man. This was far worse than any of the warnings from her sister and her mother. She was cruelly disappointed. After existing for years in quiet desperation in a marriage without tenderness, she had grasped at what seemed to be her last chance.

And she had confessed her every private thought and hope to someone who wasn't at all what she believed "him" to be. She was angry, but most of all she was heartbroken at the loss of someone who never was.

"Guess I should have known you were too good to be true," she wrote. "Like you said last night, didn't I suspect anything? NO! I believed in you. Guess I should have known. I am an idiot!"

Chapter Twenty-One

November 2004

JENN'S HOPES LAY IN ASHES. There was nothing for her to look forward to. Bart was urging her to stay in their marriage, but he was still involved with Dara. Jenn had long accepted that her marriage was based on a fragile foundation that could crack and crumble any moment. And, finally, it had. Only now it didn't matter to her. She had no one at all to love, and Dara could have Bart.

The working balance in the Corbins' marriage had shifted. Jenn had been the first to bring up the subject of divorce. And that triggered a conditioned response in Bart. It was imperative that he be the one to walk away from a relationship with a woman. Gradually, with Jenn, he had lost control, and control was everything to him.

Jenn didn't tell her mother, her sister Heather, or her best friend Juliet that she had discovered "Chris" was really "Anita." She was too embarrassed to admit that they had been right all along; she had been deceived. They sensed something was wrong, but she couldn't bring herself to convey how devastated she was. She had kept the depth of her feelings for his virtual stranger secret. They had certainly known she was happy and excited about the new person in her life, but Jenn's love for Chris had been far more intense than anyone knew.

Jenn's family had seen for themselves how moody Bart could be, and observed traces of the rage that often smoldered just below the surface. Although they empathized greatly with her unhappiness, they still considered Bart a member of their family, albeit one who would move out of their close inner circle after the New Year. There had been so many happy times together, and all in all, their holidays together had been warm and serene.

Now they were all saddened to think that Jenn and Bart might actually get divorced, and that their little boys might grow up without both parents there for them. Bart had been with her family for every holiday since 1995. At least Jenn and Bart had agreed to celebrate the holidays as always—together. And perhaps it was still possible that they would make up their differences as they went through the family traditions.

But as Thanksgiving 2004 approached, Jenn confessed to her mother that she was sometimes afraid that Bart was capable of hurting her physically. She said he was so angry with her that he frightened her. But physical violence? No, that seemed impossible to Narda. She assured Jenn that, whatever she chose to do, she and Max would stand behind her. That was a given.

Jenn tried to act cheerful for Dalton and Dillon. She knew now why her "Sir Tank" had been so hesitant to come to Georgia, or send a photograph, or even call her on the phone. Heather and Narda had warned Jenn that she couldn't possibly know who a stranger she had met on the Internet really was, and she had brushed aside their qualms. Worried, Heather had done her best to find out who Christopher really was. She had searched the Internet, EverQuest, tried to find a phone number—but she never found him. From the beginning, Heather was afraid that Chris might harm Jenn. Now, she knew something was wrong—but she had no idea what Chris had done to make Jenn so unhappy.

*   *   *

IN 2004, Thanksgiving fell on November 25, and Heather and Doug Tierney were hosting dinner at their new house in Dawsonville. As always, Jenn and Bart and their boys were expected.

Jenn had a great deal on her mind, most of it dealing with her correspondence with Anita Hearn. She still wasn't clear about her feelings. She kept remembering Chris—as if he still existed somewhere in St. Louis, and might suddenly come forward and say, "It was all a joke." She had erased many of the thousand or more emails that had flown through the Internet between herself and "Christopher." She didn't want to leave them on the computer for fear that Bart might discover them and use them against her to prove to the court she was an unfit mother. Bart had warned her if she ever tried to leave him, that he would take her boys away from her.

Before they left for Heather and Doug's house Thanksgiving afternoon, Jenn placed some special emails she'd printed out and saved in her knitting-bag-sized purse. That seemed to her to be the safest place to hide them until she read them again to figure out what she should do, and to come to some kind of resolution. Only a week had passed, and her mind was jumbled with scenarios. But, above all, she didn't want Bart to read the emails. She took them with her as they left for the Tierneys' house, hooking her purse over the headrest of the driver's seat of their SUV.

Jenn drove, with Bart in the passenger seat. Dalton and Dillon sat in the backseat, excited about the holiday. As they were on their way, Jenn's cell phone rang. It was her mother, asking if they could stop at a store and pick up a turkey baster. She had looked all over Heather's kitchen and couldn't find one. It was probably still in the boxes that weren't unpacked yet.

"No problem—of course, we can," Jenn said. "We'll stop at the next store that's open. I think Kroger's is."

It was such an innocuous errand. While Bart waited in the SUV with the boys, Jenn ran into the supermarket and grabbed a turkey baster, waiting in line behind all the holiday shoppers buying last-minute items. She wasn't gone long, but as she slid back into the driver's seat, she could almost smell rage emanating from her husband. She wasn't sure what might have happened until she saw that Bart held her empty purse in his lap, its contents on the seat, the floor, and on him, too. He had dumped it all and found the very emails she had tried to hide from him.

Suspicious, Bart had begun to search the SUV the moment she left. He had opened her purse and rifled through it, pocketing her cell phone. With a sense of horror, Jenn realized that he must have read the emails from Anita Hearn. Without allowing herself to think of the ramifications of Bart's discovery, Jenn put the vehicle in gear and drove on to Heather's house, the blood roaring in her ears as she waited for an onslaught of accusations from Bart. He was so angry that it seemed as if the front seat was actually vibrating. Jenn was relieved to see the turn into Heather's neighborhood ahead.

Bart hadn't said a word to her. As soon as he walked through the door at the Heather's house, he headed for the bathroom and everyone in the house could hear him vomiting. When he finally came out, he was as pale as death itself.

It was a horrible afternoon. Besides their own family, some of Doug Tierney's relatives had also been invited for dinner, yet Bart made no effort to be civil to anyone. It was impossible not to notice that he was furious about something. He downed two bottles of wine, pacing back and forth in the basement, and then sat on the back deck, glowering. The more he drank, the blacker his mood became.

Usually, Bart would have spent time visiting with Max, and talking to Jenn's mother and sisters. But on this Thanksgiving he was avoiding everyone, and he looked like a thundercloud, his jaw clenched as he grew steadily more intoxicated.

They all sat down around the dining room table, and ate the turkey dinner, but their conversation sounded tinny and self-conscious, and they often lapsed into awkward silences. Dessert hadn't even been served when Bart stood up and announced that he was going home. He ordered Jenn and the boys to get their coats and get in the car. Dalton and Dillon pleaded to stay longer to play with their cousins, but Bart ignored them. Jenn had no time even to make apologies. She hurried after Bart.

They were no sooner outside than Bart began shouting at Jenn. Everyone inside could hear him.

"Slut!" he shouted at her. "Are you going to tell me what you've been doing on the Internet? What sordid little game have you been playing? You might as well tell me because you know I'm going to find out all about it."

White-faced, Jenn urged him to keep his voice down. She touched her finger to her lips in a "hushing" motion: "Not in front of the boys. We can talk about it when we get home."

As always, she tried to protect their children from seeing them argue. But this was far beyond an argument. She lifted the boys into the backseat and drove off, still begging Bart to lower his voice. When Bart saw her shake her finger at him, he erupted. He no longer cared if his sons heard him. When Jenn turned toward him, he hauled off and hit her square in the face. She was shocked; as cruel as some of his verbal taunts had become, he had never struck her.

"I never touched you," Bart sneered, anticipating that she would tell someone. "It's your word against mine."

Now the car was silent except for the sound of Dalton sobbing. Amazingly, through all of this Dillon had fallen asleep in the back seat. The boys had heard their father shout and swear before—but neither of them had ever seen him hit their mother. Jenn attempted to stifle her own tears, trying desperately not to scare Dalton any more than he already was. She watched the road ahead. It was dark out and visibility was poor. All she could think of was getting Dalton and Dillon home without anything worse happening. Bart was so out of control that she was afraid he might grab the wheel and send them plunging off the road.

Jenn was relieved when they finally pulled up into their own driveway. Bart stalked into the house, leaving Jenn to follow with the boys. She didn't try to talk to Bart until she had Dalton calmed down. Then Jenn called Heather and told her what had happened.

"Call Dad," Heather said.

Jenn did call her father, who urged her to grab the boys and what clothes she could, and drive back to Heather's house. He didn't think she would be safe if she stayed in her own house.

"Take the back roads," Max warned her. "Don't come the way you usually do, in case he decides to follow you."

Bart made calls, too, using his cell phone to call the Tierneys to explain his side of the fight. He spoke to Doug, and denied adamantly that he had hit Jenn, telling his brother-in-law that she was only being dramatic.

"She might get the boys to say they were witnesses," Bart complained. "But they're children. No one would believe them over me."

Bart had an explanation for what had happened. He said that Jenn had been trying to choke him, and he had hit her accidentally as he tried to get her hand off his throat.

Jenn's parents and sisters and their husbands had never known Bart to be any danger to her. But they had all been concerned from the moment he'd walked into the Tierney's home that afternoon. He had acted so strange all day. This was an ugly ending to Thanksgiving.

Jenn scrambled hurriedly to get pajamas for the boys. As she ran out to her SUV, Kelly Comeau called out, "Happy Thanksgiving!"

Kelly would remember that night. "Well, Happy Thanksgiving to you, Kelly," Jenn called back bleakly. "Bart just punched me in the face."

Kelly ran across the street and helped Jenn get the

boys in her car, and she drove off before Bart could stop her. Bart told Kelly, too, that Jenn had been trying to choke him and he'd had no choice but to try to get her hands off of him. He swore he hadn't meant to hit her.

Jenn drove the back roads as Max suggested but kept looking in the rearview mirror to see if he was following her. Fortunately, he was nowhere in sight. But they had passed through a safety barrier into a kind of insanity. And nothing would ever be the same again. As frightened as she was, Jenn Corbin had no idea what lay ahead.

*   *   *

IT TOOK QUITE A WHILE for Jenn to get Dalton and Dillon settled down for the night, at the Tierneys' house. Finally, exhausted, they dropped off to sleep. Jenn sat on the couch, talking quietly to Doug. She was very upset, but she seemed resolute that she was going to leave Bart. She told her brother-in-law how frightened Dalton had been when Bart hit her in the face, and that he had screamed and cried. Even Dillon, awakened when they got home, caught the panic of the moment.

Now, Jenn didn't seem afraid—only disappointed at the path her life was taking. She told Doug that she just didn't love Bart anymore.

Their marriage had been going downhill rapidly since midsummer, Jenn explained. Bart was jealous of the time she spent on the Internet, and increasingly suspicious. Their home life had become unbearable, Dalton and Dillon sensed the tension, and Jenn said she was finally at a place where she didn't want to try to patch up her tattered marriage. There was nothing left to save.

In fact, she confided that Bart had been sleeping upstairs in a bedroom next to the boys' room for a month. Jenn said she'd moved all his clothes up there to their guest room.

Feeling safe in Doug and Heather's house, Jenn finally relaxed enough to be able to sleep.

*   *   *

IN THE MORNING, the sun came out and nothing seemed quite as awful as it had the night before. Jenn told Heather that she was going back to her own house; she didn't want to have to sleep on someone else's couch or live in a tiny apartment. She felt she could figure out a way to make a new life with her sons. Despite her sister's misgivings, she packed up her boys and drove home.

In his business as a computer expert, Doug worked with a number of legal firms, and he gave Jenn the name of a divorce lawyer to call: Judy King. When Jenn replied that she had no money to pay an attorney, Doug told her that he would give her $5,000 to help with a divorce if she decided that was best.

Heather assured her sister that she could share their home. There was plenty of room in the new Dawsonville house that they'd moved into only two weeks before. The whole basement could be fixed up as an apartment. Even so, the Tierneys and the Barbers still hoped that there might be the possibility of a reconciliation between Bart and Jenn.

For the next six days, Bart went to his clinic, but returned home every night. Jenn kept up her part-time job at the Sugar Hill church preschool, and she saw to it that their house was as neat as always. The family ate dinner together each night, but mealtimes were stressful, with

Bart and Jenn usually exchanging harsh words. Most things rolled off Dillon's back, but Dalton had become Jenn's shadow, with his eyes darting constantly between his father and mother; he was only seven, but he took on the job of protecting his mother. As frightened as he was of his father, Dalton had become a small but stubborn force. He would not allow anyone to hurt her—not even his father. That annoyed Bart even more.

Bart was now his own private eye. He was obsessed with discovering everything he could about Jenn's life. He stole her cell phone from her purse and methodically called every number listed in its directory, hoping to connect with the "Chris" in Jenn's emails.

Most of the calls he made connected him to someone he knew, and he made excuses for why he'd phoned—usually telling people he was "reprogramming Jenn's phone for her."

"He even called me at work," Narda said, "and he felt kind of foolish when he realized he'd dialed one of my numbers."

*   *   *

WHEN BART GOT A NUMBER that rang and rang without an answer, he jotted it down and kept calling.

In between checking on Jenn's secret life, Bart called friends and relatives to learn what he could. He phoned Heather, wanting to talk about Jenn. "She just wants my money," he complained. "I've done nothing wrong."

Heather thought that was classic Bart; with him, it was always money, money, money.

"Bart. You punched Jenn in the face—and Dalton saw it."

"Yes," he argued, "but I didn't hit her hard."

"I saw how red her face was," Heather snapped.

When he realized that Heather wasn't on his side, Bart switched tactics and began to call Doug Tierney more often. He acted now as if Doug were his close buddy, and he expected his brother-in-law would pass on any information about Jenn. Bart also consulted Doug as a computer expert.

"He wanted to know where he could take the hard drive in the computer that Jenn had used," Doug recalled. "He was looking for all the emails she had written or received."

Doug did his best to avoid referring Bart to a technician who could do that, but as Bart kept hounding him, he finally mumbled the name of a small firm in Norcross, Georgia. Doug hoped Bart wouldn't pursue his almost pathological curiosity. But Bart was fanatical as he tracked Jenn's every movement.

*   *   *

BART CONTACTED A NUMBER of people he had met during his marriage, and a very few he knew before he met Jenn. He was building an increasingly complicated network of those who had the potential to help him unveil all of her secrets.

One couple—Jenn Grossman and her husband, Rob—had considered themselves close friends of Jenn and Bart Corbin for more than five years. In 1999, Rob Grossman had a satellite-dish company and he installed one at the Corbin home. Rob and Bart quickly became friends, and they soon bartered back and forth, with Bart providing dental care to the Grossmans in exchange for satellite dishes on his houseboat and in his dental offices. The two Jenns got along well, too, and the couples started spending time together on a regular basis, having dinner at one another's house and going out to restaurants on birthdays and holidays.

As for Jenn and Bart's relationship, it seemed like a typical happy marriage to Rob and Jenn. Certainly, they never fought or argued in front of the Grossmans.

Jenn gave Jennifer Grossman the baby clothes and equipment that she'd saved after Dillon's birth. With Bart's vasectomy, she knew there would be no more babies for her.

Jenn Grossman had noticed that Bart swore a lot when he was working on her teeth, but thought he was simply more relaxed around her and Rob because they were personal friends. In the fall of 2004, they had a falling out with Bart regarding a dental bill, and stopped talking, although the Grossmans assumed that sooner or later, they would work it out.

To his dismay, Max Barber had inadvertently revealed information to Bart about an item on the Corbins' credit record. Despite his financial problems, Bart didn't hesitate to spend money on things he wanted. In the fall of 2004, he bought himself a classic 1978 yellow Mustang convertible, and, as always, he had gone to Max to handle the sale. What Max didn't know was that, unbeknownst to Bart, Jenn had taken out a single credit card in her name alone. The card had only a $2,000 limit. It showed up on the couple's joint marital credit record and Bart's finger stopped as he traced down his family's report.

For a man who demanded that his wife account for every item on her grocery list, the information about a credit card he didn't recognize had to have been jolting.

"This is a mistake," Bart said. "It isn't mine."

He asked Max to check to see if the surprise credit card had incurred a legitimate debt. Unaware that he was giving away his daughter's secret, Max ran the card through again, and told Bart that the charge was accurate.

Max could read Bart's reaction as if a lightbulb had gone on over his head. He started to speak, but his son-in-law was already dashing out the door.

Jenn hadn't bought anything even vaguely incriminating with the card, only household items. But they were duplicates of things that already existed in the house on Bogan Gates Drive. On Monday, November 29, when Jenn arrived in Lawrenceville to work with Narda, she asked her mother if she could store some things in the Lake Arts warehouse.

"She had wiped out the balance on that credit card," Narda recalled. "She backed her car around and unloaded things she thought she and the boys would need if they had to leave their home: towels, dinnerware, salt and pepper shakers, a vacuum cleaner, even Band-Aids and aspirin tablets—just the very basic stuff she might need to set up a house. I don't know where Jenn planned to go—maybe she didn't either. She had taken a $500 cash advance from that card—that's about all. She knew that she was welcome with Max and me, and with Heather and Doug, but we all lived in a different school district, and she didn't want to take the boys out of their school."

Bart continued to call every number stored on Jenn's cell phone, trying to find out whom she might be talking to that he didn't know about. Once Anita had confessed her real identity to Jenn, they had exchanged phone numbers, although Jenn wasn't sure what, if anything, would happen in their future. When Bart stole Jenn's cell phone on

Thanksgiving Day, Anita's number was in it—albeit without a name. Jenn alerted Anita not to answer any calls from numbers she didn't recognize or blocked numbers— just in case.

On Tuesday, November 30, Bart took the hard drive from his Hewlett-Packard computer into ACR Data Recovery Inc. in Norcross, and asked the technician there to pull out all of the information possible on emails that had been sent to and from his wife.

He was determined to unearth everything he could about Jenn's secrets, and it seemed he was only a few steps behind her.

Jenn was living day to day, fearful enough that she was prepared to run if she had to, but still ambivalent. Would Bart really hurt her? Before he hit her on Thanksgiving, she would have said absolutely not. Now, she wasn't so sure.

She had never found her cell phone, so she arranged to get a replacement for the one Bart had stolen from her purse. Jenn needed the security of having a phone of her own at all times. She replaced the journal that was missing, too, but kept it with her always.

Judy King, the divorce attorney Doug had recommended, explained to Jenn that, if at all possible, she should not move out of the house. If she left, that could be construed as "abandonment," and it would give Bart a stronger case. He could claim that Jenn had deserted him. Bart had told Jenn that he didn't want a divorce, but if she went ahead with her threat to file, he intended to go for full custody of Dalton and Dillon, and he would keep the Bogan Gates Drive house, too.

Jenn's teaching job at the preschool would barely support them, and she was already looking for a full-time job.

She had applied at the Harmony School where the boys attended. Jenn didn't want to argue over money, but she suspected Bart would fight her all the way.

Jenn felt suspended between the life she no longer trusted and the life she had longed for with Chris. All of her hopes had vanished like smoke in a sudden gust of wind. She would stay with Bart at least over Christmas, no matter how uncomfortable it might be.

Surely she could make it through until 2005.

*   *   *

JENN WAS TORN by aching indecision. Although she knew intellectually that there was no Christopher and never had been, she was unable to let go emotionally of the mind-picture she still had of him. He wasn't real, but he still existed for her.

Chris—Anita—Hearn had fashioned her emails so that Jenn would believe they were on the same wavelength as far as their interests and concerns. Anita sounded as if she was as devoted to "her sister's children" as Jenn was to Dalton and Dillon. She had written about taking care of her ill mother, and she was seeking to live a life with someone who was kind and gentle. Although Anita had carried out what many people would consider a cruel hoax, Jenn found it in her heart to forgive her.

She told her mother and sister only that she hoped to meet "the person" she had met online in person. She would deal with the dicier truth about who Anita really was later.

Part of Jenn Corbin still loved someone who was, in truth, neither Chris nor Anita but rather a figment of a desperate imagination. As she was going through the chaos of living with an enraged Bart, Jenn started answering the messages that Anita still sent her. She still had a friend. She even considered Anita's suggestion that they might share a home together as they struggled to raise their children.

Cautiously, they started exchanging emails again, sometimes as often as before. The New Year would come in a few weeks, and Jenn didn't know what she was going to do or where she would be living. And so she continued to stockpile household items in her mother's warehouse and to write to Anita in Missouri when Bart wasn't around.

And Bart continued his fanatical exploration into every corner of Jenn's private world. He would not allow another woman to leave him. It did not matter that he had emotionally abandoned her years earlier. He was a man on fire.

Chapter Twenty-Two

December 2004

Jenn had once mused to her sister that there might be things about Bart she didn't know. And, of course, there were many. Jenn might have known that Bart once dated another dental student, but she certainly didn't know that woman had "committed suicide," and she had never heard her name. So she could not have imagined his shock when he received the report that the hard drive he took in to be examined had emails from someone named Hearn. He had also gleaned a phone number for that person in Missouri, but his calls to that number were never answered. He had relegated Dolly to the past—but now her family name was surfacing in his life again.

* * *

FIVE DAYS AFTER THANKSGIVING, on the Wednesday morning of December 1, just before 6 A.M., the war of the Corbins escalated once more. Jenn was in their recreation room running her usual mile on her treadmill, and she assumed Bart was upstairs taking his shower. But when she walked into the master bedroom, she saw her purse lying on the floor, its contents once again strewn all over. When she checked to see if anything was missing, she saw that her new cell phone, new journal, and her only credit card were gone.

Now, she was angry. She confronted Bart as he walked from the bathroom wrapping a towel around his waist.

"You were in my purse again!" Jenn said accusingly. "You took my phone and I want it back."

"I have no idea what you're talking about," he said dismissively, and brushed by her.

"I want what you took out of my purse," Jenn demanded.

Bart walked out of the room, ran down the stairs, and jumped into his yellow convertible. He was virtually naked—wearing nothing but the bath towel.

Jenn could see that he was out of control.

"Bart," she warned, grabbing a cordless phone, "stop! I'm calling the police. Please don't make me do this!"

He ignored her. Jenn punched 911. Bart had no business being out on the road nearly nude. As angry as he was, he might kill somebody. With the phone in hand, she followed him out to the driveway, and stood behind his Mustang to stop him from leaving. Although Bart's behavior had become increasingly bizarre, she had never seen him quite like this.

Jenn didn't want a public fight—a "scene." She had tried throughout her marriage to avoid that. There had to be a way for them to split up with the least damage possible, but this certainly wasn't it. By now Dalton and Dillon were awake and crouched inside the door, watching with horrified looks on their faces.

Jenn planted her bare feet firmly on the driveway as Bart steadily backed the car toward her. She was talking to the 911 operator, asking for a patrol car to come by. Jenn fully expected Bart to stop, but he kept coming. At the last moment, she tried to jump clear, but it was too late. She was still on the phone when Bart deliberately backed over her foot and drove off.

"Husband taking off with her personal belongings," the 911 dispatcher radioed. "Vehicle is '78 yellow Mustang . . . Hear female screaming—think I hear child crying in the background. He took shotgun out of the house—she doesn't know where gun is now . . ."

Jenn gasped that she had been run over.

"Officers are on their way, Ma'am," the dispatcher said. "Are you hurt badly?"

"I don't know," Jenn said. "I'm not sure."

While she waited for the police, Jenn called Narda. Then she called Heather. Jenn was crying hysterically, something that was completely out of character for her. Heather couldn't believe it—Jenn was always the one who took charge, calmed people down, and made everyone feel better. Finally, Jenn calmed down enough to tell her sister that Bart had just deliberately run over her. No wonder that Jenn herself was in shock, injured, and stunned by Bart's behavior. Heather could hear Dalton and Dillon in the background, and they were crying loudly, too.

When the Gwinnett County patrolmen pulled up a few minutes later, they saw the bruise blooming on Jennifer Corbin's foot, and took her to the emergency room.

Although the injury to the soft tissues was painful, the X-rays revealed no broken bones in her foot.

Although Jenn was the one who had asked for a divorce four days earlier, Bart had already sought out an attorney and filed for divorce on November 29. Bart had instructed his attorney to file a petition seeking the divorce, preempting Jenn.

He wanted everything: the house, the furniture, full custody of Dalton and Dillon, his attorney's fees, and a restraining order against Jenn. The only thing he was willing to split was responsibility for any marital debts. In his view, she should pay half of those.

Bart had also set about liquidating their bank accounts, and doing whatever he could to block Jenn from getting any more of what he considered his money. He took the largest cash advance he could on his main credit card—almost $40,000. Not only was he protecting his assets, he wanted to make if financially impossible for her to leave him. He remained unaware of the preparations she had made for her new life. Jenn had moved a few more things to her mother's warehouse: lamps, flatware, a new medicine chest. None of it was expensive. Actually, it was quite utilitarian.

When Bart returned home after he'd run over Jenn's foot, he found the house empty. Jenn and their sons were gone. She had taken enough clothes for herself and the boys to be away for a while. They had gone back to Heather and Doug's house.

Bart was not arrested for assault; Jenn had declined to press charges, feeling it would just lead to more trouble.

Jenn told her sister that Bart had been harassing her constantly about the "person" she had written to online.

"Heather," Jenn said with a sigh, "all this person has

done is show me that I don't have to be unhappy—that there could be a better life out there."

Bart was on the phone constantly now—to Doug, and to Heather. He alternately begged for help to get his wife to come back to him, and expressed scorn that she would even try to leave him. "I'm going to make sure that she gets absolutely nothing," he said. "I don't know where she thinks she's going to get the money to divorce me."

"Well, Bart," Heather finally said. "I guess she's going to get it from us."

Annoyed, Bart didn't try to talk further to his sister-in-law; she was clearly on "Jenn's side." But he continued to call Doug for advice. Finally, Doug explained to Bart that he didn't feel comfortable talking to him any longer since Bart's conversation had changed from asking how he could mend his broken marriage to questions that were obviously phrased to gain private information about Jenn.

"Heather doesn't think it's a good idea for me to talk with you about Jenn anymore," Doug said. "And I have to agree with her."

After Jenn went to work, Heather phoned Bart's brother Bobby. She was worried now about what Bart might be capable of, and she asked Bobby how he thought Bart was doing.

"Well, I've seen him a whole lot happier." Bobby said.

"Do you know that Dalton told us that he is afraid his daddy is going to kill his mom?"

Bobby Corbin drew his breath in sharply, and Heather could tell he was shocked. She explained how Dalton would not leave Jenn's side, and that he continually voiced his fear of what his father might do. Running over Jenn and racing off in nothing but a bath towel weren't exactly the actions of a rational man. The boys had witnessed all of that.

Heather recognized that Bart needed someone to talk to, and she and Doug just couldn't do that anymore, not after what Bart had done to her sister. Even so, there was something pathetic about her estranged brother-in-law, and she urged Bobby to get in touch with Bart.

Bobby said he was already trying to spend time with Bart. He thought Bart was also talking with some of his male friends, including Kevin Lyttle, who was the man they called "Iron"—both because he worked at an iron works, and because he was one of the more muscular men at BodyPlex, the gym where Bart worked out each morning. Brian Fox was another friend of Bart's. Like most of the men Bart knew, Kevin and Brian weren't his close pals but they could see he was having a rough time and were attempting to bond the way males do—drinking beer and watching football, usually at the Wild Wing Cafe in Suwanee.

While Heather had voiced her fears to Bobby, Narda called Bart's mother, Connie, to tell her about what Dalton had been saying. Narda was so frightened for Jenn that she found herself in tears as she spoke to Connie Corbin, but she met with a blank wall. Connie said she wasn't going to interfere. "I tried that before," she said succinctly, "and I was told to mind my own business."

Narda didn't know what "before" meant. Bart hadn't been married before; perhaps she was speaking of his twin, Brad, who had divorced. At any rate Connie gave no credence to Dalton's warning that his father was going to kill his mother.

Narda and Heather tried to convince themselves that Dalton's fears were groundless. He was a very worried little boy, but he was only seven, after all, and he'd seen too much arguing and violence in the last week.

Dalton refused to play with Dillon or his younger cousins, Max and Sylvia; he wanted to be right next to Jenn constantly, as if he could protect her from anyone who might try to hurt her. Jenn wasn't that worried. She explained to Heather that no matter how angry Bart might be with her, he would never seriously harm her. "He wouldn't do something so devastating to his own children," she told Heather. "Even for Bart, that's unthinkable."

"I wish you were still in my neighborhood," Jenn added. If only Heather hadn't moved to Dawsonville, she and Doug would still be in the same school district as the Corbins and she could take Dalton and Dillon to school. Then it would have been easier for Jenn to get a full-time job.

Almost certainly, Jenn's boys would adjust to a different school if they had to; Max and Narda had moved many times and their girls had been fine. But Jenn had always been the kind of mother who wanted her sons to have as perfect a childhood as she could provide.

* * *

ADVENT CALENDARS HUNG in homes and churches, their little doors opening as the days wound down toward Christmas. Jenn carried out the holiday activities she had planned for the youngsters at the Sugar Hill church preschool, helping them make presents for their parents.

On December 2, she and her boys were still safely ensconced at Heather's. Doug and Heather took turns talking with Jenn, listening to her plans to "just get through the holidays." Their home was a kind of oasis for her, and they urged her to stay. Seeing her sister wrapped in her old pink flannel robe made Heather feel as though, somehow, she could always keep her safe.

"I gotta go home, you know," Jenn told her.

"I don't want you to go back there."

"Heather, no. I have to. If I don't go back, he's going to take my house."

The sisters were both emotionally drained. They had talked about problems, solutions, new starts, closed doors that could never be opened again, what Bart might or might not do, and they had kept assuring each other that everything would work out for the best.

Heather and Doug Tierney had virtually put their lives on hold so they could help Jenn. They didn't want her to move home, but they needed a little "time out" from her marital problems so they could concentrate on their own family. The last few weeks had been so up and down and disturbing. Maybe Jenn was right about going home. It was a moot point, anyway. Once she made up her mind, there was no talking her out of it, and she was determined to go back to Bogan Gates Drive and finish decorating her Christmas tree.

Even though Bart seemed to grow angrier and more hyper every day, she was no longer afraid of him. As long as he didn't try to have sex with her, she thought they could get along in the same house. She had suggested he live on their houseboat until he found an apartment, but he complained that it would be too cold there at that time of year, and she relented.

Jenn had confided in her sister that she felt she had never loved Bart and never had a satisfactory sex life with him. He cared only about his own sexual drive and didn't bother with foreplay or romance. "Heather," she once said, "when he touches me, I just shiver and go 'ewwww' inside."

Heather didn't know how to respond to that. It broke her heart that her sister who had always been the one who was "so comfortable to be around, who made people feel good, who was kind and nonjudgmental" could be this unhappy.

At 9 A.M. on that Thursday, December 2, Heather watched Jenn drive away. Thinking they would talk later, Heather turned to catch up on the chores she still had to do to settle into their new house. She and Jenn would have time to get together, drink coffee as they always did, and work things out.

*   *   *

IN THESE EARLY DECEMBER DAYS, Bart was usually in his dental offices, although moving his clinic to Hamilton Mill wasn't drawing enough patients to keep it afloat financially. He was gone somewhere most nights after they ate supper—probably out drinking beer with his brother or his friends. Both Jenn and Bart had their own lives now. Most of the time, she didn't know, or care, where he was.

One discovery, though, had puzzled her. When she was doing the laundry, she had found a parking lot stub in the pocket of one of his shirts. It looked to be from a library in Birmingham, Alabama, and it was stamped November 29. Bart had apparently made a quick trip there a few days earlier. She had no idea what for. Jenn mentioned it to her good friends, Juliet Styles and Jennifer Rupured. The drive to Birmingham and back would have taken him more than six hours.

She was only vaguely curious, just enough to tell her friends and then forget about it. Jenn's biggest concern was the same as it always had been—that her sons were doing okay. She hoped she could keep Bart from yelling at them. Sometimes she wondered if she could ever find a way to undo the negative effect he had on Dalton.

*   *   *

ALTHOUGH BART RESENTED that Heather and Doug were supporting Jenn as she pulled away from him, he made one more phone call to Heather on Friday morning, December 3. "He kept asking me about why Jenn wasn't with him," Heather said, "and was she going to get a divorce? He kept saying he didn't really want a divorce. He wanted to work it out with her.

"And then he said, 'I can't change who I am. I'm going to do what I have to do to protect myself—and I should have been doing it all along.' "

That was odd, Heather thought. He had *always* protected himself. She knew that a year earlier, when he was besieged by creditors, Bart had put all of his assets in Jenn's name. And it was the third time he'd done that. They had barely any equity in their house—Bart had taken out a second mortgage. The juggling he had done, "robbing Peter to pay Paul," according to his in-laws, was about to catch up with him because he refused to compromise on what he needed or wanted. Sure that he could trust Jenn, he made her responsible when his debts were called in. Now that he realized she was about to leave, he had taken back what he considered his, emptying his accounts of all the liquid cash he could take out, putting everything back in his name.

On that Friday, Jenn was scheduled to work with

Narda. But first, she had a meeting with Angie Smith, who was president of the PTA at Harmony School; when she applied at Harmony, she had been encouraged to hear that she more than met their requirements.

Smith found her cheerful and upbeat. "Like a woman looking forward to her future."

When Jenn arrived at her mother's warehouse a little later, Narda saw that she was very happy, optimistic and positive about her life. Jenn had been to Target and spent almost $500. She had loaded up her SUV with her final purchases for her new home, wherever that was going to be. She was smiling as she stacked packages in the empty cupboards of Narda's warehouse.

It was great to see Jenn so happy. Narda was planning to meet a couple of her women friends that evening for drinks and dinner and she asked Jenn to come along, but Jenn said she couldn't; Dalton and Dillon had basketball games, and they wanted her to take them. Dalton was still saying to anyone who would listen, "Daddy's going to kill Mommy," and he didn't want to go anywhere with Bart.

It was disturbing to hear Dalton talk like that, but Narda and Jenn agreed it was a phase. Earlier that afternoon, Bart had insisted on taking Dalton to the park to ride his bicycle, and that hadn't turned out at all well. Dalton had stopped at a curb to wait for a car to go by, and apparently Bart had shouted at him, *"Go!"* He had come home very upset, saying his daddy tried to push him in front of a car.

Jenn had always told her sister and her mother that she would never keep Bart from seeing his sons after they were divorced. He was, after all, their father. But she still wanted to be sure that Bart stopped shouting at Dalton, and belittling him. That was something they would definitely have to work out. But she didn't believe that he would hurt their children.

Narda would remember watching Jenn back out of her driveway. "She was smiling, and she was going to Starbucks to get a Caramel Macchiatto and say hi to Rajel's son, Joey, who worked there. I didn't even hug her goodbye."

December 3 was the first day in months that Heather and Jenn hadn't talked—not even on the phone. "I was exhausted," Heather would remember, her voice full of tears. "Jenn's troubles were occupying so much of my time. I needed a break, and I didn't call her. The last time I saw her was the morning before when she left my house, and I couldn't stop her. I guess it was like giving a drunk driver car keys."

And yet, Jenn hoped that she and Bart could just get through Christmas. They were so close to going their separate ways. Only three more weeks.

It was Friday night, December 3, 2004.

PART FIVE

The Investigation

GWINNETT COUNTY

Chapter Twenty-Three

December 4–10, 2004

EVEN AS HER FAMILY was bracing for her funeral, the probe into Jenn's death was widening. Investigators had learned early on that the last few weeks of her life had been marked by dissension and shocking revelations. They knew that her mother had seen her on the late afternoon of Friday, December 3, and, according to seven-year-old Dalton Corbin, that the couple had eaten together with the kids in their home on Friday evening. Dalton, who was a very intelligent little boy, related that his father had gone out somewhere. He and his brother had watched television and gone to bed. They hadn't heard anything during the night and slept peacefully until Saturday morning when Dalton discovered his mother dead in her bed.

It was vital now for detectives to find the locations of people who were part of Jenn's life at the time she died.

They knew that she had been emailing and phoning someone in a suburb of St. Louis, Missouri—someone that
even those closest to her had never seen. Actually, as far
as anyone knew, Jenn herself had never seen this person
who might be named "Christopher Hearn," or was possibly named "Anita Hearn." No one close to Jenn Corbin
could say absolutely whether this person was, in actuality,
a male or a female. Jenn had been secretive about her email
correspondent—even with her sister. Was it possible that
Jenn had been set up by a deadly con artist who had traveled to Georgia to harm her? It seemed outlandish, but
then so did the idea that she had become so involved with
a stranger.

Jenn and Bart had been locked in an ugly divorce and
custody battle, so it was also very important to know
where Bart Corbin had been in the early morning hours of
December 4.

And there was another woman in the picture—Bart
had had at least one mistress since before he was married
to Jenn. Dara Prentice had apparently loved him for more
than nine years, and the only obstacle between Dara and
Bart had been Jenn. However, Dara didn't seem to be a
likely suspect; if she wanted Bart and was privy to most of
the details about his personal life, she would have known
that he was soon to be divorced. She wouldn't have had to
kill her lover's wife so she could have him.

It appeared that Jenn had no real enemies. Her killing
might have been a random thing. Perhaps she had wakened to find a burglar in her home—and been shot when
she surprised him. She was a striking woman whom men
noticed. Although her sisters and her closest friends didn't
recall that she had spoken of being harassed or stalked by
a man, Jenn herself might not have realized that someone

was watching her and waiting for a time when her husband wasn't home.

Steve Comeau had heard a truck coming down their street early Saturday morning—during the period that Medical Examiner Dr. Carol Terry estimated as Jenn's time of death. He was quite sure that he had recognized the familiar sound of Bart's pickup truck as it slowed and turned into the Corbin's driveway close to 2 A.M. But Steve hadn't actually *seen* either Bart or the truck. He could testify only to an almost subconscious impression—not as an eyewitness.

Marcus Head, leading the Gwinnett County Police Department's detectives in the investigation, and Gwinnett County District Attorney Danny Porter needed to follow up all possibilities and refuse to allow themselves to be locked into any one theory on who the killer they sought might be.

Most of the public still believed that Jenn Corbin had committed suicide, but insiders knew that the physical evidence gleaned from the shooting scene made that the least likely cause of her death.

The police detectives and the two dozen DA's investigators working on various aspects of the Corbin case were very different from one another, a diversity that had worked well for them in case after case.

Danny Porter ran a remarkable district attorney's office. He was that rare prosecutor with virtually no need for ego gratification or desire to take sole credit for the cases he had successfully prosecuted—and there were many. Having won four elections, and in his fourteenth year as Gwinnett County's DA, Porter was just as happy to have his assistant DAs and investigators appear in the media—perhaps more so—than he was to garner publicity for himself. While he dressed impeccably in the courtroom, Porter usually wore cargo pants and sports shirts around his office. He was handsome in a "Humphrey Bogart" kind of way, and he spoke in a deep, growly voice. He often taught courses for cops. Once a group of deputies waiting to hear a lecture by a highly regarded district attorney didn't recognize him when he hopped out of his beat-up 1970 Land Cruiser, dressed in his preferred garb. They thought he was someone who had fallen on hard times.

That Toyota Land Cruiser, an FJ-55, was both Porter's hobby and his passion. He spent weeks in an auto mechanic course and fixed its innards before he bothered with cosmetic details.

Porter's road to become one of the outstanding DAs in the state of Georgia was as dissimilar from the usual approach as his vehicles and clothing were. His father rose from being a TV antenna installer to top management in the Space Control program, and during those years the family lived in Utica, New York, in the Bahamas, in Florida, and eventually in Atlanta. During the elder Porter's offshore assignments, there were no accredited schools, but Danny Porter read constantly, and, back on the mainland, he was always ahead of his class. He began college at the University of Georgia majoring in architecture and ended up in law school—which he hated.

"Lawyers should solve problems," he commented. "Law school wants you to think in a circular pattern."

Porter became a Gwinnett County assistant district attorney on September 8, 1981. Early on, one of his main concerns was for victims of crime and their families. Jack Burnette, Porter's right hand, who supervised the twenty-three investigators in the District Attorney's Office, had Porter's support from the beginning. "Danny has a little cop inside screaming to get out," Burnette commented. Porter prosecuted some of the more bizarre cases in the South. His first homicide scene was in a pet store where exotic birds flapped overhead.

Often, Porter had to take his small son, Kyle, with him when he was called out to a murder scene. "Jack took care of Kyle for me. And he held ladders for me while I clambered over cold roofs in the dark."

"Each case had its own twists," Porter recalled. Some of the "twists" involved threats against his own life. A school bus driver was once furious when a search warrant of his home produced 150 guns, and Porter ordered them all destroyed. The berserk man threatened to cut Porter's throat.

"Luckily, he was wearing a GPS monitor," Porter recalled, "on the night they tracked him to within three miles of my house."

Never concerned for himself, the DA worried continually about his family. In 1992, Porter successfully prosecuted one of the first murder cases in Georgia where no body was ever found. Later, while most of America was watching the O. J. Simpson trial, Danny Porter was in court on the kind of case any prosecutor dreads—a homicide involving a dirty cop. A dead woman was found shot in her parked car at midnight as a fierce thunderstorm raged. Everything pointed to her grown son as the killer, but something didn't quite fit. She had come into $14,000 in an insurance settlement, and half of that was missing from her trailer after a break-in.

Porter and Burnette found ten witnesses who had seen a police car driving behind the woman the night she was shot. The hugely popular cop who responded to her burglary complaint hadn't filed a report on it. He was identified as the cop witnesses had spotted the night of her murder, but that wasn't enough to arrest him. Burnette searched the suspect's police car, and found a small amount of blood on an arm rest. "It held the victim's DNA," Porter recalled, "and we got a conviction. He was sentenced to two life terms."

Sometimes criticized for being too tough on criminals, Porter shrugged it off; he had seen too much tragedy for victims. Raised Catholic, he was not a churchgoer but he was a devout man, often troubled by the unfairness of life. "My job makes you see things that would absolutely make you deny the existence of God," he once told an *Atlanta Journal-Constitution* reporter. "Then there are other times with no other explanation but the hand of God. I accepted a long time ago that we'll never know why some of these things happen. I used to agonize over that."

For Danny Porter, who once found law school onerous, his job was endlessly fascinating. He never knew what challenge was coming next. Porter quoted the Roman poet Juvenal: "The people that once bestowed commands, consulships, legions, and all else, now concerns itself no more, and longs eagerly for just two things—bread and circuses!"

Bread and circuses. The Atlanta-area media responded to the public's insatiable curiosity about the Jenn and Bart Corbin case with headlines that served to titillate. There was, indeed, a rather morbid circus going on. But Danny Porter was deeply concerned with the survivors' emotional pain, and he made himself available to them whenever they needed to talk.

Jack Burnette and Porter *did* go way back, and Burnette spoke in the Georgia drawl that most people expect to find in Southern cops. Burnette was once a road deputy and then a detective for the Gwinnett County Police Department. He was a big man, standing about six feet five inches tall. He was absolutely devoted to his wife of thirty years, whom he called "Miss Marian." They lived a very happy life together in Social Circle, Georgia, and doted on their children and grandchildren. When asked how they first met, Jack Burnette tried to avoid the subject, but finally admitted that his once macho attitude toward female officers almost guaranteed that Marian would dislike him intensely.

Burnette was on patrol out in the county one night and a violent rainstorm came pounding down in blinding sheets. Burnette underestimated the amount of water on the road and didn't realize his police car was hydroplaning. He skidded off the road and ended up down in a field. He radioed for assistance, and the first unit responding was driven by Miss Marian. She rolled down her window and called out to ask if he needed help.

Burnette opened his mouth and put his foot squarely inside as he answered, "I don't think there's a thing in the world a woman can do for me right now."

She lifted her hand, gave him a familiar gesture of disrespect with one finger, and drove away, leaving him standing in the rain on the interstate.

After that, it took a couple of years for her to even speak to Burnette—except for business—and another year before she would accept his invitation for a date. But she changed his way of thinking about what women could do, and he considered himself very lucky when she finally agreed to marry him.

Burnette's wife was the first female officer in his department, and turned out to be one of the best cops they had for many years.

Burnette never again cast aspersions on the intelligence and capability of women in law enforcement. He held his female investigators in high esteem. "Always hire people smarter than you," he advised, "never dumber."

Burnette followed his own advice. And although he might have seemed the quintessential good ol' Georgia boy, he was as well versed in forensic science as anybody on his team. He could be wonderfully crafty and sly when he needed to "play dumb." He would fill a number of roles in this investigation. Now, he dispatched several of his investigative team to find out more about Jenn and Bart Corbin, while Marcus Head moved ahead on the Gwinnett County Police's probe into Jenn's death.

Jack Burnette's twenty-three investigators were a fascinating cross-section of personalities and demographic origin; the only things they seemed to have in common were an intense desire to find answers where there appeared to be none—and their satisfaction in their jobs. There were both men and women in a 75–25 percent ratio. They were intellectuals, seemingly rough cobs who flew by the seat of their pants, computer experts, techies, careful and patient plodders, rapid thinkers, streetwise veterans, and young Turks. Some of Burnette's investigators worked from home by computer and some worked in the DA's office. They were all given a great deal of freedom to do what they did best.

Morale in Porter's office ran high. That would be important as they embarked on this investigation. Even as they worked alongside the Gwinnett County Police Department's Marcus Head; District Attorney Danny Craig of Richmond County in Augusta and his investigators; and Richmond County sheriff's detectives Scott Peebles and De Wayne Piper, it would be a very long time before the person who killed Jenn Corbin might finally be headed for trial.

Two days before Jenn's funeral, Danny Porter's investigator, Kevin Vincent, drove to Bart Corbin's dental office at 3617 Braselton Highway in Dacula. Corbin's practice was housed in Suites 102 and 103. Vincent found the office closed, with a sign posted saying there had been a death in the family. There were no phone numbers listed to call in an emergency—not even for an alarm company.

An attorney whose office was in Suite 104 told Vincent that he'd last spoken to Bart on Friday, December 3. It was his understanding that Bart had either bought—or was buying—the section of the commercial building that housed his dental practice. The lawyer said that he and Bart occasionally bartered legal advice for dental work. He knew from personal experience that Bart Corbin was a man of volatile temperament. He said he could often hear Bart shouting at his staff—"right through the walls."

The attorney said that Bart had asked him "nervously" on the afternoon before his wife was shot about which of them would be legally responsible for paying the mortgage on their home if he and his wife were to divorce. "I told him that it would be the one of them who could most afford to pay."

There was no question who that would be. As deep in debt as Bart Corbin was, he made far more money than Jenn could make teaching part-time in preschool.

The lawyer observed that Bart had been acting strangely that Friday afternoon. "He said to me, 'Everyone told me not to marry her. I should have listened, but it will all be over soon.' "

At the time, the lawyer took that to mean Bart was speaking about their upcoming divorce.

Kevin Vincent talked to a number of people in the Buford-Dacula area who had called in to say that they might have information. One woman said that she had been standing in a long line waiting to vote in a Bogan Park precinct in November when she overheard a conversation between two men ahead of her. She was startled to hear one of the men complaining about his wife, "Jennifer."

"He was telling the other man that Jennifer was a bitch, and that she was lazy and useless. He said she spent most of her time on the computer and she wasn't bringing in as much money as she used to. I got the impression that he was either in the midst of a divorce or that he was planning to divorce this 'Jennifer.' "

The man had spoken of being a dentist, and she had listened for his name as he gave it to the precinct worker. "It was Corbin. I only listened because I wanted to make sure that I never went to him!"

She didn't know the other man's name, but he had talked about his job, which had something to do with natural gas.

In a door-to-door sweep of the Corbins' closest neighbors, DA's Investigators Kevin Vincent, Eddie Ballew, and Brad Wiley found that the disintegration of the Corbins' marriage was fairly well known—as were Bart's explosions of temper. It hadn't always been so, but lately his fuse had seemed to grow shorter. A nearby neighbor said that on one occasion he had felt it necessary to step in to protect Dalton from Bart's temper.

In the first few days of December, Bart Corbin seemed to have gone out of his way to discuss his marital problems, always painting himself as the injured party. He stressed to neighbors that he would do anything to avoid divorce. He had called both his family and Jenn's family, sobbing on the phone, and begging for advice.

Wanting to believe his sincerity, Narda Barber had suggested that he might make one last attempt at a reconciliation. Maybe he could write a "sweet letter" to Jenn? And he had done that—eager to create a written record of a man with a broken heart.

The detectives learned that Bart had lost fifty to sixty pounds over the last few months, and he now looked almost skeletal, a man ravaged.

He had filed secretly for divorce, but still seemed consumed with pain and rage during the days before Jennifer died. The DA's investigators continued to find both acquaintances and strangers who were witness to that.

Bart was pulling ahead on the original list of possible suspects. If they needed to find someone with a motive for murder, he was a likely candidate. He had been obsessed with getting his wife back. The question was, What might have set him off? They weren't going to find out from him; he still refused to talk with detectives and he had hired attorneys to represent him. He had not, however, authorized them to release any statements quoting him.

On December 9, Ballew and Wiley assisted Kevin Vincent in locating Bobby and Brad Corbin and two other men said to have been with Bart that Friday night before Jenn Corbin died. Although Connie Corbin said that she hadn't seen her sons lately and appeared distraught to be asked about them, she wrote down Kevin Vincent's number and said she would pass it on to Brad if she heard from him.

Only a few minutes later, Vincent got a phone call from Bart Corbin's twin, who said he and Bobby were at the Men's Wearhouse at the Mall of Georgia being fitted for suits for Jenn's funeral. Brad agreed to meet with the investigators, who served him with a subpoena requiring him to appear before a grand jury that DA Porter had called for. Bobby had already left.

The DA's investigators went next to the gym where Bart worked out each morning: BodyPlex. They were looking for Bart's friends, Kevin "Iron" Lyttle and Brian Fox, to serve them with grand jury subpoenas.

That was accomplished, but it wasn't until Jenn's services the next day that Jack Burnette, along with Manny Perez and Tom Davis, was able to locate Bobby Corbin. He was considerably disgruntled that he was served, however discreetly, at the Sugar Hill Methodist Church.

"Why here?" Bobby asked. "You could have called me, and I would have come in."

But they had no assurance of that; the Corbin brothers weren't being particularly cooperative with the detectives and continued to form a protective barrier around Bart. Now legally served, they would have to appear before the grand jury on December 15.

*   *   *

JUDY KING, who had been prepared to represent Jenn in her divorce petition and was now the Barbers' attorney, told the media, "The family was highly suspicious [of Bart]. When they heard about the circumstances in Augusta, they became even more suspicious."

She meant, of course, the gunshot death of Dolly Hearn so many years before. The Atlanta-area media kept abreast of any new information on the investigation and had quickly reported the information about the Hearn case. The public also knew that Dalton had blurted out that his father had shot his mother, although DA Danny Porter didn't feel that the seven-year-old's certainty would be enough yet to draft an affidavit for an arrest warrant.

There was physical evidence—mostly ballistic—that indicated homicide, but that wasn't official yet. The rest of the evidence that investigators were gathering was more ephemeral. If this did prove to be an "intrafamily murder," finding more physical evidence would be tough. The usual things left behind by a killer—blood type, DNA, hairs and fibers, body fluids, and fingerprints—wouldn't be nearly as convincing to a jury if they had come from a family member rather than a stranger. This kind of physical evidence was expected to be found in a household where they had all lived. (Both of the .38 revolvers—Dolly's and the mystery gun used to kill Jenn—had been wiped clean of fingerprints!)

Circumstantial evidence was a bit more convincing. The Corbins' marriage had fallen completely apart, and there were numerous witnesses who would testify to that. And Dalton had talked of seeing his parents arguing during November and December, although a child his age could have easily assumed that had led to murder. Rather than long for his surviving parent, Dalton was clearly afraid of his father.

Already, there was a tug-of-war between Bart's and Jenn's families over the boys. Everyone was traumatized, of course, and Heather and Doug Tierney were doing their best to protect the youngsters from any more stress, but it wasn't easy. They wanted to establish legal precedent that would ensure that the boys would stay with them, at least for the present. They sought to have visits with Dalton and Dillon from Bart or the extended Corbin family evaluated by a skilled counselor so that the little boys wouldn't be more upset than they already were.

"Dalton is in complete fear of his father," Narda Barber wrote in her affidavit supporting the Tierneys' bid for temporary custody of the boys. "If the doorbell rings or the dogs bark, Dalton runs into the bedroom and hides behind the door."

Doug Tierney agreed, recalling the first phone conversation between Bart and Dalton. They had spoken for only moments when Dalton began crying and refused the phone. He said he was afraid and did not want to talk to his dad.

Even so, both Dalton and Dillon were fearful of displeasing Bart. He was the punitive parent who shouted at them whenever they failed to live up to the standards he had set for them.

Both of the Corbin boys were seeing a therapist to help them deal with their loss. It was fortunate that Heather and Jenn had spent so much time together, while the four cousins played. The Tierneys' home was almost as familiar to the Corbin boys as their own.

*   *   *

THERE WAS MUCH TALK about guns. Jenn had said a shotgun was missing from the house on Bogan Gates Drive when she called 911 after Bart ran over her foot on December 1. It had always been in the back of a closet, unloaded so that the boys weren't in danger, and she had suddenly discovered it wasn't there any longer. It was still missing. And during the funeral, someone had broken into Narda and Max's house in Lawrenceville and stolen, among other things, Max's shotgun. No one yet knew where the .38-caliber pistol that had killed Jenn had come from, although detectives were certainly working to find out.

Chapter Twenty-Four

DECEMBER 2004

THE INVESTIGATION into Jenn Corbin's death was becoming increasingly complicated. There were literally dozens of people who knew something about Bart Corbin that they wanted to tell to detectives. Some had helpful information, and some had only general comments, or repeated unfounded rumors. The media was anxious for anything new that might give them an edge in their daily coverage. Certain aspects of the probe into Jenn Corbin's death had been quickly made available to the public, something that Bart deplored.

Bart stayed away from his dental offices for several days, but ultimately he went back to work. And he was exceedingly annoyed at the photographers and reporters who seemed always to be driving by or hanging out in his parking lot. Finally, he called the police because of the reporters congregating in his parking lot. Patrol officers checked, and did observe the media presence, but told him they were breaking no laws.

District Attorney Danny Porter, his investigator, Kevin Vincent, and Detective Marcus Head were intrigued by one aspect of the dentist's behavior. They had read over the Richmond County file on Dolly Hearn's still-unsolved case. One detail in the Augusta file didn't seem all that interesting on their first reading, but they were looking for more similarities, however slight, between two cases where women involved with Bart Corbin had died of .38-caliber gunshot wounds to the right side of the head.

Fourteen years earlier, part of Bart's complicated alibi for the afternoon of June 6, 1990, when Dolly was shot was that he had gotten a haircut that day in Augusta. That was true enough. But it struck the investigative team as more than a coincidence when they learned Bart had made a barbershop appointment for December 4, 2004. Getting a haircut wasn't usually suspicious, of course, but they had to wonder if Corbin was following some kind of pattern that had worked for him once before.

In December 2004, the owner of a high-end barbershop in Duluth, Georgia, called detectives. Dr. Jon Paul Zaleski, who was also a dentist, informed them that earlier in the week, Bart Corbin had made an appointment to have his hair cut at 11:00 A.M. on Saturday, December 4. He was a first-time client, referred by another dentist. However, at 8:30 P.M. on Friday, December 3, Bart had phoned to say that his oldest son had a ball game the next day, and asked if he could come in after 1:00 that afternoon. His request to change his appointment would have taken place an hour or so before he was to meet his friends at the Wild Wing Cafe in Suwanee. And approximately six hours before Jenn was shot.

Of course, the Corbins' world had changed overnight, and Bart hadn't shown up at Jon Paul's at all on Saturday; he had been instead on his way to police headquarters to have a gunshot residue test on his hands.

Four days later, on Wednesday, December 8, Bart Corbin called Jon Paul's hair salon again close to 5:30 P.M., and left a message on the answering machine asking for an appointment. "I need to come in," he said, "because I have to attend a funeral tomorrow."

In that same message on the answering machine, he added, "I'm widowed and I need a new look."

The receptionist called back and gave him an appointment two hours later that evening. Since it was his first visit and he arrived early, he was given a "client information" form to fill out. Under the question asking marital status, he circled "No," and wrote in "widowed."

The receptionist noted that he seemed tired and looked like a man who had "had a bad week." When she commented sympathetically about that, he had answered that he had "family problems."

She offered him a glass of wine, which he first refused, saying, "My brother doesn't want me to drink."

But after Cathy Zaleski, who was Dr. Zaleski's wife, began to cut Bart Corbin's hair, he said he'd changed his mind and would like a glass of wine. As barbers and beauty operators often do, Mrs. Zaleski made conversation, and asked him if the person who had died was someone close to him. She had not connected him to the headlines and news bulletins, and had no idea that it was his wife's funeral he was going to the next day.

"I don't want to talk about it," he answered, and she quickly dropped the subject.

"Why did you marry Jon Paul," Bart suddenly asked her.

"Oh you know," she joked. "The second time around is for money."

"I think my wife married me for my money," he said.

She didn't know whether he was joking or not.

The hair salon's answering machine tape was handed over to Kevin Vincent. The message left on Jon Paul's tape on December 8 mentioned only that Bart had to go to a funeral. Bart's voice was very calm, almost cheerful as he said he needed a "new look."

Apparently he liked the way his hair looked, because he made another appointment for a month later, on January 7, 2005.

Rob and Jenn Grossman, his friends in the satellite business, had an even more unusual situation. Bart called Rob on Sunday, December 5. He didn't mention their estrangement; he wanted Rob's help in getting some information off his computer. When Rob called him back to ask what was going on, Bart told him everything and everyone was fine, but that he and Jenn were getting a divorce and he needed Rob's help to get the info from his computer so he could prove she was cheating on him. Rob told him he really did not want to get involved.

Rob turned to his wife and said that the Corbins were getting divorced, and she was "shocked" at that news.

But Jenn Grossman was about to have a bigger shock. "Later in the day, Rob was going to work and he heard on the radio that Jenn was dead, and he called me to see if anything was on the news—and if it was really Jenn Corbin. We couldn't believe it, but sure enough, I turned on the TV and saw Jenn's beautiful face all over the news saying that they suspected suicide!"

The Grossmans realized then that Jenn Corbin had already been dead when Bart had called Rob earlier in the day saying everyone was fine at his house. "He knew she was dead and he was still trying to get info that Jenn was cheating on him," Jenn Grossman said.

*   *   *

DETECTIVES THOUGHT they knew what Bart was looking for in his computer. One thing that had not become instantly available to the public was the information about Jenn's online relationship with someone in Missouri.

Anita Hearn had been in daily—perhaps hourly—contact with Jenn at the end of her life. Within a few days of Jenn's death, Narda and Heather had discussed what, if anything, they should do about contacting this person who had meant so much to Jenn.

"All we knew," Narda remembered, "was that, next to her sons, and our family, this person seemed to have meant more to Jenn than anyone. I can't remember now if we were even sure whether 'Chris' was a female or a male. I don't think we knew. Would he be wondering why he could no longer contact Jenn? What if he never knew what had happened? We decided it would be the kindest thing to call him and tell him what had happened."

The Gwinnett County Police had seized Jenn's T-Mobile cell phone—her newest cell phone—as evidence when they found it on the bed where she died. Narda and Heather looked through the list they had made of the numbers in Jenn's phone address book. They found a phone number for someone in Missouri. That was where Jenn said her correspondent lived, and there were no other numbers in that state. This was probably the person Jenn called "Chris." There was evidently someone named "Anita" at this number, too.

Jenn's mother and sister weren't sure just how they felt about Jenn's Internet friend; for so long, they had pictured "him"—and now, perhaps "her"—as a negative influence in Jenn's life, but they had gradually come to accept that the encouragement and friendship had made Jenn happier than they had seen her in years. In their own grief, they reached out to a complete stranger, wary of whom they might find.

Narda made the call. A woman answered, her voice cautious and evasive as if she might be expecting a bill collector or some other unwelcome caller. When Narda asked to speak to Chris or Anita, the woman said that she was Chris's sister. "She lives next door," the woman said. "She doesn't have a phone, but I can go get her."

She? Narda looked at Heather, confused. There was a long wait, and then another voice came on the line. It was a female voice. This was Chris/Anita Hearn. Narda wasn't sure, but she suspected this was the same woman who had answered the phone in the first place, and said she was "Chris's sister."

She sounded nervous, as if she didn't know who was calling or what to expect, as, of course, she didn't.

"Chris? Anita?" Narda began. "I am Jennifer's mother, and I have terrible news to tell you—"

Narda Barber explained that Jenn was dead, possibly murdered, and she heard the woman in Missouri begin to sob and grow more and more hysterical. She said she had been trying to get through to Jenn on the phone, on the Internet, through the EverQuest game, and was worried sick that there was no response. That had never happened before, and Anita said she had known that things were reaching a crisis point in Jenn's home.

"She was absolutely devastated," Narda recalled. "She blamed herself, and I can't really say that I didn't blame her, too. It was so hard to know. Once I sorted out who she really was, I think Anita had begun something online, maybe some part of the game, and then she lost control of it—until she was in too deep—and didn't know how to back out. She must have known that the time would come when she had to tell the truth, and we found out that she had done that—and that Jenn had forgiven her."

Nevertheless, what Anita Hearn had done to Jennifer Corbin seemed a wicked deception. She had courted a vulnerable woman for months, pretending to be a man. Narda and Heather sensed that Anita had done this before on the Internet. Hiding behind the characters on Ever-Quest, anyone could be someone else, if only for a short time. But Anita Hearn's subterfuge had ended in stark tragedy. Maybe she hadn't meant to do harm, and she certainly hadn't been a factor in the eight years during which Jenn's marriage had slowly crumbled. But she had possibly been a catalyst in the final denouement. That much was inescapable, and Anita knew it.

Even as she pondered this, Narda realized that Anita must have been very lonely, too, and that in her way she had loved Jenn and that she would miss her, however impossible their connection had been. She had expected to talk to a cold-hearted opportunist, a person with his/her own agenda, perhaps even a con artist. But Narda didn't sense that in Anita Hearn. The woman on the other end of the phone line sounded completely broken-hearted and consumed with guilt.

Anita had been, perhaps, the last person to talk to Jenn on the night she died. She promised Narda that she would do what she could to help the detectives who were investigating the shooting.

Marcus Head obtained the Corbins' telephone records, and saw that Jenn had, indeed, been on the phone or online with Chris "Anita" Hearn for hours during the last evening of her life, not once but several times.

The conversations had been lengthy. Head knew that he was calling a female, and he was very curious to see what she might remember from the phone calls that night, and what her relationship to Jenn Corbin might have been.

Even as mourners were gathering at the Sugar Hill Methodist Church, Head called Anita. It was 4:40 in the afternoon of December 10. His call, too, was answered by a woman who said Anita wasn't home, and had gone over to her sister's house. She was expected back in fifteen minutes.

Anita did call Marcus Head back within that time period.

After Head's first contact with Anita Hearn, he knew that she had been very close to Jenn at the time of her death. Anita knew about Bart's running over Jenn on December 1, and she also knew that Jenn's journal was missing. She asked Head if the detectives had found it when they executed a search warrant of the house.

"We took the game, the PlayStation, and we looked for the journal—which we can't find," he said. "We knew he stole one journal, and Jennifer's sister told us that Jennifer went and bought a new one and she redrafted some of the contents from the old one into the new one, and that she took extra steps to hide it, so that he wouldn't find it this time. So then we took extra steps, too, to look for it. But we didn't find it."

"Okay," Anita said. "She never mentioned where she hid it to me."

Head asked Anita to go over the timeline for Friday night, December 3. "I've got phone records coming in, but would you verify for me that y'all were playing the game online that night?"

"Right."

"Okay—how long were you connected to the game?"

"[Until] 1:15 in the morning—her time—maybe even 1:20, close to 1:30."

Head said he had a copy of the EverQuest game, and he wondered if it was possible for him to retrieve a message that was on a screen after the players had cleared it.

"We can't," Anita said. "Do they [the game administrators] keep records of it? I'm not sure. They may very well. I know that if you delete your character, they keep it for so many months."

Anita said that Bart had left the house about 9 P.M. on Friday night while she was talking to Jenn on the phone, and that after that, she and Jenn had been on the phone with one another off and on during the evening.

Jenn had told Anita that Bart left without telling her where he was going. He had just walked out without speaking to her. Jenn had been aware that night that Bart had filed for divorce. But she hadn't been upset about it at all, just a little surprised that he had filed first. She had told Anita sometime in the past week or so that she had to delete some of her email, because Bart was coming home to talk with her.

"And they talked that night," Anita continued, "and she called me that night, and she said, 'That totals it.' "

Jenn had confided in Anita, saying that she knew in her heart that even if she tried and went to marriage counseling, it just wasn't going to work. She had told Bart that she had a new friend she cared for in another state, but Anita was quite sure that Jenn never told Bart that Anita was a woman. She had wanted to end her marriage amicably, because of her sons.

"And he was gonna be in her life for the rest of her life," Anita said, "and she wanted things okay for the kids."

Jenn had hoped that Bart would be moving out that night, but he had decided to stay, or, possibly, he had asked Jenn if he could stay because he didn't have anywhere to go, and he didn't want to go to his mom's.

That was when Jenn had suggested he move to their houseboat, and he had refused, saying it was too cold.

"So she told him: Okay, he could stay until he found somewhere—"

"Tell me about the plans you and she had made—that you agreed to talk again?" Head asked.

Anita said that she and Jenn had agreed to wait to meet until after Christmas to decide what they were going to do. At that point, they would consider moving in together with their children and seeing if they could afford a place if they both pitched in.

Anita Hearn seemed anxious to have Head read all the correspondence between herself and Jenn Corbin, almost as if she wanted to validate her friendship with a dead woman she had never met. Anita's family were still unaware of any plans she had to move to Georgia. She didn't know how much Jenn's family knew, but told him she had spoken with Jenn's mother and sister. Her conversation was strangely matter-of-fact and tightly controlled, until she asked Head if anyone knew if Jenn had been awake or asleep when she was shot.

"We don't know," Head said. "There's some suggestion, but it's only a suggestion . . . about the way she was found that suggests she may have been asleep."

"Okay, that's what I'm hoping for. And do you know who has her cell phone?"

"I have it. It's locked up in evidence."

Anita offered to email all of the correspondence she had had with Jenn, whatever was left on her computer. At this time, Head had no idea what a landslide of emails that would be. He asked her again if she felt Jenn was really planning to share a house with her in Georgia.

"Yes, I mean in our conversations, yes. I mean at first—when she found out I was a woman and stuff, everything kind of changed a little bit. But, after that, she was okay with it. We were still—she said she wanted to be a mom to my kids, and things like that."

It was difficult to tell if Anita Hearn was convincing herself that she had not pulled off a hugely dark deception on a woman who was now dead—perhaps even dead because of Anita's lie. Maybe she truly believed that the man she had pretended to be—the masquerade she had carried out for month after month—was no part of Jenn's death. Everything she said, however, had a tinge of guilt to it.

"It is kind of weird," she continued. "My last name—Hearn—the woman he may have killed before—had the same name. Did you guys get the letters he had?"

"No. We can't find them. He cleaned the house out. We also think that he may have taken a lot of things that belonged to Jennifer, that Jennifer had documented."

There was so much missing beyond the journals that Jenn's family knew she always had with her. Head suspected that Bart had taken them, and hidden them or destroyed them to save himself embarrassment or to hide things that might incriminate him.

"I know he had my name," Anita said. "Because he called me twice on my cell phone. I never answered."

"Do you know what number he called from?"

"His home phone as far as I know. I can tell when I get my phone bill."

Anita said that Jenn had told her, too, about Bart's mysterious trip to Alabama. "All she said was she found a receipt that basically showed he had been in Alabama that day—a few days before she died. She goes 'Well, I thought maybe somebody just told him there was a good lawyer in Alabama.' "

Anita Hearn told Head that Jenn had been particularly worried about something that occurred on Thursday, December 2. "She had gone to work that day and she forgot her Christmas gift, so she went back home to get it. When she got there, it was weird because Bart's brother was there sitting in his truck, and then Bart was sitting in his truck, warming it up. And then the Mustang was gone. She asked where the Mustang went, and he said he'd loaned it to a friend named Iron. She said it was weird because Bart would have kept the Mustang and loaned the truck."

Head realized that Jenn must have been frightened that morning. She would have just come from Heather's house after being there overnight after her foot was injured. She may have felt that Bart or his friends were going to do her harm.

Anita didn't know which of the Corbin brothers was at the Bogan Gates Drive house that morning, but Jenn was afraid. And that wasn't like her.

Head thanked Anita for her help.

"Not a problem," she said. "I hope we can do something about him."

Was she grieving? It was hard for Head to be sure. When he found hundreds upon hundreds of emails on his computer, sent by Anita, he read them all. For months, they had been from Christopher, until two weeks before Jenn was murdered. And suddenly, they were from Anita. It was a good thing that he had verified where Anita Hearn was on the night Jenn was killed because one of the later emails was truly bizarre.

Anita had asked Jenn if she had ever thought about putting a bullet in the cylinder of a gun and then holding the barrel against Anita's head and pulling the trigger at the very instant Anita had an orgasm.

"No, no," Jenn had written back. "I would never do that."

Evidently, Jenn's online seducer had been into masochism, and found a version of Russian roulette and sex fascinating. But Anita went too far, and it had troubled Jenn Corbin. Still, this was the kind of thing that a defense attorney would grab and run with, planting the suggestion in jurors' minds that Anita was asking Jenn to shoot herself. A clever defense lawyer could argue that Jenn was suicidal.

Jenn had clearly been involved in something that was out of her league, and she was trapped between a jealous, punitive husband and, possibly, a masochistic game-player.

Jenn died without ever having seen even a picture of Anita. However Jenn had pictured this stranger in Missouri, she might have been surprised had they ever met. The woman who had written to her had long, straight, black hair, and very dark eyes, rimmed with black eyeliner. She had a rather sharp, pointed nose and Slavic flat cheekbones, slightly pitted with acne scars. She was short and thin, and neither particularly pretty nor homely. Whatever "magic" she possessed for Jenn had to have been in her false persona, in that image she painted of a tall, handsome man. There was a certain darkness about Anita—so different from the warmth that characterized Jenn.

Anita had been very accomplished in portraying Sir Tank. Now she seemed sincere in wanting to make sure that Bart would not walk away without being punished for Jenn's death.

CHAPTER TWENTY-FIVE

DECEMBER 15–16, 2004

IT WAS EASY ENOUGH to check on the whereabouts of Anita Hearn on the night of December 3–4. She had been in Missouri, talking on the phone with Jenn. And Bart had been in his home until about 9 P.M.

The big question was, Where did he go after that?

That was answered when the Gwinnett County grand jury met on December 15. District Attorney Danny Porter had subpoenaed four men to testify at that legal proceeding: Brad Corbin, Bart's twin; Bobby Corbin, his younger brother; Kevin Lyttle, his friend, the man they called "Iron" or "Iron Head"; and another acquaintance, Brian Fox. Although they were clearly uncomfortable at having any role at all in the investigation into Jenn Corbin's murder, Bart's brothers and friends had no choice but to appear before the grand jury.

The investigation thus far had brought forth the information that Bart Corbin had spent at least some of the missing hours between the time he walked out of his home—until he was notified of his wife's death the following morning—with these men in the Wild Wing Cafe in Suwanee. None of them were particularly forthcoming when they were served with subpoenas or at the grand jury hearing. According to Bart, who spoke occasionally now through his attorneys, he had been some distance away from his house on Bogan Gates Drive after he left late in the evening of December 3. He said he hadn't gone home at all that night, and that he slept at his brother Bobby's house.

Kevin "Iron" Lyttle told DA Porter that he had known both Bobby and Bart Corbin for about thirteen years. He said he had "in-depth" conversations with Bart, but asked to describe them, the only specific topics he mentioned were football games and the time his car was stolen. Lyttle said he knew Jenn Corbin only as his friend's wife. In the recent past, however, Bart had begun to discuss his failing marriage with him.

"We were at Bob's house watching the game, and he just blurted out during the halftime show that he'd found she had a second cell phone."

"Did he tell you that he had called numbers on that second cell phone?" Porter asked.

"Right . . . I really don't get involved in other people's relationships. I don't ask, you know. If they talk about it, you know, I listen, but I don't dig into anybody's personal business."

"And I understand that," Porter said. "But what I'm trying to get you to tell me is what has Bart Corbin told you specifically about his relationship with his wife, and how that relationship began to end, and what did he find that led him to believe she was having an affair?"

"I guess he found some notes, and I guess he found the cell phones and then he called the numbers on the cell phone."

"Now when he was describing this, what was his demeanor? What did he act like?"

"I guess he kinda suspected she was having an affair because she was on the computer all the time. And I guess [his] finding the notes—would probably confirm it."

"Was he angry?"

"I wouldn't say he was angry, no."

Lyttle said he had learned that Jennifer was dead in a phone call from Bobby Corbin about 9:15 on Saturday morning, December 4. But Bobby hadn't said how she died, nor had Lyttle asked.

"That was sort of back to your 'Don't get involved in other people's business' [approach]?" Danny Porter asked.

"No. I was kinda in shock and he asked me, 'What time did he leave?' and I said, 'I don't know.' "

Kevin Lyttle was one of the last people to see Bart Corbin late on Friday night.

"Since that conversation with Bob, have you had a conversation with Bart about the death of his wife?"

"No."

It seemed that Lyttle had been either the soul of tact or just wasn't very curious. He assured Porter and the grand jurors that he had never seen Bart Corbin angry during their thirteen-year friendship.

"Were you aware in the days after Jennifer Corbin's death that there was some question about Dr. Corbin's involvement?" Porter asked next.

"Yes."

"Why didn't you come forward this week?"

"I was working at that job and if I missed a day, or any time at all, I would have been fired."

"So you couldn't come forward, you couldn't even call the police, and say, 'Corbin was with me that night'?"

"I figured they'd be at my house sooner or later."

According to Lyttle's testimony, he, Bart, and another friend, Brian Fox, were to have had dinner at the Mexican restaurant and bar Dos Copas, in Hamilton Mill, on the Friday night Jenn was shot. But Bart hadn't shown up. At about ten, Brian had called Bart, who assured him he was on his way. Bart did arrive shortly thereafter, and Lyttle hopped into his truck. The three men then drove to the Wild Wing Cafe.

Both Fox and Lyttle noticed that Bart was quiet and that he seemed "a little stressed." That didn't surprise them since they both knew he had filed for divorce from his wife that week. The three men drank beer and watched a football game.

Fox told the grand jurors that Bart had brought up his marital situation a couple of times, but that both he and Lyttle had told him they didn't want to know his personal business. "We told him," Fox said, "we just want to relax, blow off a little steam, watch a ball game."

Neither man knew Jennifer Corbin any more than to wave hello to her once in a while.

Investigator Kevin Vincent had obtained a copy of the bar tab from the Wild Wing, a $35 bill Brian Fox paid with his Visa card. The three men left the café at 1:07 A.M. Over their three hours there, they downed fourteen bottles of Miller Lite beer. Kevin Lyttle, who was to have been the designated driver, testified that he had had one beer, Brian

Fox admitted to eight, and said that Bart had had about six before they switched to water.

"I wouldn't consider myself very intoxicated at all," Fox testified. "Or him" (meaning Bart).

Nevertheless, they had agreed that Bart would stay at Kevin's house rather than drive on to Bogan Gates in Buford. As Kevin Lyttle took the wheel of Bart's Chevy pickup, he realized he was out of coffee for breakfast, and he and Bart had stopped at the Wal-Mart in Hoschton to buy some. By the time they got to Lyttle's house, it was 1:35 A.M.

But Bart had changed his mind. He didn't want to spend the night at Iron's house, and no amount of arguing from his old friend would dissuade him.

"I took his keys so he wouldn't drive," Lyttle told the grand jury. "It wasn't that he was sloppy drunk or nothing. He had more than one beer—so he's probably gonna get a DUI or something. I took his keys and he wanted to leave. I went into the master bedroom and put his keys in my dresser, so he wouldn't get up and leave—and I went to the bathroom. And he was—the whole time—he was 'I wanna go, I need to go.' I told him to stay on the couch, and I was going to bed, and then I went to the bathroom. As I was coming out of the bathroom, I heard him say he had his own keys—another set of keys.

"And he left."

*   *   *

AS THE GRAND JURY HEARING continued, the timeline was narrowing. Jenn Corbin had probably died somewhere between 2 and 3 A.M. that morning. Steve Comeau had heard the sound of what he thought was Bart Corbin's pickup truck approaching close to 2 A.M., and then heard a truck leaving about fifteen minutes later.

Bobby Corbin was next. He was more expansive than the men who had gone to the Wild Wing Cafe with Bart, and more at ease on the witness stand. He recalled that he had met Jenn first—at Barnacle's where he was the door-man and she was the bartender. "She kind of met Bart through me when he came to see me."

Bobby said he lived in Auburn, Georgia. He gave his place of employment as a car dealership in Braselton, a job he'd held for nine years.

Danny Porter hastened to inform the grand jurors that he and Bart's younger brother knew each other, and Bobby agreed that he and the prosecutor were members of the same gym, although they were mere acquaintances.

Bobby said he was close to Bart, although they didn't see each other as often as he would like. They played golf, watched football games—usually at Bobby's house. He had been aware of the difficulties in Bart's marriage, and he had talked to Heather about it. Both of them had wanted to be sure that Dalton and Dillon were okay, but he hadn't wanted to meddle in someone else's marriage.

"She [Heather] said when she listened to Bart, then she was mad at Jenn, thinking she was being an idiot, and then next time she was talking with Jenn and [then] Bart was being an idiot. I told the same thing to Jennifer when she told me they were not talking. I said, 'Bottom line is you either want to fix it or you don't—if you want to fix it, you need a third party because neither one of y'all are opening up in any shape or form.' "

Bobby testified that as far as he knew, Bart had never

stayed away from his home overnight, not even as he filed for divorce. And Bart told him he needed to move his truck to Bobby's house because it was in his company's name, and he didn't want it sitting in the driveway at Bogan Gates. "So I came by before work, picked him up, went to get his truck, and drive it over to my house, and she happened to drive back up."

There had apparently been nothing ominous about that encounter. He had asked Jenn how she was, and she said "Okay," and that she was doing fine, and walked inside the house. Bobby had never seen her again.

"When did you learn that Jennifer Corbin had been killed?" Danny Porter asked Bobby Corbin.

"That would have been the 4th, I believe, between 8:30 and 9:00 A.M. Mama called me."

"Where was Bart when your mother called?"

"Sitting across from me at the breakfast table."

"When your mama called, what did she tell you?"

"She was a little upset, obviously, and she said 'They are calling you,' and I said, 'Who is calling me?'

"Steve, which is the neighbor across the street. He said that Jennifer was dead—that she had been shot and they were saying that Bart did it. I said, 'Well, he is sitting right here with me.' "

Bobby Corbin said he had been "flabbergasted," and didn't know what to say, that he and Bart had just been talking about going to Dalton's basketball game at eleven that morning.

"I looked at my brother and asked, 'You have something to tell me,' and he says, 'No,' but I knew something wasn't right."

Bobby told Danny Porter that he had asked his wife to take his children upstairs, and then he called Steve Comeau.

"I said, 'Steve, what is going on?' and he said, 'Well, Jennifer is dead.' [And I said] 'Yeah, my mama said that, but what is going on?' "

There was little question that things had been chaotic in Bobby Corbin's house. Bart had run upstairs, and was vomiting, something he always seemed to do when he was upset. Bobby testified that his own plan was to drive with Bart over to the house on Bogan Gates, but then Heather called and accused Bart of shooting Jenn. And then Doug Tierney called, and asked where Bart was.

"Right here."

"When did he get there?"

"Early this morning."

"How did he look?" Doug asked.

Bobby said he had looked fine.

Danny Porter said, "Let's talk about that. What time did your brother arrive at your house on the morning of December 4th."

"My dog barked, and that is when he probably got there. My wife said about 2:30. I cannot look at the clock, and say when he came in."

"Did you even get out of bed?"

"Initially, no."

"He came into the house?" Porter pressed.

Bobby explained that Bart hadn't come in at that point. He could have entered the garage, because since the problems with Jenn had escalated, he'd given Bart the code to his garage door so he always had a way to get in, but he apparently couldn't unlock the door to the house itself because he didn't know where the spare key was.

"He said he went around back to see if another door was open, and that's when the dog barks again. He told me he didn't want to wake me up, so he was going to sleep in my Suburban, which was parked in the garage. When it started getting cold, he called me on my cell and I went down."

"About what time in the morning?" Porter asked.

"The phone call was at 3:23."

"He called you on your cell, you woke up, and where was he?"

"When I came down, he was at my garage door."

"Did you let him in?"

"Yes."

"And what would you describe as his demeanor at 3:23 in the morning?"

"He had been out with the guys, but he wasn't—I mean—walking—staggering. I mean his demeanor was fine. He'd had a few beers, but that was about it—nothing drastic."

"He didn't seem agitated or upset?"

"No—no."

Bobby said he had pointed toward a recliner, given Bart a blanket, and gone back to bed. They both slept until about seven. Except for the fact that Bart had shown up in the middle of the night, everything was normal until Steve Comeau called. Bart was calm until he heard Bobby's voice change when he heard the news about Jenn. Then he had begun to shake, and Bobby was afraid he was going into shock. He wasn't sure which of them had decided not to go over to Bart's house and talk to the police, but once Bart heard that his sons were with Steve and Kelly Comeau, he felt they were okay. The more the brothers discussed what they should do, the more reluctant they were to go to Buford. Feelings were running high, and Jenn's family were already pointing fingers at Bart by then.

* * *

"WHERE DID YOUR BROTHER tell you he was between 1:40 in the morning and 3:30 when he showed up at your door?" Danny Porter asked.

Bobby repeated his earlier testimony about the two times his dog had barked, and Bart's explanation that he couldn't find the spare key. As far as Bobby knew, Bart had slept in the Suburban in his garage until he got cold. He wasn't sure about when Bart left the Wild Wing Cafe or parted from Kevin Lyttle.

"So," Porter pushed. "In other words your brother has not discussed the specifics of that event with you that night? Your brother denied to you that he had any involvement in the death of his wife?"

"He said he had nothing to do with it."

"But his only story is that he left Kevin's and drove to your house?" Porter continued.

"Um, hum."

Asked to estimate the time it would take for Bart to make that drive, Bobby said his brother had a "lousy sense of direction," and would likely have taken the long way from Kevin Lyttle's house to his own. "Probably about thirty minutes."

Then where was Bart during the almost two hours when no one saw him in the wee hours of December 4? Any convincing alibi virtually depended on his whereabouts when Jenn was shot. The investigators would have to chart time and distance precisely. It was certainly possible that Bart had gone directly to Bobby's garage, and, half-drunk, had crawled in the Suburban and gone to sleep. Maybe Steve Comeau had heard a stranger's truck at 2 A.M., just before Jenn died.

And maybe not. Comeau was frank that the only sense he used that made him believe it was Bart had been aural; he had heard, but he hadn't seen.

Now, when Danny Porter asked Bobby Corbin if he knew the name "Dolly Hearn," he replied that he had read it recently in the newspapers.

"You were not aware your brother had a girlfriend that died under mysterious circumstances?"

"I am aware of it—I just didn't know her name. I never met her. If I met her, it was only once and I don't remember."

"Have you ever discussed that circumstance with—"

"I was down there," Bobby cut in. "I mean I was called down there. I got a call from my dad, I believe. Old memories here. And he [Bart] was depressed and upset about the fact that this had happened. So I went down there and stayed with him through his medical boards."

"Did he ever discuss the circumstances, or how this happened?"

"No—any other than the fact that he thought it was suicide—that was the only thing we knew, as I can recall."

*   *   *

BOBBY CORBIN HAD BEEN extremely considerate of his older brother's feelings, never pressing Bart about where he had been when Jenn was shot, never speculating on what might have happened. He hadn't asked much about Dolly Hearn's apparent suicide, either.

If Bobby's approach was hands-off, Brad Corbin, Bart's fraternal twin, had been even further removed from what had happened eleven days earlier. It appeared that the connection among the three brothers was almost un-emotional, more like that of casual acquaintances. Perhaps they had been raised to respect each other's privacy.

Or perhaps they didn't ask questions because they didn't want to know the answers.

Brad told the grand jurors that he and Bart had shared a "womb and a room" for twenty-three years—until they went in different directions after they left the University of Georgia in Athens in the late '80s. Like Bobby, Brad recalled having a friendly relationship with his sister-in-law. He had been quite fond of her. The last time he'd seen Jenn was on November 12, when she and Bart came to Connie Corbin's birthday party. Brad said he was aware that Jenn and Bart were having some marital troubles and knew that both the Corbin and Barber families supported their getting counseling. Brad continually stressed in his testimony that he wasn't an expert on emotional problems—even in his own family.

"It seemed like they were at least trying," he said. "[Jenn] said basically she didn't know what she was going to do—that she had not been out in the work place before."

"So she really expressed," Porter asked, "that she didn't know how she was going to support herself and the children, and how she and the children would go on? And when you had a conversation with Bart about the divorce, what did he express?"

"The same. I mean I think it was a combination of sadness, remorse—again I don't want to sit here and say I'm a psychiatrist."

"Did he ever express to you specifically the reason he was pursuing the divorce?"

"He did not give me the details, but he did say she

might be having some sort of Internet affair—some sort of Internet gaming thing, possible addiction, as far as that goes."

Brad said he knew that his twin had taken the hard drive from his computer to find out what was on it. He didn't know what—if anything—Bart had learned about that. Brad recalled that he had not seen Bart on Friday evening. He hadn't learned of Jenn's death until about nine on Saturday morning, when his mother called him. He had gone to his mother's home and "walked around in a fog" like the rest of his family were. They had all been in shock, including Bart.

He described Bart's demeanor as "disheveled, numb—blank."

"Was he agitated?"

"No."

Danny Porter asked Brad if he had ever asked his twin about Jenn's death. No, he hadn't at that time, nor later in the day when he and Bobby had accompanied Bart to the police station for the gunshot residue tests on Bart's hands. By that time, Bart had hired an attorney.

"Since then, and later that day, did you have conversations with Bart about the death of Jennifer Corbin?"

"I have had none."

"You have not spoken to him about the death of his wife?" Porter asked with incredulity in his voice.

"No, sir. But have I asked? Yes."

"Have you asked?"

"Yes."

"What was his response?"

"He said, basically, it was like his lawyer told him he could not say anything—and he said for us not to take it personally."

"So he has said he was not even to talk to you?"

"Um, hum."

It seemed odd, considering the bond that most people expect twins to share. But as Porter's questioning continued, Brad Corbin seemed not to have been privy to his twin's life. He knew no more about what had happened on the morning of December 4 than anyone who read a newspaper in Atlanta did—if that much. He acknowledged that he had heard Dolly Hearn's name, but said he had never met her. He'd never questioned Bart about her strange and sudden death.

One of the grand jurors asked Brad if he and Bart were, indeed, twins. He nodded and said yes. The woman looked a little confused, perhaps even a bit dismayed.

Bradley Corbin was dismissed.

*   *   *

KEVIN VINCENT AND EDDIE BALLEW met with their boss, Jack Burnette, and set out to drive the Gwinnett County roads that Bart Corbin and Kevin Lyttle had traveled on December 4. Investigators clocked time and distance both at 9 A.M. and, again, at about 1 A.M. The early morning test showed that Lyttle's house was 15.5 miles from the Wild Wing Cafe, and it took twenty-one minutes to get there. When Bart reportedly left Kevin Lyttle house's shortly after they argued about his car keys, his departure time would have been between 1:40 and 1:45 A.M. The 9 A.M. reenactment probably took longer than the drive would have shortly after midnight when few cars were on the road.

The detectives suspected that Bart had driven from

Lyttle's house on Marshview Court in Hoschton directly to his own house on Bogan Gates Drive, and that he had spent about fifteen minutes there. And that during that time he had shot and killed his wife.

The distance between Kevin's house and Bart's house was 10.5 miles, and it took them twenty-three minutes during daylight hours, and sixteen minutes at 1:47 in the morning. That would place Bart at the murder scene between 2:03 A.M. and 2:15 A.M.

If Bart had then walked out of his house, leaving his small sons asleep and his wife dead, at approximately 2:30 A.M. and then drove to his brother Bobby's house, he had 14.9 miles to travel. And the time elapsed during that drive would have been between twenty and thirty minutes. He would have used Bobby's code to open the garage door there sometime between 2:50 and 3:00 A.M.

Bobby Corbin's dog often barked during the night for any number of reasons, and Bobby hadn't gotten up until 3:23 when Bart called his cell phone and said he was cold sleeping in the garage.

To be fair, Burnette and his investigators checked out the distance that Bart would have traveled if he had, as he claimed, driven directly from Kevin Lyttle's house to his brother Bobby's house. It was a short drive—only 6.2 miles, and it took twelve minutes. If Bart hadn't gone to his own house during those early morning hours, he should have arrived at his brother's at approximately 1:47 A.M. And Bobby had testified—albeit by hearsay— that his wife, Suzanne, had heard their dog bark at 2:30 A.M.

But neither of them had checked to see why.

In the end, there was no way to determine absolutely

where Bart Corbin had been for the vital period of nearly two hours. No one saw him. All the detectives had to go on were sounds: the barking of a dog, the roar of a truck's engine. Neither would fly in court; there had to be some other way to track Bart Corbin.

PART SIX

The Investigation

RICHMOND COUNTY

CHAPTER TWENTY-SIX

DECEMBER 2004

WHILE THE GWINNETT COUNTY DETECTIVES were working to determine how and why Jennifer Corbin had died, the parallel investigation into Dolly Hearn's death was taking place in Augusta at the Richmond County Sheriff's Office. The detectives in each jurisdiction kept in constant touch with each other, and they were discovering more and more similarities in the two shootings.

Detective Sergeant Scott Peebles in Richmond County was the son of Ron Peebles, one of the first investigators on the scene of Dolly Hearn's shooting in June 1990. Scott had just graduated from high school that week. And that was also the week Dolly had attended her brother Gil's graduation in Washington, Georgia.

"My high school was across the street from where

Dolly Hearn died," Scott recalled. "I remember standing at my school and I could see her apartment."

Although the younger Peebles recalled the mystery of Dolly's death, he never expected to revisit it. But he grew up wanting to be a cop like his father, and he moved up rapidly in the Richmond County Sheriff's Department. And now, almost fifteen years later, he had just been assigned to be the lead detective on the newly revived investigation into Dolly's case. He was *literally* following in his father's footsteps.

Scott Peebles pored over the thick, tattered files of the original Hearn investigation, reading words his father had written and recognizing his dad's scribbled additions in now-faded ink. He saw that each incident Dolly had reported—either to the Medical College police or to his own department back in 1989 and 1990—had been checked out. She had told officers she was afraid of her ex-boyfriend, Bart Corbin, but, in the end, she had backed away from prosecuting him. Caught somewhere between feeling sorry for him, remembering the good days they had shared, and being afraid of him, Dolly had finally decided that she didn't want them to arrest Bart.

Without a complaining witness who would testify in court, there was no point in filing charges against him.

Forensic science techniques had steadily advanced in sophistication since 1990, and Scott Peebles could see that the investigation that took place then had some holes in it, most of them not the fault of the men working the case in the weeks after Dolly died. While it was still standard procedure for patrol officers to remove weapons from locations where someone could be hurt, it bothered detectives to reach a crime scene and find that it had been disturbed.

"If they can just take photographs first," Peebles said

firmly, "we have a chance to reconstruct the scene—but once a gun is removed, we can't be sure just where it was."

Reading over Bart Corbin's two meetings with detectives in 1990, Scott Peebles wondered why Corbin hadn't been pushed a little harder in these interrogations, particularly in the second interview where he admitted that he had lied.

"I realized that they were hoping to get him on a polygraph," Peebles said, "and they felt that going a little easy on him might make that more likely—but, in the end, he balked at being hooked up to the lie detector."

Now, Bart was refusing the lie detector test in Gwinnett County, too, and this time, he wasn't willing to talk to detectives as he once did in Augusta.

And so, in the last days of 2004, Scott Peebles, his fellow investigators, District Attorney Danny Craig and Senior Assistant District Attorneys Parks White and Jason Troiano were faced with reopening an old case that many had believed was a suicide. They didn't have a lot to work with. They had only a thin folder of photos of Dolly Hearn's body and her apartment, some follow-up police reports, the old autopsy reports, and a list of witnesses, half of whom were probably scattered all over America. The Augusta team realized all too well that memories dim as the years pass and new experiences are superimposed over them. But they would have to work with what they had, and somehow take another look at what had happened to Dolly on that June afternoon just before graduation ceremonies at the Dental School at the Medical College of Georgia.

One man that Peebles turned to early on was the investigator who had trained him in crime scene investigation: DeWayne Piper. They were both young men—under forty—but, between them, they had years of experience in criminal investigation and training in the newest advances of forensic science.

DeWayne Piper had come to a career in law enforcement after four years in the U.S. Army, during which he had been stationed in Washington, D.C. In the two decades since, Piper had undergone intensive training, read voluminously, and honed his skill until he became, arguably, one of the outstanding experts in this country in a relatively new discipline of forensic science: bloodstain pattern analysis. Piper was also an expert in fingerprint analysis. He worked as a crime scene investigator for Richmond County.

"Scott and I kind of went in different directions," Piper recalled. "He loves following suspects, finding out everything about them, matching up circumstantial and physical evidence—and he's very, very, good at it; I love looking at a crime scene or photographs where blood has been shed, and figuring out what happened. You might say we each have special talents.

"I know it might sound strange," Piper added. "but blood patterns are almost an art form and you have to have a predilection for it. It's like learning to play a musical instrument. I have a guitar and music scores, and I've studied all of that—still I can't make music the way I want to. But I can see things in bloodstains that other people often can't see."

He wasn't bragging; he was simply stating fact. Blood found after a shooting is different from blood shed in a stabbing, or flung off when a bludgeon has been swung with great force. Given body positions, weapons, velocity, and a dozen other variables, it is quite possible for blood pattern experts like Piper to re-create what has happened as if they had actually been present when attacks occurred. Many times, suspects are shocked to learn the telltale secrets they left behind in scarlet testimony. There are splashes, streaks, drips, spatters, spray, smears, and even transfers of blood stains, and DeWayne Piper could read them all.

"DeWayne looked at the photographs of Dolly's body, sitting there on her sofa," Scott Peebles said. "He saw things I didn't—but once he showed me, it was so obvious."

Piper took the negatives Scott Peebles found in the old Hearn file to have them developed. There weren't many—perhaps two dozen—but he had them enlarged and gave one set to Peebles. There were a dozen pictures of Dolly Hearn's body, a lovely woman sitting cross-legged on her nubby-textured plaid couch. She might have appeared almost relaxed were it not for the dried blood that coated her entire face and then left stains on her clothing and certain portions of her bare skin. She wore shorts and a black and white blouse. The expression on her face was tranquil, as if she had died without ever knowing she was in danger.

For the next two days, Piper spent all of his time silently studying the pictures of Dolly's body, the surrounding furniture, and the everyday items in the photographs.

He had his own thoughts about what had happened, but he wanted to compare his opinions with experts who had done postmortem evaluations. Almost immediately, he had doubted that she had committed suicide. Now, he wondered if anyone back in 1990 had had similar suspicions.

The autopsy report was signed by Dr. Sharon G.

Daspit, M.D., M.E., and there were neuropathological notes added by Dr. Farivar Yaghmai, M.D. Luckily, both physicians were still in the Augusta area.

Dr. Daspit told Piper that she had "vivid recall" of the Hearn case, and even though she was told Dolly's death was a suicide, she had questioned that. That was why she ruled the manner of death as "Undetermined."

When asked about what the immediate effect from a gunshot wound to the head would be, Sharon Daspit said that the victim would have been rendered unconscious immediately. Her breathing would have stopped at that moment, too. "It was a contact wound," she offered, "and there should have been some blowback of her blood into the barrel of the gun."

Could Dolly's body have moved—either consciously or by reflex after being shot? The answer was no. But Dr. Daspit suggested that Piper talk to Dr. Yaghmai since that was more in his area of expertise.

With Sergeant Scott Peebles, Piper went to interview Dr. Yaghmai. Both detectives were convinced that Dolly hadn't been found in a position that she should have been in just after she was shot. As Peebles and Piper asked Yaghmai questions, they were careful not to reveal their own suspicions. They hoped for validation of what they believed—but they wanted to glean information from the neuropathologist without planting any suggestions in his mind.

Yaghmai reviewed his notes and looked at the photos Piper presented. He, too, remembered this case even though he had been called in to consult on numerous violent deaths since he had last thought about Dolly Hearn.

He explained that the bullet through Dolly's brain had cut such a destructive path that all brain activity would have ceased immediately. "Her heart might have beaten for seconds," Yaghmai said. "But the only possible movement in her body would have been an immediate 'jerking' motion, or a very brief trembling."

When DeWayne Piper asked if she would have been capable of moving into the position her body was discovered in—at the end of the couch, with her head and upper torso leaning slightly over the arm rest—Yaghmai shook his head. He felt someone had changed her body position after she died.

And that was exactly what DeWayne Piper thought, too. There was much too much blood on her left thigh for the position she was found in. And there was a transfer stain on the skin of her right leg that could not be explained.

Dr. Yaghmai opined that while he could not completely rule out suicide as a possibility, he didn't think that was probable.

But even at this point, Piper wasn't ready to submit his report. He decided to replicate the scene as it had been on June 6, 1990, and to do that he needed fresh blood. He knew that his own blood was healthy, not inclined to clot—neither too thin or too thick. He was about to make a blood donation to the cause of justice.

"My niece is an RN," he recalled. "So I asked her to remove a pint and a half of blood from me."

To keep Piper's blood at the proper viscosity, a small amount of heparin was added. He began some of his tests within an hour or so and continued the next day.

With the help of his thirteen-year-old son, Ryan Piper, DeWayne arranged a couch and end table—and even a piece of cardboard with fourteen clothespins clipped to it that had been on the floor next to Dolly's couch—so that they had virtually re-created a possible crime scene of fifteen years earlier.

The Pipers, father and son, also constructed boards in their garage that would catch blood at varying velocities. Although Piper felt Ryan was still too young to be present when his dad's blood was used, Piper enlisted him to participate by sitting on the couch just as Dolly would have.

DeWayne manipulated Ryan's arms, legs, and torso into the most likely position Dolly was in when she was shot—and then into the position in which she was found, slightly leaning against the cushions near the left arm of the sofa.

In that final posture, there was simply no possible way that a cascade of blood could have fallen on Dolly's lower left thigh near her kneecap. Nor was there any explanation for the smear of blood transfer on the skin of her other leg—not unless someone else had moved her body.

Even some of the stains on the clothespins and cardboard warred with the original supposition that Dolly was a suicide. They were stained with low-velocity spatter that would have dripped from her head when she was slightly moved by someone after her death.

Although he was now positive that Dolly hadn't shot herself, DeWayne Piper asked for a peer review on his findings from Senior Criminalist John Black at the South Carolina Law Enforcement Division Headquarters in Columbia. He didn't know Black personally or professionally, nor did he know any of the other special agents—Steve Derrick, Vicki Hallman, and Eddie Porter. Piper provided the basic details of the Hearn case and the 8x10 photographs of Dolly's body.

The South Carolinians came to a unanimous conclusion that matched Piper's. The bloodstains in the photos could not be explained unless someone else had been present to manipulate her body and the scene.

Back in 1990, there weren't many bloodstain pattern analysts. And no one had detected the telltale patterns that would have proved Dolly was no suicide. But now, Scott Peebles moved forward with this information, and reviewed witness statements about the relationship between Dolly and Bart Corbin.

With his father's approval, Peebles was starting from scratch, as if this suspicious death, unresolved for fifteen years, had never been investigated before.

Chapter Twenty-Seven

December 2004

WHILE DETECTIVES ON BOTH SIDES of Georgia continued to gather and evaluate evidence and the public speculated about media coverage of the Corbin case, Dr. Bart Corbin appeared to have gone back to work full-time. In mid-December, he put up a sign at his clinic on Braselton Road in Dacula: "New Patients Accepted." Jenn's funeral was over, and he was ready for business as usual. When a reporter appeared at his clinic seeking an interview with him, Bart quickly turned away, saying, "This conversation is not taking place."

He did give one short quote to a reporter from WAGA-TV, but only to complain about being harassed: "I've been persecuted by the media in the last ten days," he said. "I'm anxious to speak, but have not because of legal advice. The truth will come out in the end."

He arrived at his clinic that morning, but locked the doors as he left at noon, and did not return. He still refused to talk to the police or to the district attorney's investigators.

Danny Porter confirmed to the media later that day that Jenn Corbin had been engaged in an Internet correspondence with a subject in Missouri, and that computers in the Corbin home had been seized during the execution of a search warrant.

A hundred people gathered outside the Corbins' empty house in Buford for a prayer vigil. It was a cold night, and the winds whipped down the street, bending trees and blowing out the candles of those participating.

Said to be living with relatives, Bart Corbin had not asked to have his sons come home to be with him. Maybe he was simply too emotionally upset himself to cope with taking care of them. If Bart Corbin had regrets—and surely he must have—answering the questions of his sons would be extremely difficult.

Bart was not without his supporters; aside from the Comeaus and other close neighbors, most people who had known the Corbins as a couple still tended to believe that they had been happily married. They were baffled to learn that Jenn and Bart had been arguing in the last few months. Friends that the Corbins had socialized with still felt that whatever was wrong, it couldn't have been anything so bad that it led to divorce. And they couldn't understand the gossip that said Bart might have killed Jenn.

Jenn's family members were convinced otherwise, and they were adamant that the best place for Dalton and Dillon was with Heather and Doug Tierney. None of them wanted to turn the boys over to Bart, or to his family. The fact that Bart was avoiding a conference with the investigators who only wanted to sit down with him and explore who might be responsible for Jenn's death, reinforced her relatives' doubts about him.

Even before Jenn's funeral, Heather and Doug had petitioned for an emergency hearing to seek temporary custody of Dalton and Dillon. They offered affidavits and the youngsters' psychological test results to support their contention that their home was the safest place for the boys.

Their attorney, Judy King, explained to the media that the Tierneys wanted to keep the boys safe and unafraid. At the moment, she said, they continued to be "very fearful."

Bart and his attorneys were not notified of the custody hearing until two hours before it was to take place. None of them were present when the judge ruled that, for the moment, the Tierneys should continue caring for their nephews.

Bart countered by removing his sons from his health insurance coverage. He was working feverishly to raise money to pay his lawyers. There was the cash advance of $40,000 from his credit card, and he had also phoned the insurance agent who had written the policy on Jenn's life four years earlier. Patricia Murphy, an insurance agent in Lawrenceville, was one of Jenn's longtime friends. Bart and Jenn had gone to her on November 16, 2000, and applied for an insurance policy on Jenn's life. The policy—a term life with Lincoln Benefit Insurance Company—was issued shortly thereafter. It insured Jenn's life for $250,000.

Both Jenn and Bart had signed the application, and Bart had opted to have the yearly premium paid in automatic monthly payments of $19.91. The premiums would not go up for twenty years, and would increase thereafter as Jenn aged. She would have coverage until 2066, when she was ninety-five.

Jenn seemed a good risk; she was a healthy twenty-nine years old at the time and had no history of ill health. Bart was listed as the principal beneficiary, with Dalton and Dillon in the second spot.

Detectives found it interesting that Bart had called Patricia Murphy on Sunday morning, December 5, a little more than twenty-four hours after Jenn's death. He left a message that Jenn had been in a "terrible accident," and asked Patricia to return his call. Indeed, he left several more messages on that Sunday.

Patricia Murphy wasn't at her phone, and she hadn't heard about Jenn's death. However, on Monday morning, she was driving to work and listening to the news on her radio when she learned that Jenn was dead—that she had been shot. Later, Patricia told Jenn's family that she "cried all the way to work."

When Murphy played back her answering machine messages, she thought that Bart Corbin's voice sounded remarkably calm for a man who had just lost his wife. She was instantly suspicious. Bart should have been grieving, and he was already trying to collect on Jenn's insurance. Patricia called Judy Laxer, the staff claim representative at the Lincoln Benefit Insurance Company headquarters in Vernon Hill, Illinois. She urged Laxer not even to think about paying out on the policy, no matter what Jenn Corbin's widower said.

Bart's Sunday call to Patricia Murphy had taken place about the time he'd called Rob Grossman, the satellite salesman, and he sounded just as calm.

It would be two more days before he called his sons.

*   *   *

HEATHER AND DOUG TIERNEY now had four children, three little boys and a girl, two dogs, three cats, and a guinea pig. Looking back, they realized that taking care of their own two children had seemed like a walk in the park compared to the chaos with their newly blended family. Heather hit the ground running every morning. Someone was always coming down with one childhood illness or another, laundry piled up endlessly, and the noise level threatened to knock the plaster off the walls. Still, all the activity was a blessing. Being busy and needed made Heather feel somewhat better, and when the kids went to their Aunt Rajel's house or to stay with Max and Narda, they brought joy to everyone.

Without blinking, the Tierneys took on the financial responsibility for Dalton and Dillon, too. Whatever it took, they would find a way. Whenever Heather felt overwhelmed, she asked herself: "What would Jenn do—if I was the one who died?"

So alike in many ways, the sisters also had had different personality traits. In her emails to Chris, Jenn had once lamented that Heather was "disorganized," and recalled that, when Heather packed to move to her new house, she was likely to pile things from her pantry, her laundry-to-do, and her makeup all in one unlabeled box. But Jenn said it in a noncritical way.

Now, when Heather remembered Jenn, she said, "If she was in my place, she would take charge, and get going to solve problems. She was the neat freak. She would grieve for me, but she'd handle it."

Heather handled it, too, although it would be years before she could bring herself to open to some of the packing boxes that held the things Jenn planned to use in her new life without Bart.

*   *   *

JENN'S BOYS HAD THEIR BLEAK MOMENTS where they grew suddenly silent in the midst of raucous play. Dalton and Dillon understood as much as small children could that their mother was gone, but they could not visualize "always." They had bad dreams and missed her terribly. They still held out hope that she would find a way to come back to them. It broke Heather's heart when they spoke about Jenn. They did not ask about their father.

Christmas was bearing down on them, though, and all the Barbers realized that, for the children's sake, they couldn't just skip the holidays, as much as they wanted to. All their long-cherished family traditions for Christmas were agonizing to contemplate now, making them miss Jenn more than ever. The funeral was over, and the years ahead without her yawned emptily. The reality of loss and grief bloomed as painfully as a toothache when the Novocain wears off. Only the little children left behind were still looking forward to Christmas with joy and excited anticipation.

Friends and strangers delivered presents for Dalton and Dillon—and for Max and Sylvia, too. This helped the adult survivors tremendously.

"We decided to make it a 'kids only' Christmas," Heather recalled. "None of the adults could bear having to go Christmas shopping. The kids would have plenty and we would get joy from seeing them tear into their presents."

Dillon and Dalton were adjusting well to living in a new home, happy to be with their cousins, Max and

Sylvia. Their Aunt Heather had always been a large part of their lives, and so had their Uncle Doug. Heather and Doug were rapidly growing used to their expanded family. There was never any question that they would take Jenn's little boys, just as Jenn would have looked after Sylvia and Max if something happened to them. Heather hadn't forgotten the pact she and Jenn had made years before, never really thinking that tragedy would visit their lives. Now, it was the only thing Heather could do for Jenn, and she felt her sister's presence often, her spirit approving and looking over all of them. Heather woke from happy dreams where Jenn came back and told her everything would be fine, but she had just as many nightmares when she wept in her sleep and awakened to a sodden pillow.

They decorated a Christmas tree. How could they not have done so? All the children would have been bereft without it. Maybe next year, Heather would be able to unpack Jenn's tree ornaments and Christmas decorations, or maybe they would just start over with new things.

All of the presents that Jenn had bought and wrapped for her sons were still in the house on Bogan Gates Drive, and Bart refused the Barbers' requests to be allowed to remove them, along with more clothes for the little boys.

Max finally took matters into his own hands, crawled in a window, and retrieved the last presents his daughter would ever buy her sons. When Bart called police to make a burglary report, Max shrugged his shoulders. It was the least important problem facing the family. Somehow, they were going to have to get through the holidays and keep smiles on their faces so that all the grandchildren could have some happy memories of this terrible year.

Gwinnett County police did not bring charges against Max Barber.

Heather had begun a website. It helped her to talk about Jenn, report how the boys were doing, and how her whole family was coping with the loss of an integral family member. Before long, her weblog became a touchstone for people everywhere, and it helped Heather when she felt overwhelmed with sorrow. One day, Heather's web pages would have 400,000 posts from people all over the world.

Heather wrote about a dream that Dalton had—so real that she hoped somehow it might be true. He came down to breakfast one morning, really happy for the first time. "He said he was leaving church and he saw his mommy standing outside by the flowers. She gave him hugs and kisses, and they went to a carnival. Dalton said they played lots of games, and had all the tokens they needed. They rode the roller coaster."

The mommy in his dream had taken him to a toy store and bought him a little street bike. They fed Zippo, Dalton's dog, and then she tucked him into bed, told him how much she loved him and that she would always be with him.

"She told him not to worry," Heather wrote. "Everything would be okay. I asked him if Jenn knew where we were living, and he said, 'Mommy is an angel and she is everywhere.' "

For a seven-year-old boy, it would be enough for a while, but he still carried a huge load of guilt and regret that he hadn't been able to protect his mother when she needed him.

CHAPTER TWENTY-EIGHT

DECEMBER 2004

TO GIVE BART CORBIN the benefit of the doubt, Marcus Head agreed with Corbin's attorneys that Dalton Corbin may very well have leapt to an erroneous conclusion that his father had killed his mother. He was, after all, only a child, and he had witnessed his parents violent arguments in recent weeks.

"We need to talk to Corbin," Head told reporters, explaining that the dentist's own reluctance to talk with the police made them wonder more about what he might be hiding.

Bart had become what police call a "person of interest," a euphemism for "suspect." He was aware that his movements and reactions on December 3 and 4 were the subject of grand jury hearings in both Richmond and

Gwinnett counties, and he must have realized that at some point he would have to submit to questioning.

Each day when Bart arrived at his clinic on Braselton Highway, he had to walk a gauntlet of reporters and photographers. The one employee he'd always been able to count on—Dara Prentice—was there for him as he tried to attract new patients despite his growing notoriety.

He was under constant surveillance—both by the media and by Gwinnett County investigators. As the pressure grew, there was the feeling among law enforcement officials that he might cut and run.

Whether Bart realized how many eyes were watching him, only he knew. He was aware of the reopened probe into Dolly Hearn's violent death in Augusta, and he remarked scornfully to one friend that "that bitch in Augusta" was still causing him trouble.

Sergeant Scott Peebles continued to peruse the 1990 case file. Given the state of forensic science at the time, he wasn't surprised when he found no physical evidence that might have convinced a jury that Bart Corbin had shot her. They had the blood pattern evidence now, but Peebles and DeWayne Piper had to agree with District Attorney Danny Craig that they needed more before they sought an arrest warrant.

Back in 1990, one of Dolly's female cousins worked for the FBI. At that time she suggested to a now-retired supervisor in the sheriff's office that the FBI lab might be able to review Dolly's file and the notes and pictures of the crime scene and come up with a new approach, but only if he requested federal assistance.

"Now, why would I want to do that?" he asked her in a condescending tone, as if to pat her on the head for being a good—but deluded—little girl.

J. Edgar Hoover, the first director of the FBI, held that post for forty-eight years, until his death in 1972, and never encouraged his agents to exchange information with local police agencies. Even in the 1980s and 1990s, city and county police departments remained reluctant to share the results of their investigations with the FBI, recalling the old days when they could send "the Feds" information—but it wasn't a reciprocal relationship. Fortunately, by 2004 that distrust was a thing of the past.

Scott Peebles read the old reports that traced Bart's and Dolly's movements during the week before she was shot—particularly the last twenty-four hours of her life. Once again, he studied the two interviews with Bart Corbin where he had given an almost minute-by-minute description of how he spent June 6, 1990. Scott's father, Ron, sat in on those interviews, and he had harbored doubts at the time about Bart Corbin's honesty. Could the younger Peebles go back after almost fifteen years and winnow out more information?

Beyond tracking reported witnesses, Scott Peebles had other, somewhat distracting, leads to follow. When people learned of Jenn Corbin's death, rumors began to circulate, and Peebles received phone calls from informants who said they had heard that Bart Corbin had admitted that he'd lied about Dolly's death. When the Augusta detective followed these rumors back to their sources, however, the leads had evaporated. One man, who was now a practicing dentist, had not yet heard that Bart's wife was dead, and possibly murdered. He told Peebles that Bart had never admitted any guilt in Dolly's death to him.

"Back when we were in school," the one-time MCG dental student said, "I told someone that Bart admitted to me he had had 'a very rocky relationship' with Dolly, and that surprised me at the time—because I always thought they got along fine. But that was the only 'admission' he ever made to me."

Another dentist was baffled when his name came up in the investigation of Bart Corbin. "I didn't know him or the girl who died," he told Peebles. "I graduated seven years before Corbin did."

Back in 1990, Carlton and Barbara Hearn, frustrated when there was no arrest in the death of their daughter, had retained their own attorney and hired a private investigator themselves. Now, Scott Peebles phoned Barbara, who said the female PI was a young woman named Sarah Hargett Mims. Barbara was confident she could find Sarah Mims and also provide Peebles with the PI's old investigative reports.

Barbara Hearn wanted Peebles to understand that Dolly had been on academic probation for only a short time—and that was because Bart had stolen and possibly destroyed her patient records and projects. "Those projects were to be what she was graded upon—and they were gone."

Dolly had, in fact, been so convinced that it was Bart whose thefts were designed to make her fail, that she had secretly recorded a conversation with him. That tape was in the old file, and Scott Peebles listened to it, although the sound was not very clear. He heard Dolly's voice asking Bart if there was any way she could get her dental charts back. And then Bart's voice said, "I don't know if you've got a recorder or something."

She continued to question him about where her charts were and he finally said, "What do you want me to say? How do I know you're not recording this?"

"I just want to know if they're at the bottom of the city dump," Dolly's voice prodded.

Again, he told her he suspected she was recording what he said. There were long gaps of silence and garbled conversation on the tape, with Bart Corbin skittering on the edges of her questions. The closest he came to an admission on the tape was when he bluntly told her that there was no way she would ever get her dental charts back.

The tape from Dolly's answering machine was also in the old file, frozen in time. Bart's seemingly contrived message about breaking a date with her remained. In his first interview with detectives in 1990, Bart had denied going to Dolly's apartment the day she died. In the second, he had done everything he could to make it look as though he saw her for only a brief half-hour at 1 p.m.

Peebles wondered why Bart had said he'd gone there to ask her to have dinner that night. That warred with his message on the answering machine, where he broke a party date with her. Why had he done that? And why had Bart said on the answering machine, "I guess you're at work." He obviously knew she wasn't.

Almost eerily, Bart had ended the message: "I love you." Peebles suspected that Dolly was no longer alive when the phone message was recorded.

As Peebles read through the voluminous reports written by Sarah Hargett Mims, the private investigator whom the Hearns had hired, he saw that Bart's reasoning was apparent. He must have realized that he had been seen on Parrish Road that day. Sarah Mims had talked to dozens of people who knew Dolly at the MCG Dental School or at the apartment complex where she was killed. Mims had done an exceptional job, but some of the people in charge of the death probe (not Ron Peebles) hadn't been very receptive to what she discovered.

Now, when Scott Peebles compared Bart Corbin's recall of the day Dolly died with statements made by others who had been close to her, he found many discrepancies.

DeWayne Piper was positive that Dolly's body had been moved after she died, and he had the pictures and reports to prove it. In addition to asking his father, Scott Peebles asked Lieutenant John Gray and Sergeant Paul Johnson if they had moved her body at the crime scene. They had not. Johnson had lifted the gun from her lap but hadn't touched her.

So far, the younger Peebles had been able to locate everyone who had been at the scene so long ago. Angela Garnto, Dolly's roommate, was sure she had touched Dolly only lightly to check for a pulse, but not nearly enough to move her body even slightly.

When Peebles asked Angela about Dolly's relationship with Bart, she told him it had begun shortly after she had moved in with Dolly at the Parrish Road apartment. In the beginning, the couple had gotten along well. Neither seemed to be more in love than the other. But by the fall of 1989, Dolly had begun to chafe under Bart's insistence that she not talk to any other men. The couple had many arguments—almost all of them over Bart's possessiveness. And soon, Bart had begun to stalk and harass both Dolly and Angela.

On June 6, 1990, Angela said goodbye to Dolly in the morning. "She was standing in our kitchen," Angela recalled. "When I came home late that afternoon, I know I put my key in the door and turned it out of habit—but I don't know if the door was locked or unlocked."

Angela said she became hysterical when she realized

Dolly was dead, and she had run next door where two girls shared an apartment. They called 911, and shortly thereafter Dr. Lyndon "Lindy" Steinhaus, a resident in psychiatry who lived in the complex, arrived home. "He went in and pronounced Dolly dead," she finished.

Angela remembered that, later, she found the sacks of groceries in the kitchen—still unpacked—as if Dolly had just come home from the store. There were also some items that Dolly must have taken from their freezer, and they had thawed on the counter.

For Angela, as for almost everyone Scott Peebles talked to, time had telescoped; Dolly's death might as well have occurred only a week before. Angela told Peebles that she had never believed that Dolly killed herself. "She wasn't depressed. She ate. She slept well. She was happy, even though she was getting more aggravated with some of the things Bart did. And Dolly was a very considerate person; I know she wouldn't have shot herself on our couch for me to find her."

Step by step, Scott Peebles reinterviewed everyone he could locate who had had any connection to Dolly Hearn's alleged "suicide." Technically, this was the third time witnesses were questioned. Fifteen years earlier, Richmond County investigators had talked to a number of people; Sarah Hargett Mims had spoken to even more possible witnesses some weeks later. And now Peebles was interviewing, reviewing, asking the same probing questions again. He noted that the answers didn't change.

When he wondered about something, Scott Peebles consulted with his father to check on the older detective's recall of certain events.

Some artifacts of Dolly's death survived, perhaps because there had never been a definitive conclusion to the case. The Hearns still had the .38-caliber revolver that Carlton Sr. had given to Dolly. Dennis Stanfield, Dolly's landlord and friend, had some ledger books in his files that were still stained with a few drops of Dolly's blood.

One of the last people to see Dolly alive was someone who had scarcely known her: a young woman named Sandra Lake.* Bart had mentioned a woman who had stopped by Dolly's apartment on June 6 while he was there talking to her. He'd even recalled that he was in the bathroom. But Peebles saw that Sarah Mim's report on his story was somewhat different.

In 1990, Sandra had just begun working at Dennis Stanfield's company—Stanfield Home Builders. On Monday, June 4, Dolly had come into the office to get some check stubs so she could enter the information into Stanfield's business ledger. The two women met and talked briefly. Dolly called later, saying she needed more check stubs to complete the job. Since Sandra didn't know her, she was concerned at first when Dolly said she would come over to the office to look for them, but it was soon apparent that Dennis trusted Dolly. While Dolly sat on the floor, going through files, the women talked about Sandra's job and her child. Dolly had remarked, "I'll be an old lady before I have any children. Lots of guys propose to you, but it's not easy to find the right one."

They chatted again on Tuesday. On Wednesday, Dennis delivered the last of the check stubs to Dolly. When Sandra came back from lunch shortly before 1 P.M. that day, she discovered that she had inadvertently locked herself out of the Stanfield Homes office. She knew Dolly had a key, so she drove the short distance to the parking lot in front of the wing where Dolly's apartment was. There were no cars parked there, but when Sandra turned down the side road to the lower lot, she saw Dolly's Trans Am. A silver Monte Carlo was parked next to it, and Sandra noted it had no license plate. A work truck of some kind was parked at the far end of the lot. Bart told detectives in his 1990 interview that he drove a silver Monte Carlo.

Sandra had never been to Dolly's apartment, and had to ask a neighbor where it was. When she knocked, Dolly, carrying Tabitha, opened the door, and said, "Come on in!"

"Oh no—I just need a favor," Sandra demurred. "If I could borrow your office key—"

But Dolly urged her to come in, insisting two or three times. Sandra stepped inside, just far enough so that the door would close. The TV was turned to a soap opera. Sandra saw that the bathroom door under the stairway was slightly ajar. As she glanced at it, she could see a man through the crack where the hinges were. She told Scott Peebles that he appeared to be quite tall, had brown hair cut in layers, and he was bare-chested.

The man had been standing very still, and he said nothing. Sandra wondered if he was watching her in the bathroom mirror. Dolly didn't mention the man or glance in his direction. She seemed to take a lot of time retrieving her Lucite key ring, and then took several more minutes to remove two keys, commenting that she wasn't sure which one worked in the office door.

Sandra told Scott Peebles that Dolly was very eager to have her stay and visit, even to the point of acting as if they were old friends.

"She didn't seem stressed, and she wasn't really acting strange—just overly friendly."

Sandra said she had been worried about being late to work because she'd only recently started her job. While

Dolly chatted with her, she was anxious to leave, and hadn't even sat down.

And the man in the bathroom hadn't moved at all. Surely Dolly must have known he was there. If he was a welcome boyfriend, why had she wanted to chitchat with Sandra? He was half-dressed, so it wasn't likely he was a stranger. He just stood there, apparently listening. Peebles wondered why.

When Sandra was finally able to slip out the door, she said she had expected she would hear from Dolly during the afternoon. Sandra knew she was anxious to get more of the material she needed to finish her work for Stanfield. Yet Dolly didn't call even once.

Sandra told Peebles that when she heard late that afternoon that Dolly was dead—shot in the head—she did not believe it was suicide. She wondered if Dolly might have been trying to persuade her to stay in her apartment because she was afraid—because something was wrong.

But Sandra hadn't known Dolly well enough to pick up on some signal Dolly was sending. And she had never seen the brown-haired man's face.

Bart had undoubtedly been at the Wintergreen section of the apartments that day. He had admitted it himself. But he'd insisted he hadn't taken a shower there, and said he'd only sat on the couch and talked to Dolly. Why then had his shirt been off?

Peebles suspected that Bart hadn't expected a witness to his visit to Dolly. Most of the other residents in the front row of apartments facing Parrish Road had been away in the early afternoon of June 6.

Only one, Russell Leffler, who lived in the first apartment, had been home for lunch that day. When someone knocked on his door, he had looked through the peephole in his front door and recognized the man as someone he had seen with Dolly Hearn. Although he had seen him drive a gray "Camaro-ish" car before, he hadn't seen the car in the front parking lot that day. The man outside his door was leaning against it as if he was listening to see if anyone was home.

When Peebles showed him a photo of the way Bart looked in 1990, Leffler said he was sure it was the same man. Just as he was about to open the door, Leffler's phone rang—and he had turned away to answer it. When he came back, the man was gone.

Shortly after that, a woman had knocked—asking where Dolly lived. Peebles knew that would have been Sandra.

Dr. Lindy Steinhaus and his wife, Sue, who were close neighbors of Dolly's, were very aware of the sometimes strained relationship between Dolly and Bart. In the last few weeks before her death, the Steinhauses had noticed that Bart often visited Dolly's apartment on the weekends when Angela Garnto was away. They suspected Angela didn't know. Whether Dolly was happy to have Bart there was debatable. When Sue commented to Dolly that she was very thin, Dolly said she had lost twenty-three pounds.

"She said it was because of 'boyfriend problems,' " Sue told Scott Peebles.

The walls in their apartment house were thin, and they had often heard Bart yelling loudly, but never heard anything that would indicate physical violence. As Steinhaus pulled into the parking lot shortly after 5:00 on June 6, Angela Garnto had come running up the driveway, screaming that Dolly had shot herself, and was dead. She asked him to go into their apartment and take her pulse to be sure. He had done that, but he knew she had been dead for hours; her skin had been very white and very cold, and her massive blood loss had dried. He had seen the gun in her right hand at that time, and noted that the coffee table had been moved away from the front of the couch.

Both Sue and Lindy Steinhaus told Peebles that Dolly was a woman who was always smiling, not someone who would have killed herself. Her neighbors had gathered together that night in 1990, trying to understand what had happened. Like Angela and the Steinhauses, none of them believed she had killed herself, and several remarked that they had asked her if she was still dating Bart Corbin.

"Kind of," she had answered obliquely. "Until he goes away to residency."

There had been almost the sense that she was playing it safe, biding her time and trying not to set off Corbin's volatile side. He would be gone soon enough.

The Steinhauses knew that Dolly's parents had given her the gun that killed her, and remarked that she surely wouldn't have used their gift to kill herself. Those who had known Dolly well didn't think it odd when one woman added: "And she never would have shot herself in front of her cat. When they wheeled her body out on the gurney, Angela was holding Tabitha, and that cat just went nuts when the stretcher passed."

Scott Peebles knew that Tabitha was still alive after all the years between the Richmond County sheriff's two investigations. That aging cat was probably the only living witness to Dolly's death. But Tabitha couldn't say what she had seen—not then and not ever.

Chapter Twenty-Nine

DECEMBER 2004 AND SPRING 1990

As SERGEANT SCOTT PEEBLES continued to interview people who had never forgotten Dolly Hearn, he was particularly interested in a statement that one of Bart Corbin's closest friends, Dr. Eric Rader, had given to Sarah Mims, the Hearns' private detective. Like almost all of Corbin's friends from his days at the dental school in Augusta, Rader was married. Bart appeared to have sought out happily married couples, and was apparently anxious to be in a similar situation himself. Moreover, when his fragile emotional state began to disintegrate, he found his married friends and their wives were sympathetic listeners—even when he called late at night.

Eric Rader had, of course, been Bart's office partner at MCG, and they spent a lot of time together at the dental school. Peebles noted that it was Rader who had insisted that Bart admit to Dolly that he had stolen her cat and show her where he'd dumped it off.

Sarah Mims had caught up with Dr. Rader on October 18, 1990—some four months after Dolly Hearn's death. The Hearns' private investigator had found Rader most informative. Eric Rader told Sarah Mims that Bart had complained to him that Dolly was so busy that she wasn't paying enough attention to him. But when Bart asked Rader for advice, his friend and office partner Rader shook his head, insisting that it was none of his business and he didn't want to be involved in Bart's romance. Rader remembered that, shortly afterward, Bart had broken up with Dolly, later admitting that he had done it without thinking it through. Bart had been very upset when he discovered Dolly wasn't taking it very hard.

"He thought she would be heartbroken," Rader said, "and she apparently wasn't."

Eric Rader said he had realized early on that Bart Corbin had a negative and unstable self-image. Bart told him that he'd been fat in high school, and that, in college, he'd made conscious efforts to lose weight, work out, wear the right clothes, and have a nice car. A beautiful girlfriend was necessary, too, to bolster his confidence.

Sarah Mims's report quoted Eric Rader's comment that, after Bart broke up with Dolly, he regretted it. Eric recalled being with Bart and their fellow dental student, Tony Gacita, at the Tip-Top, a popular college nightspot, when Dolly arrived with a number of her classmates, mostly males. Bart had grumbled and started swearing, but he and Tony were able to persuade him not to approach her that night.

The next notation on the Rader report made Scott Peebles sit up straight. According to Eric Rader, there was a night during the late winter or early spring of 1990 when Bart confessed to him that he had come close to killing Dolly. "He said he waited in the parking lot of Dolly's apartment," Rader recalled. "And he had a gun. He told me he was planning to shoot her."

Moreover—although this was hearsay—Eric Rader had heard from Tony Gacita that Bart had told him he had planned "the perfect murder."

Both of these admissions had come out during one of Bart's tearful sessions with his trusted friends.

While Eric had driven Bart around, trying to comfort him, on the night Dolly's body was discovered, he could not help but notice that Bart didn't seem as distraught as one would expect. Bart had taken pains to point out that Dolly committed suicide with a gun her father had given her for Christmas.

Of course, Scott Peebles knew that Bart had told Lieutenant John Gray and Scott's father, Ron, that he didn't know Dolly had a gun, and that he'd never been upstairs in her apartment. But Peebles figured he had known full well that the .38 revolver was in a box under her bed.

Eric Rader had subsequently told the 1990 team of detectives that Bart had indeed known about the gun. He also said that when Bart found out what Eric had revealed about that gun to the Richmond County sheriff's investigators, he'd been really angry with him. But Rader's tip about the gun had apparently gone unheeded by the detectives, who were convinced that Dolly's death was a suicide.

The Hearns' PI had phoned Dr. Tony Gacita in Pennsylvania to ask him about Bart's brag that he knew how to commit the "perfect crime." Gacita verified that Bart made the remark during a weepy 3 A.M. call on February 24, 1990, during Dolly's date with Jon Everett—when she was so terrified by Bart's pounding on the door that she had finally called the police. And Bart had kept Tony Gacita on the phone for two or three hours until just before dawn. He had asked Tony to come over, and when he arrived he had found Bart holding a gun, threatening suicide.

Bart had sobbed that he had "cheated his way through life," and wanted to die. He said his friends didn't know him, and he couldn't live with that. Gacita recalled to Mims that Bart was all over the place emotionally, suddenly switching gears and saying that he knew how to "commit the perfect crime."

Gacita had managed to get the gun away from Bart and he later hid it—and a second gun—at his own house. He took Bart home with him to spend the rest of that night in February 1990, and Vicky, Gacita's girlfriend and soon to be his wife, had arranged for Bart to see a psychologist.

Three and a half months later, Bart had come for his guns on the night Dolly died, but the Gacita-Martins hadn't given them to him. Instead, they had taken them to Bart's father, who was staying at a nearby motel.

Tony Gacita had told Sarah Mims that Gene Corbin was angry with Bart for admitting to police that he had been at Dolly's apartment on the day she died, and had admonished his son for being stupid—telling him that people had been convicted of murder with nothing more than "circumstantial evidence."

Scott Peebles felt that there *had been* ample circumstantial evidence in 1990 incriminating Dr. Bart Corbin in the murder of Dolly Hearn, and now, in mid-December 2004, with DeWayne Piper's blood pattern evidence that proved someone had moved Dolly's body after her death, there was physical evidence, too.

Peebles located Dr. Eric Rader at his dental clinic near

Atlanta, and phoned him. He asked the dentist who had once been Bart's officemate in med school if he remembered making a statement to Sarah Hargett Mims. He did, indeed.

"Was her report accurate—where Bart told you he waited in Dolly's parking lot, planning to shoot her?"

"Yes," Rader said. "I remember distinctly that he told me that."

Next, Peebles faxed a copy of Mims's report on her interview with Dr. Tony Gacita to Gacita's dental clinic in Pennsylvania. Gacita, too, agreed that his statements about Bart's early-morning phone call were accurate. But, after fifteen years, he was a little unsure of every detail that led up to Bart's claim that he knew how to commit the "perfect murder" or the "perfect crime."

Tony and Vicky Gacita said they had spoken to Bart only once after he left Augusta. He had called them late one night in September 1990, but they told him they could not talk. Like many of the people who had known him when Dolly Hearn died, they had become a little afraid of him.

*   *   *

DANNY CRAIG WAS the district attorney of Richmond County, an affable, intelligent man who seemed completely comfortable in his own skin. His job sometimes put him at risk, however, and after threats were made on his life, the county provided him with a car that he could unlock and start with a remote key from many yards away. His supporters didn't want him to have to fiddle with a car door when he encountered sudden danger. He and his counterpart in Gwinnett County, DA Danny Porter, had both been threatened; it was something they shared, just as they shared the same first name. Each had enraged opponents who were either crooked, delusional, or who didn't care where their income came from. Whether the death threats were real or meant to intimidate them, they didn't want to hang around and find out.

Craig was an Augusta native, descended from Augusta natives, and he loved his city. With good reason, for Augusta is a beautiful and gracious city with wide boulevards, abundant flowers, historic churches, and rich traditions. He especially enjoyed giving tours of Augusta. From the narrow streets down in the flats with their tiny houses huddled close together to the splendid mansions in the Summerhill neighborhood less than a mile away, to the paper cup factory and on to the manicured golf courses that attract thousand upon thousands of spectators at the Masters' Tournament each April, Craig knew his way around his native city like the lines on his own hand.

Danny Craig had personal stories to tell about every spot. Crossing over a bridge, he would point to the wide canal that rushed beneath, as he recalled a boating trip when his wife, Crystal, who was very pregnant with one of their three daughters at the time. She fell out of their boat into deep water after some teenaged boys threw stones at them and swamped the boat. Craig rescued her and then chased the culprits down and marched them to the police.

By 2004, Danny Craig had been the district attorney in Richmond County for several terms, and from his optimistic approach toward life, it would have been easy to believe he had no problems beyond the next case he would prosecute. He had a devoted wife, who was a registered nurse, three pretty and smart daughters, and a warm and welcoming two-story house on a wide, treed lot. But the

Craigs had suffered a tragedy a few years earlier that only other parents could fully understand.

One evening as the sun was setting, their eighteen-year-old middle daughter, Sarah Elizabeth, had driven only a short distance from home to pick up a friend so they could help each other deal with the sudden death of one of their classmates. She was a little late in calling home when Crystal Craig heard sirens keening less than a block from their house.

She was devastated when she learned that her own daughter had been terribly injured in a car accident. Sarah had come to a stop at the intersection of the street where the Craigs lived. Blinded by the orange setting sun in her eyes, she didn't see the truck approaching to her left, and she pulled directly into its path.

One of her two passengers, Lydia Guntharp, seventeen, was killed, and Sarah came very close to dying, but prayers and her family's constant presence called her back to life, but not to full consciousness. It was a stellar day when she was able to leave the hospital. An absolutely brilliant student before her accident, Sarah Elizabeth lay in bed at home for years, all of her plans and hopes for college seemingly gone. Her progress was agonizingly slow, but someone was always with her, and in the evenings it was her dad.

As he plunged into the Corbin investigation, Danny Craig went to work every weekday as the district attorney of Richmond County, but each night he sat next to Sarah's bed, talking to her, reading, occasionally doing paperwork. By 2006, she was able to respond to questions by wiggling her right foot, and her mother knew what colors and songs Sarah liked.

Devout Catholics, the Craigs refused to weep about

what their family had lost, but continued to hold out hope for a happy future for Sarah Elizabeth.

It's doubtful that the criminals he investigated and later faced in court ever saw the other, tender, side of Danny Craig's life. People had to know him well before he would speak of his daughter.

*   *   *

SCOTT PEEBLES CONFERRED with Danny Craig, Assistant District Attorneys Jason Troiano, and Parks White, presenting his case and explaining all the reasons he was convinced that Bart Corbin had shot Dolly Hearn.

The men in the District Attorney's Office agreed that it was time to take the case before a grand jury. Danny Craig jotted down a list of the compelling factors that stamped Bart Corbin as a guilty man:

The breakup
The criminal behavior
Burglary
Theft of cat
Hair spray in contact lens solution
Theft of files
Things he chose to steal, e.g., "Dolly's favorite tuxedo outfit"
The recorded admission by silence
Knowledge of the gun gained in burglaries of apartment
Approach to neighbor's apartment
Presence of defendant's car
License tag removed from car

Stands "frozen" behind bathroom door while Sandra L. is there

Recorded message to stage an alibi

Later admission of his presence

Effect of his (later) admission—he staged an alibi

Innocent people don't stage alibis

Dolly was preparing food for family vacation

Female shot in the head—unusual for suicide

Specific bullet trajectory—destroyed pons at top of brain stem

Blood spatter evidence

Absence of blood on handle of gun

Negative gunshot residue test (not compelling as isolated fact)

Wound immediately disabling

Dolly's fear of defendant—Tip-Top incident

Defendant's midnight visit to Jon Everett's apartment

Retrieval of his personal gun after "suicide"

It wasn't a particularly long list of evidence and circumstances that suggested murder rather than suicide, but it was more than enough to remind Danny Craig of the case against Bart Corbin. Each phrase and ramification stamped him as a clever, enraged, premeditated killer. And, thank God, they still had the witnesses who would back up the physical evidence. DeWayne Piper and Scott Peebles had been the ideal investigative team.

Craig felt that the Augusta grand jury would have enough variables to consider, and return with an arrest warrant for Barton Corbin for the shooting death of Dorothy Carlisle Hearn.

Chapter Thirty

December 3–22, 2004

Detective Marcus Head had every reason to feel confident that Bart Corbin wasn't going to flee. He was at his dental clinic every day and went to lunch each day with Dara Prentice, who appeared to be very supportive of him. Although Dara was married, the investigators had heard a flood of rumors about her personal relationship with Corbin. Teams of deputies and investigators were keeping track of him, much to his apparent annoyance. News crews were also nearby, waiting for something to happen.

The officers tracking Bart were in plainclothes and drove unmarked vehicles. They waited outside his mother's house in Snellville on Tuesday evening, December 21, and then followed him to the Frontera restaurant on Highway 78, where they observed him meet a short man, who wore a black leather jacket. The men shook hands, and then walked down to Ruby Tuesday's. One of the undercover investigators was standing just behind Bart when the tall dentist said to the man. "We need to sit somewhere secluded so we can talk serious business."

Unaware that there was a cop just behind him, Bart glanced over his shoulder four or five times to see if anyone was listening.

At that point, they moved farther away, and the undercover officer couldn't hear what they said. It was a short meeting; six minutes later, Bart Corbin walked out, got into his tan truck, and drove away.

On December 22, Bart's forty-first birthday, Scott Peebles notified Marcus Head in Gwinnett County that an arrest warrant charging Bart Corbin with murder had just been issued by Richmond County in Augusta. Head assured Peebles that there were already surveillance teams following Corbin, and that he believed an arrest could be accomplished before the sun set.

While they had waited for the Richmond County grand jury to hand down an indictment, Gwinnett County police officers had always hoped to arrest him at his office. Confronting him in a relatively private venue would give them the opportunity to control the situation. Corbin had made it very clear he didn't want anything to do with the police, and no one knew how this man, who was given to violent rages, would react.

On that Wednesday morning three days before Christmas, Bart was seeing patients in his clinic on Braselton Highway, apparently conducting his practice as usual. Investigators G. R. Thompson and M. A. Lester were part of a four-man team assigned to surveil Bart Corbin, and, as always, they waited outside his dental office in Hamilton

Mill. Suddenly, they were notified that Corbin had just been indicted in Richmond County and were told to stand by.

At about ten minutes to noon, Bart and Dara Prentice left the clinic and walked toward a white Chevy Suburban. Bart looked up at the sky at a low-hovering helicopter with the logo "11 Alive," and slipped quickly into the passenger seat. Dara drove the SUV, heading slowly toward the parking lot exit, and then turned onto Jim Moore Road.

Although the plan had been for Marcus Head to come to the office to arrest Bart, he instructed Thompson to stop Dara's car before it could disappear into traffic. "Then move in and make the arrest," Head said. "I'm headed your way now."

Fortunately, Dara's SUV was caught in heavy traffic at the intersection of Braselton (Georgia Highway 124) and Jim Moore Road. The day shift team from the Gwinnett County police decided to move in. Detective C. T. Fish wore a sweatshirt with "POLICE" written across the chest and back as he approached the driver's door. He asked Dara Prentice who was in the car with her, and she answered, "Dr. Corbin."

Fish shouted to the surveillance team that Corbin was, in fact, in the car. Thompson and Lester blocked the white vehicle in the front, while G. Linder pulled in close behind. Thompson and J. R. West approached the passenger door where Bart Corbin was sitting, and the other three officers—Lester, Linder, and J. Carter stood by. West shouted to Bart to raise his hands, and he complied. He was clearly surprised, and he put up no struggle as he was removed from the car, put on the ground, and handcuffed, although he insisted it wasn't necessary to handcuff him.

Bart was even more surprised when he found he was

under arrest on a warrant—not out of Gwinnett County—
but from Richmond County. The grand jury in Augusta
had handed down a sealed warrant charging Corbin with
"felony and malice murder" in the death of Dolly Hearn.
He had almost expected to be arrested in his home county,
but he thought he had left his problems in Augusta in the
distant past.

Marcus Head arrived to transport Bart to jail. As
Head lifted the prisoner off the ground, Bart asked him to
please pull up his collar, which Head did. The hovering
Channel 11 helicopter followed Head's gold undercover
car as it headed toward Hi Hope Road in Lawrenceville.
The two men made small talk as they drove toward police
headquarters, conversation that men fall into easily—
sports, the weather, avoiding any discussion of the charges
against Bart. He would not talk without his attorneys present, and Head respected that.

The fact that it was Bart Corbin's birthday was only
accidental—the grand jurors in Augusta were unaware
that the date meant anything. It wouldn't be his best, although it might not be his worst, either. Film footage and
whatever details the media could gather of his arrest were
aired over and over on television stations in the Atlanta
area, with announcers breaking into regular programming
with news bulletins.

*   *   *

BART DIDN'T STAY LONG in the Gwinnett County police office. An hour later, Richmond County detectives Scott Peebles and Don Bryant arrived in two unmarked cars to
transport him east to Augusta. He would ride in one police
vehicle, while the second car would follow behind to avert

any attempt on his part to escape. He didn't look like an escape risk, but he was certainly a man capable of desperate acts, and the extra precautions might be needed. In Augusta, photographers caught the image of a tall, very thin man, handcuffed and manacled as he walked next to Bryant in a shadowed area near the Law Enforcement Center, headed for jail.

Bart fully expected to be released within a short time.

*   *   *

DARA PRENTICE WASN'T ARRESTED, but Detective D. P. Henry interviewed her as Bart was taken away. She said she had known Bart for more than nine years. Asked about Jenn Corbin, she said she didn't know a "whole lot" about the Corbins' marriage because she tried not to get involved in any family problems. However, she said she was friendly with Jenn and her family, and they went to each other's children's birthday parties and ball games.

"I knew Bart was filing for divorce, and Jenn asked me a couple of things—as far as did I know that he had hit her? One thing I told him when he asked me something was to try to work it out 'cause you've got kids involved."

Dara said Jenn had had an appointment for Monday, November 29, in Bart's office, the Monday before her death. Dara said she had called Jenn on the previous Tuesday to tell her that her dental crown had come in, but Jenn said she and Bart weren't on speaking terms, and she wouldn't be in. Dara said she hadn't asked any questions about that.

Bart had been more voluble about what was going on, explaining to Dara that he was living at home but sleeping in a separate bedroom. He had also told Dara that Jenn was corresponding with someone on the Internet, and that he'd talked to his wife about that since he "wasn't happy" about her corresponding with a strange man.

Dara was a difficult interview. Although she said a lot of words, they were evasive and she never quite answered Detective Henry's questions. She gave herself away as she said "Ummmmm" before every answer, and in between many words. She didn't know of any woman Bart might have talked to a lot on the phone—besides herself.

"Okay, let me ask you this," Henry began, "and this is for investigative purposes only. We've heard rumors—"

"*I've* heard rumors," she echoed.

"Okay, and that is that you were having an affair with him."

"I've heard rumors, ummmmm."

"Is there any truth to that?"

"No, we have been good friends, and like I said, ummmmm, we go to lunch just about every day together because we work together."

"You're not in any type of relationship at all?"

"Friendship." Dara refused to discuss anything more about what she and Bart Corbin were to each other. She was clearly torn, and trying to protect her boss by minimizing his temper tantrums, and insisting that he could not have shot Jenn in the head. He'd sworn he hadn't done that when he spoke to Dara on December 4.

That information had not been released on the day Jenn died, and Henry jumped in and asked, "He knew she'd been shot *in the head*?"

"Right. He knew that *after*." She realized her mistake, and tried to make up for it. "I don't know when he knew that, but you know—I know he'd found that out, but he didn't know where—"

In the end, Dara struggled with what might be the truth. "I've just gone back and forth, 'cause I sit there and look at the stuff on the news. I look at that other case in Augusta, and like it doesn't look good. But then I try to think that I've known him a long time. I would hate to think my judgment's that bad."

Henry tried to make it easy for her to give her frank opinion: "Things like this happen in the blink of an eye, just for a fraction of a second. Then everything's back to normal, and somebody loses their temper and their cool for just a couple of seconds and they do something that normally they would not do, and then it's something they have to regret for the rest of their lives. I deal with it all the time, because I work Homicide, so I see really good people that do things not in their normal character . . . Sometimes everything is aligned just right, and something happens, and then it's over with and the chances of its happening again are a million to one."

"I feel bad for her family," Dara said, "and I feel bad for the boys. I really hate it for the boys."

Did Henry really believe that Bart was unlikely to hurt anyone again? Hardly a possibility. Henry knew all about Dolly Hearn. And it seemed that the odds involving what harm Bart Corbin might do were much lower than "a million to one."

Later, Dara would admit to investigators that Bart had called her on either December 2 or 3 and asked her to come to his dental clinic to help him clean up broken glass. He said he had discovered that someone broke out a back window, although he wasn't yet sure what was missing.

As always, she had done what he asked without question.

When the investigative team learned of that, they had

discussed their suspicions with one another. They concluded that Bart had accidentally locked the .38 revolver in his office on December 3, and broke in to retrieve it.

* * *

MARCUS HEAD AND HIS CREW and DA Danny Porter's investigators were uncovering more and more parallels between Dolly's and Jenn's murders. Bart had created an alibi when he left the message on Dolly's answering machine breaking a date with her—ironically ending it with "I love you." But he had to adjust his alibi when Sandra Lake saw him in Dolly's bathroom. With an eyewitness coming forward, he had no choice but to admit in his second interrogation that he had visited Dolly's apartment on the afternoon she died.

He had also set up several alibis in Jenn's murder. Some, like making a haircut appointment, were almost identical in both murders. However, he hadn't left a phone message for Jenn. Instead, he had written in his journal, probably expecting that the Gwinnett team would find it.

They did, and they read the three carefully composed pages he had written, beginning on December 1. Bart portrayed himself as sensitive and loving, while painting Jenn as unstable and confused, the kind of woman who might well commit suicide. He'd done it with Dolly, and now, he'd done it with Jenn.

His phrases were flowery and overdone, his style part Edwardian, and part Harlequin romance.

On Wednesday, December 1, he wrote, "Hardest but most cleansing discussion Jenn and I have ever had. I am proud of the discipline I displayed externally, but it disguises a man torn apart."

Bart described how Jenn had allowed him to comfort her, as she seemed to be the "sweet, sensitive woman" of their early days together.

"As we became 're-introduced' to some comfort level of long ago, we delved into deeper waters of emotion. I wished not to feel again, but sadistically drawn to [her] as a moth to a flame. I tried in vain to kiss away her tears of pain, repressing memories, long, hard passionate kisses. Her great pain fed by a grotesque false sense of inadequacy she has endured. Her demeanor became more cold, matter of fact, and stoic. Was this an instrument to deliver retaliation with confessions admitted to me? Necessity or purge? Benefit or consequence? Pain as I would hesitate to lay upon my worst counterpart, my cross to bear faithfully in sacrifice to cease my lover's anguish. I questioned not enough; she spoke not enough. Can I conjure the strength and courage to weather the storm? I know not now. Time will tell. Jenn is my only love."

The Gwinnett County investigators might have found Bart Corbin's first journal entry more convincing if he had not dated it on the day that he had begun by stealing his wife's purse, journal, cell phone, and then running over her foot. And when was this soul-searching conversation supposed to have taken place? Jenn had stayed Wednesday night at her sister Heather's home.

The detectives knew it was all a faked journal entry. And they noted the repetitive use of I . . . I . . . I . . . I. Bart wrote continually of his own feelings, stopping only to describe Jenn as a mixed-up, neurotic woman in pain.

His journal entry on December 2 was almost pure pornography, something one might expect to find in XXX-rated magazines in plain wrappers, kept behind the counters of convenience stores. Bart wrote about being lasciviously seduced by Jenn in their shower, suggesting that he had been shocked at her immodesty. He—the honorable man in the journal—had been extremely disturbed that the mother of his children had been so sexually demanding.

But Jenn had told her mother, her sister, and her best friends that she could not bear to have her husband touch her. More indicative that Bart's version was not true: Jenn wasn't even home during the time he described. She was still at Heather's house, trying to explain why she had to go home or lose her house in the divorce action to come.

After his description of wanton sex with Jenn, Bart wrote on December 3 about how Dalton had asked to ride bikes with him—so he had agreed. He had also agreed to "let" Jenn take Dalton to basketball practice. Then Bart wrote that he had cooked supper, and played a SpiderMan game and the Candy Land game with Dillon.

Continuing to burnish his image as the perfect father, Bart described how he'd helped Dillon brush and floss his teeth. "He asked me to sleep with him [as he does frequently] until he fell asleep close to 9:30 p.m. Jenn returned from practice, [but she] contrived to finish housework, then retreated to the master bedroom to watch television."

The rest of Bart's last entry in his journal was taken up with his continuing complaints that Jenn was too sexually aggressive, while before she "was always angelic to me." He wrote that he would have much preferred to sit quietly with her and hold her hand.

Bart had never cooked dinner in anyone's memory. The rest of his "journal" was equally suspect.

The December 3rd entry was the last.

*   *   *

AS HE CONTINUED to interview people who had been important in Jenn Corbin's life, Marcus Head discovered how frantic Bart Corbin was on that last Friday night. Head doubted that he would have been capable of cooking supper or playing games with Dillon. When Head interviewed Juliet Styles and her husband, Darren, he found that Bart had called them on Friday night, too. Bart had reached Juliet on her cell phone, and she was surprised because she didn't think he had the number, and he called her only rarely—usually when he was looking for Jenn. Later, she learned he had stolen Jenn's phone and was calling everyone whose information was stored there.

"I'd been talking to Jenn earlier," Juliet told Head, "but Bart was sorta popping in and out of the house, and she would say, 'Bart's here—I've gotta go.' "

When Bart called Juliet on that last Friday night, December 3, he had sounded rational at first, but she could hear a hoarseness in his voice that sounded as though he'd been crying. He asked her, "Do you think there's any hope?"

She had tried to soothe him and said that Jenn was going to go to marriage counseling, and that could be a good sign. But Bart kept harking back to Jenn's Internet relationship. Had Juliet ever seen a photograph, and had she ever met the man? She told him "No"—which was true—and said that as far as she knew, the person was out of state. And Juliet had tried to lighten his mood by saying, "He can't be any better looking than you."

"Is she only staying with me for financial reasons?" Bart pressed.

Juliet had admitted that that was certainly one of the reasons. "But she's scared to leave you, Bart. Besides throwing away her marriage, she's like me—a stay-at-home mom, and she's worried about how she's gonna support herself."

Later, Juliet wondered if she had told Bart too much, but he'd sounded in fairly good control of himself. She knew that her best friend was leaving her husband, but she thought he would adjust to it in time. Juliet told Marcus Head that she'd invited Jenn to her house the next day, Saturday, when they planned to discuss Jenn's plans in depth.

"She did tell me," Juliet said, "that she wasn't leaving her husband for this Internet person; she was leaving because this person had opened up her eyes that she didn't have to walk around on eggshells, and fear Bart, you know—his sharp words and stuff, anymore."

Of course, it had been far too late for Jenn. Marcus Head now knew that, at that point, Jenn Corbin had approximately five and a half hours to live.

Chapter Thirty-One

BART WAS SITTING in the Richmond County Jail in Augusta, charged with the murder of Dolly Hearn. That was somewhat ironic because both Danny Porter and Danny Craig felt that Gwinnett County had the stronger case for a murder conviction. But it had only been eighteen days since Jenn's murder, and Porter's case was embryonic; they had many avenues to explore before they would have it tightly knit.

The Gwinnett County investigators had an avalanche of circumstantial evidence, but they still needed to trace Corbin's movements after he drove off from Kevin Lyttle's house during the early morning hours of December 4. They had yet to find any witnesses who had actually seen him before he appeared at his brother Bobby's house. Steve Comeau was sure it was Bart's truck he'd heard come down Bogan Gates Drive. But that was merely supposition.

Comeau figured it was Bart and that he'd probably had a few too many drinks. Whoever it was who had turned into the Corbins' driveway had stayed no more than thirty minutes—if that. Comeau didn't remember anyone else on the street during that time. No one else in their neighborhood drove a Chevy truck with a 350-horsepower engine and dual exhausts.

How could the investigators place Bart in his own house at the vital time?

One member of Jack Burnette's team, Russ Halcome, had an idea about that, but first he had to check out how Jenn and Anita Hearn had corresponded.

Halcome, who was one of the top forensic technology experts in the DA's office, drafted two search warrants that enabled detectives not only to search the Corbin house on Bogan Gates Drive, but also to seize the computer there.

Halcome maintained his "own little computer lab" in the Gwinnett County District Attorney's Office. Whenever he began an evaluation of a suspect computer in an investigation, he looked first into the tower case, which held the hard drive and other computer components. He searched for signs that someone had recently been in there, and might have attempted to modify the computer components. Had any screws been changed or replaced? That would indicate that the hard drive had been in and out, or even that a booby trap such as a device with an electromagnetic force had been placed inside the tower case. In this instance, there was no hard drive at all, but Halcome detected where it had once been by traceries in the dust patterns.

It was frustrating to look into the empty case, but

often there are other ways to get around such blank walls, and Halcome got lucky. A day or so later, an *Atlanta Journal-Constitution* reporter wrote a feature article about computer forensics, a relatively new—but powerful—investigative tool. It was common knowledge in Atlanta that emails were somehow involved in the Jenn Corbin probe, and the reporter used the Corbin case as an example of how detectives utilized computer forensics. That was fortuitous for Russ Halcome.

"I got a phone call in early January from a guy who read that article," Halcome recalled. "He wondered if I'd be interested in what was on the hard drive that had been in the Corbins' computer."

Suppressing his excitement, Halcome replied laconically. "Yeah, I would."

The caller was the computer technician in Norcross who had worked on the hard drive that Bart asked him to look at.

"I happen to have a copy of the hard drive that Bart Corbin brought in," he said. "My practice is always to make a copy before I start working on it, and I use that copy to work from."

Bart had told the computer expert that he was filing for divorce because his wife was having an affair on the Internet. She had printed out some of the emails sent through his Bell South provider, but he said he hadn't been able to find anything after September. He said he'd discovered that she had a Yahoo email account, but he didn't know the name she was using or the password. He did know that she was writing to someone named "Chris" or "Christopher" with an email address of sirtank1223@yahoo.com. Corbin had wanted copies of any emails or correspondence—including instant messages—that might exist on the hard drive.

The computer technician told Halcome that Bart Corbin returned on December 8, nine days after he left the hard drive. He had come back "in a rush and a huff," demanding to have it back at once. The computer expert said he had handed it over, but he still had the copy he'd made of the contents on that hard drive. He hadn't gotten around to destroying it yet.

Halcome could no longer hide his enthusiasm, "Where are you? I'll be right over."

The technician wasn't sure what he should do, and asked if he could talk to an attorney first. Although he hated to wait, Russ Halcome said, "Sure."

On his attorney's advice, the computer whiz asked that the DA's office send him something official, asking for the evidence. Assistant DA Tom Davis wrote up a subpoena, and Halcome presented it, and then took the hard drive into evidence.

Russ Halcome knew that once the hard drive was out of the Corbins' computer, Jenn would have lost a key way to communicate with Anita Hearn, because she had lost her basic Internet connection. However, her PlayStation II had a keyboard and was online so Jenn had been able to instant-message on that, though IMs, by their very design, have to be short.

In Jenn's last days, she had written scores of brief messages to Anita, and from eight hundred miles away, Anita had been virtually an "eyewitness" to Jenn's murder. They had instant-messaged and phoned each other throughout the evening of December 3.

And then, suddenly, Jenn was no longer there. Not on her PlayStation. Not on her cell phone.

* * *

CELL PHONES ARE one of the richest sources of information for forensic technology experts to mine. The normal investigation procedure is to determine if a suspect has a cell phone. If he does, detectives want to see phone records. Halcome had numerous contacts with phone companies, and he filled out phone requests for "call detail" reports.

"We were looking for calls in and calls out," he explained. "In this case, the original investigators had already identified certain cell phone numbers."

Russ Halcome turned next to checking on Bart Corbin's cell phone usage, and was pleased to find that Corbin was a cell phone addict. Between December 1 and December 22, when he was arrested on the Richmond County warrant, Bart had initiated 851 calls on his cell phone. Sixty-five of them were on December 4 and 5. Corbin had apparently felt naked without his cell phone, and his obsession with it had increased over the previous few months. He had used it to try to trace and trap Jenn Corbin, but also to create alibis for himself.

Now it occurred to Halcome that that sword could cut both ways. Bart's cell phone could be used to trace *his* activities as well. Following his footsteps would require a lot of research and cross-connections, but Halcome was a man who loved the challenges in each new case.

"I haven't had to work a day in my life," he said cheerfully. "This is all great fun."

Halcome focused now on Bart Corbin's cell phone calls, charting the "towers" and "sectors" where Corbin's calls had leap-frogged from their origins to their final destinations. Most people don't notice the cell phone towers that rise from the landscapes of America like skeleton trees whose bones are made of metal. And yet the towers are virtually everywhere, bouncing signals that connect our wireless networks. These networks can be searched for phone records, but they also can be used to chart the comings and goings of the humans who make those cell phone calls. Cell phones are actually far more accurate for this purpose than calls made from an ordinary phone wired to one location.

Armed with a list of Bart's telephone calls, Halcome set to work, believing he could make a map of exactly where Bart Corbin had been at particular times. It was all dependent upon how often he had used his cell phone, and with those sixty-five calls he'd made shortly before and after Jenn Corbin's murder, Halcome had more than enough information. He shared his findings with Jack Burnette and DA Danny Porter.

"When we found out where he was—at the Wild Wing Cafe, and then at Kevin Lyttle's house—we charted out the tower locations, and drew up maps to follow his route and times on the night of December 3rd and 4th," Halcome explained. "The guys at Nextel gave me a key—or a code—to figure out physical addresses, sectors, latitudes, and longitudes. Then I put that information into Microsoft's 'Streets and Trips' software. And there was Bart Corbin driving through small towns in Gwinnett County.

"We could see Hamilton Mill Road where they hooked up.

"I am on my own cell phone a lot, working out my 'to do' list as I'm driving. Bart apparently did the same thing."

Russ Halcome put his spreadsheets on a computer disk, and he read all the police reports from his fellow investigators, and from the Gwinnett County Police file that Marcus Head had prepared. He read all the witness statements. Everything tracked for the first part of the evening.

Bart's calls were hitting on the towers that matched the addresses where he claimed to have been.

Halcome was prepared to testify in Corbin's trial that the defendant had, indeed, been at the Wild Wing Cafe, and buying coffee at a Wal-Mart on the way to Lyttle's house, and, finally, after 3 A.M., at a tower close to his brother Bobby's house.

"But there was no way he could have been at Bobby's as early as he said he was," Russ Halcome pointed out. "His cell phone hit on a tower close to his own house in Buford—just about the time we figured that Jenn was shot—right after Steve Comeau heard what he thought was Bart's truck coming up the street. He made a couple of phone calls that bounced off the tower closest to Bogan Gates Drive."

Believing he was smarter than any detective, Bart Corbin was unaware that he'd left a trail of cell phone tower hits behind him, hits that showed he had been in his own neighborhood for just long enough to kill the wife who wanted only to be free of him. In fact, one of those outgoing cell phone calls was at 1:58 A.M.

Could Russ Halcome explain the very technical and detailed aspects of how he had tracked Bart Corbin to a jury? He thought of how confused the O. J. Simpson jury had been as the prosecutors tried to explain DNA to them. What made perfect sense to Halcome might be difficult for a jury of laypersons to understand.

But it was enough to take to the grand jurors in Gwinnett County and get the indictment that Danny Porter and Marcus Head and their backup teams wanted so badly.

On January 5, 2005, a month after Jenn Corbin's death, the grand jury indictment came down in Gwinnett County. Barton Thomas Corbin was officially charged with one count of malice murder, one count of felony murder, and one count of possession of a firearm during the commission of a felony. The felony was Jenn's murder.

Superior Court Judge Melodie Snell Conner had issued a bench warrant to be sure there was a hold on Corbin in the unlikely chance he was able to post bond in Augusta. He would now face trials in two counties, but no one could say which jurisdiction would be the first to proceed. Judge Conner recused herself, asking to be replaced. Her reason was not—as some people thought—that she had attended high school in Snellville with Bart, but rather that she had taken evidence in Corbin's case and granted one of the early search warrants of the Bogan Gates house.

Judge Debra Turner would be the next judge to oversee matters involving Bart Corbin.

Shortly before the Gwinnett County indictment in Lawrenceville, Bart Corbin hired two of Georgia's top criminal defense attorneys, Bruce Harvey and David Wolfe of Atlanta. The two had worked as a team before, and very successfully. They had gone on the offensive immediately, asking for a most unusual order from the judge. They asked to have the grand jury hearings moved out of Gwinnett County, suggesting that the already massive media saturation might have prejudiced or otherwise tainted the grand jurors. Although the motion was not granted, Judge Turner granted a sweeping gag order. There was little question that it was necessary. Greta Van Susteren, *48 Hours, Dateline, People,* the weekly tabloids, and untold reporters were anxious to focus on each new detail of the crimes that Bart Corbin stood accused of. Turner's gag order shut down the flow of information, and the media soon found doors at least partially closed. It was frustrating, of course, to those who were seeking quotes and scoops on information that no one else had.

Bruce Harvey and David Wolfe were showmen. Wolfe was a former standup comedian whose thick gray hair grew over his collar. Harvey wore a ponytail and had tattoos peeking out below his shirt cuffs and above his collar. He was famous for his theatrics in trials, and savvy court-watchers were anxious to see what Harvey would do next as he fought for his clients. On one occasion where he represented a former table dancer in a racketeering trial in federal court, Harvey doffed his jacket and swirled it around as he performed a mock table dance for the jury. In another trial, he ripped off his tie and took a pugilistic pose aimed at the prosecutor. A peeved judge found little humor in that. Harvey blamed his behavior on nicotine deprivation because he was trying to quit smoking. That demonstration landed him in jail with a short stay for contempt.

CHAPTER THIRTY-TWO

2005

ON JANUARY 17, 2005, after less than a month in jail in Augusta, Bart Corbin was moved back to the Gwinnett County Jail in Lawrenceville, where he was housed in "administrative segregation." For his own protection, he would be kept away from other prisoners. Most men in jail and prison don't hurt women, and they take a harsh view of prisoners accused of killing them. Inmates charged with crimes against women or children who are housed in the general population are prone to "accidents" for which no witnesses come forward.

Initially, Danny Craig and Danny Porter decided that the first trial would be in Augusta, for the murder of Dolly Hearn, followed immediately by a trial in Jenn Corbin's case in Gwinnett County. Bart Corbin was arraigned in Lawrenceville on January 21, 2005, before Judge Turner.

The third Superior Court judge in Gwinnett Court, who became the permanent judge in the prosecution for Jenn Corbin's death, was Michael C. Clark. Back in 1981 when Gwinnett County was far more rural, Clark and Danny Porter were assistant DAs together. With the other four ADAs they had time then to drink beer, eat oysters, and tell war stories. Clark also went to the University of Georgia, but really mastered the law when he was a law clerk. A lifelong scholar, his chambers overflowed with books—all kinds of books. He had read them all, and was working toward his Ph.D. attending classes and seminars all over the world.

Before being elected to the bench in 1992, Michael Clark was a defense attorney for a decade. "Then, I was going through a big bottle of Rolaids every week," he recalled. "As a judge, I didn't have to take any."

Serious in trial, Clark's chambers were more whimsical. The placard on his desk read, "When in doubt, mumble." Next to that, two bronze dolphins represented another avocation: scuba diving in the Caribbean. His deepest dive was 217 feet.

*   *   *

IT SEEMED THAT A TRIAL would surely begin soon—either in Augusta or in Gwinnett County.

Newspapers in Georgia filed suit to have all gag orders in the Corbin cases dropped. On March 28, 2005, Judge Clark lifted the gag order, although he warned family, witnesses, police officers, and others to be careful of what they might say to the media. Max Barber appeared on the Nancy Grace show on Court TV, but he was cautious in what he said.

On March 29, both Jenn Corbin's family and Dolly Hearn's were in the courtroom for another hearing, wearing buttons with the dead women's pictures on them. Bart studiously avoided making eye contact with them.

Asked to speculate on trial dates, Danny Porter would say only that he expected the Richmond County case to go to trial in Augusta in the summer of 2005, and the trial on Jenn's murder in the fall.

In March, Max Barber filed a civil complaint asking that Bart be stopped from selling the house, along with other possessions that had once belonged to Jenn. In the years they had lived on Bogan Gates Drive, Bart had, of course, transferred title to their house three times to Jenn "with love and affection," meaning no money changed hands. It was a way to protect himself. Two months before her death, he had taken it back again. As it turned out, after Bart's refinancing there was no equity left in the house, nothing for Dalton and Dillon. It would eventually sell well below market value.

When Max had crawled in a window before Christmas to get the presents Jenn had bought for her sons, Bart had wanted the District Attorney's Office to file breaking and entering charges against him. No charges had ensued. Because they'd been barred from taking Dalton's and Dillon's beds from the house, Max and Narda had bought two sets of rough-hewn bunk beds so that Jenn's boys and Max and Sylvia would have somewhere to sleep—both at Doug and Heather's house and when they stayed at their grandparents' home.

* * *

AS THE FIRST SIGNS of spring 2005 appeared, Heather went to Jenn's dormant garden and dug up several of the plants

Jenn had loved, moving them to her own yard. The family planted a weeping willow tree in Jenn's memory, and Heather surrounded it with scores of tulip bulbs, Jenn's favorites. Within weeks, someone dug up Jenn's flowers. No one could say who had done that.

Heather searched constantly for signs that Jenn was somehow nearby, that she approved of the way Heather was managing all four of their children. It made her feel less lonely for her sister. She often saw a white dove whirling out of the sky to alight nearby, and ladybugs suddenly appeared where there had been none. Like Dalton, she had myriad dreams of Jenn. One morning when she had just wakened, Heather felt a sharp poke in her shoulder. She rolled over to see who had done it.

"Nobody was there," she recalled. "But I knew it was Jenn—just like the old Jenn, who was so organized— telling me to get up and get the kids ready for school."

Almost every day, Heather added something to her Internet journal, and it helped her get through the worst days. She wrote that she was grateful to be so busy with the children that she sometimes forgot her grief. And she shared the things she couldn't really explain with the thousands of people who read her website about Jenn.

One day that spring, Heather heard a faint sound, a "ping . . . ping . . . ping." It was coming from somewhere in her house, and she held her breath as she searched, hearing the insistent chime grow louder and then fading. It took Heather two days to locate its source. She hadn't yet had the heart to go through Jenn's things, but now she recognized the sound of the alarm on Jenn's watch, and she finally found it caught up in her sister's curlers, snagged on the blond hairs there. The watch, set months before to remind Jenn that she needed to pick her sons up at Harmony School, had, for some unexplainable reason, begun to chime. Its small sound was somehow comforting.

"You know your life has changed," Heather had written in February, "when you spend Valentine's Day with your husband at Chuck E. Cheeses!"

It was clear that Doug and Heather Tierney put the children—all four of them—first.

In April, a new website appeared on the Internet: "Friends of Bart Corbin." Brad, Bart's twin, was the webmaster, and the introduction of the new site said, "This web site has been created by Bart Corbin's friends to express our disappointment at unjustified assassination by private and public parties and the voyeuristic behavior of the media. Our purpose is to ask you to keep an open mind and think beyond what is published in the press and the CaringBridge.com website [host to Heather's site]."

The Corbins' site featured numerous pictures of Bart and Jenn in happier days, photos of the children, and extolled Bart's virtues, while denying any possibility of his guilt. It also requested donations to help pay for Bart's legal expenses. He had been the shining light in his family, and they were having a difficult time trying to raise funds for his defense in two trials that would surely last weeks, even months.

Dolly Hearn's brother Gil had a website, too, filled with photographs and memories of Dolly. She seemed as alive as she had ever been. Years before, her family had set up a scholarship in her name at the MCG Dental School, and many students had already benefited from it.

Soon, discussion groups on the Corbin case began to spring up on the Internet. This was a whole new venue for grieving, communicating, arguing, and politicizing. Just as the forensic investigation had moved into technical realms, so had those who cared for Jenn, Bart, and Dolly.

Would future jurors read these Internet pages? Perhaps. But although Danny Porter objected to the anonymous discussions about specifics and quality of evidence on the Corbin sites, he acknowledged that shutting down websites or home pages could violate the First Amendment. He and David Wolfe discussed problem areas and reached some agreement that certain posts should be removed.

The Internet speculation was akin to discussions about crimes a century ago among locals sitting around a pot-bellied stove at a country store—except that, in 2005, their opinions could instantly travel around the world.

*   *   *

DA DANNY PORTER and Senior Assistant DA Chuck Ross were gearing up for trial in Gwinnett County, just as Danny Craig and Jason Troiano were in Richmond County. Ideally, a prosecuting duo would have attorneys who complemented each other—one slightly more skilled at oratory and persuasive arguments, the other adept at the cross-examination. In Gwinnett County, Porter was the cross-examiner who could ask a series of questions that would lead a witness or defendant down a dead-end street, and then pounce and trip them up when their lies became apparent.

Chuck Ross was the "natural arguer." Always on the debate teams in high school and college, he had abandoned his ambition to earn a Ph.D. in political science when he became fascinated with criminal law. Ross paid his way through law school working as a bartender, and, even after he became an attorney, he invented somewhat bizarre drinks. Two of his specialties were the "Key Lime Pie" and the "Tiramisu" martinis. He was also a gourmet cook, but his remarkable knowledge of computer technology was what made him essential to the Corbin case.

Aware that their evidence might confuse a lay jury, Ross, the senior assistant DA and DA Danny Porter knew they were quite possibly in for the courtroom battle of their lives as they prepared the prosecution's case against Bart Corbin.

Everyone involved—from Bart Corbin, the defendant, to detectives and prosecutors in two counties, the families of the victims, the media, and the public—was anxious to see the case go to trial. Everyone, that is, with the exception of Bruce Harvey and David Wolfe. Corbin's defense team seemed determined to delay any trials for months— years—if they could. Some of their motions were capricious, and some were based on precedent-setting rulings in the state of Georgia.

And yet the summer of 2005 passed without a trial date, and hearings set for early September were postponed after Bart Corbin's defense team filed a motion claiming that the Gwinnett County investigators had illegally obtained evidence from the Corbins' home. They also wanted the information derived from the electronic surveillance of his cell phone thrown out.

On September 8, 2005, a first trial date was finally set: January 9, 2006. District Attorney Danny Craig in Augusta was scheduled to go first, prosecuting Bart Corbin for the murder of Dolly Hearn.

In the interim, Corbin's attorneys continued to file motions. On October 31, David Wolfe and Bruce Harvey, with a bit of bluster, asked for a *fourteen-year* delay in prosecution. Their reasoning was that it had taken Richmond County fourteen years to charge their client in Dolly's murder, so it was only fair that the trial should be put off for that long.

On December 7, a year and three days after Jenn Corbin's murder, a preliminary hearing was postponed after Harvey and Wolfe submitted a motion to have both the evidence retrieved after a search warrant on the Bogan Gates house and all evidence gleaned from Halcome's electronic surveillance barred from the upcoming trial in Augusta. They were determined not to have any evidence from the Jenn Corbin case pop up in the Augusta prosecution of Bart Corbin for Dolly Hearn's murder. If they could get it thrown out early, they wouldn't have to worry about it.

On December 14, 2005, the pretrial hearing was held in Superior Court Judge Carl C. Brown's Augusta courtroom. DA Craig listed all the similar circumstances that were part of both Dolly Hearn's and Jenn Corbin's murders, and submitted that just before Dolly's death Bart had told "a good friend" that he had planned the "perfect murder."

Again, both the Hearn and the Barber families were in the courtroom, this time for a hearing that would be exquisitely painful for them. Bruce Harvey presented a slide show. The first frame was a Harley-Davidson motorcycle, something that had nothing to do with either case. But, later, there were sexually provocative and incendiary quotes from Jenn Corbin's emails to Anita Hearn, the words hugely magnified on the screen. Narda Barber realized that the defense undoubtedly intended to use these slides in front of a jury, and her heart sank. Taken out of context, they were shocking. Her eyes filled with tears, and she dreaded the upcoming trials even more than she had before.

Next, Harvey painted Dolly as an academic failure who had been in danger of flunking out of dental school. He did not, of course, mention that Bart had stolen the projects that determined her grades for an entire quarter.

The defense position was that both women had been suicidal, and that Bart Corbin was about to be prosecuted for deaths that weren't even homicides. He suggested that Dolly had been depressed because she and Bart were breaking up, and Jenn had been shocked and saddened to find out the real identity of her email correspondent

Danny Craig pointed out that, in his opinion, Harvey's take on the dead women was completely backward; the victims had been anxious to be rid of Bart Corbin, and what Harvey saw as indications that the victims were suicidal was really evidence of Corbin's guilt.

"You don't jilt Dr. Corbin," the Augusta prosecutor intoned. "You die [if you try]."

Undeterred, Harvey and Wolfe asked Judge Brown to drop all charges against Bart Corbin in the case of Dolly Hearn. They stressed that so much time had passed that witnesses' memories had blurred and changed, and evidence had been lost. They suggested sarcastically that the state must have waited for Corbin to kill another person to advance their case against him for Dolly's alleged murder.

Craig scoffed at that. "That is preposterous," he said. "And long delays usually help—rather than hurt—the defendant's case."

Moreover, he assured the judge that the interview transcripts and police files from the 1990 case involving Dolly were intact, and that the gunshot residue test results were perfectly adequate.

Judge Brown reserved his decision on the defense motions.

*   *   *

ANOTHER CHRISTMAS HAD PASSED without a trial. Indeed, it would be a far longer delay for any trial in either victim's case than anyone involved could have guessed. But at least at the moment the one trial date was set: January 9, 2006. Shortly after Christmas, Danny Craig and his chief assistant DA, Jason Troiano, were scheduled to begin the trial in Dolly Hearn's murder.

January 9 arrived, but there was no trial. Instead, in yet another pretrial hearing, the two Dannies—Craig and Porter—announced that they had agreed that the positioning of the trials should be switched.

Danny Porter would prosecute Bart first in Gwinnett County for Jenn's death. After that, Porter hoped to move to Augusta and, as a specially appointed prosecutor in that venue, continue in a second trial, prosecuting Bart in the case of Dolly Hearn.

Danny Craig was open to that, but it would mean that there would be no trial at all in January. Now, Judge Brown postponed the first trial until April in Gwinnett County.

It was beginning to be difficult to keep track of the players and dates without a program.

As he sat in Judge Brown's courtroom, Bart Corbin's complexion was the pale yellow of prison pallor, and he appeared to be even thinner than before. His gaunt frame had lost all muscle tone; he was no longer working out in a health club. He spent his days and nights in a jail cell, avoiding other prisoners.

Bart wrote to people he had been close to in the past, including Shelly Mansfield, the girlfriend of his youth at the University of Georgia. Shelly was thousands of miles away, living in another country, married to someone else—but she had heard of his arrest and written to him, asking if there was anything she could do for him.

Bart's first letter to Shelly sounded "like the old Bart," Shelly recalled. He was hopeful that she might be a character witness for him when he went to trial. Remembering the gentle "boy" she'd known when he was nineteen, she felt sorry for him, and wrote back, telling him that she would consider being a defense witness.

But she was shocked by the acid tone of his second letter, a letter filled with vituperative and cruel criticism of his own son, Dalton. He was a grown man complaining about a little boy. She realized that Bart Corbin was no longer the person she remembered. She wondered if he ever had been. She didn't write to him again.

* * *

WITH THE LATEST TRIAL DATE coming up in April, there were motions to rule on. The most serious was undoubtedly the question of whether the startling similarities between Dolly's and Jenn's murders would be allowed in both trials. If they were, it would be a coup for the prosecution. And if they were not, jurors in Dolly's trial would not hear about Jenn's death fourteen years later. Conversely, Jenn's jurors wouldn't know about Dolly. Legally, incorporating evidence from two different homicides in one trial would be allowed only as "similar transactions."

Since the Gwinnett County trial was going first, it was now up to Judge Michael Clark to rule on the defense motions.

On Friday, February 17, 2006, Clark had a less compelling motion to deal with. It was silly enough that even the defendant didn't seem too concerned. Surprisingly, Bart appeared less drawn, and he wasn't as thin and gloomy as he sat at the defense table. Now, he had a slight tan, and he had actually gained a little weight. It was obvious that he was chewing gum, an insult to the Court, and he turned to wink at his mother, his brothers, and Brad's wife, Edwina, who were in the courtroom. He ignored Jenn's and Dolly's families, however, his eyes seeming to sweep deliberately in another direction, focusing in the distance. It was almost as if he had never known them. He had only met Carlton and Barbara Hearn once, but he had been a beloved member of Jenn's extended family for almost a decade.

Judge Clark denied the defense request to delay the trials for fourteen years. He was not amused by this pretrial motion. Even Bruce Harvey and David Wolfe would admit they had initiated the "fourteen-year delay" as a way to draw attention to the case.

Clark responded in kind, offering the defense a deal. If they would agree to a state motion that Corbin waive his right to bond and agree to stay in jail for the next fourteen years, Clark would stipulate to postponing the trials for a similar period.

Clearly, the defendant had no intention of doing that, and Clark moved ahead, setting the next pretrial hearing for March 24, 2006.

Bobby Corbin spoke to the press, saying that he wondered if Porter "really had a case. All I hear is 'similar transaction.' That's crazy.'"

He told reporters that Danny Porter's case consisted of only "smoke and mirrors," and that there was no real evidence implicating his brother.

Judge Clark's decision on allowing evidence from the

Dolly Hearn case into the Jenn Barber case could give the prosecution a huge advantage. Although the attorneys from both sides had waited to see if Clark would rule on that, he hadn't addressed similar transactions in this February hearing.

Michael Clark, with the help of his assistant, attorney Greg Lundy, pored over case law and other cases where the question had been raised. It was understandable that the defense attorneys wanted the "similar transactions" in Jenn's and Dolly's cases thrown out.

* * *

DANNY PORTER was an easy "boss," and he trusted his staff to work unsupervised at those things they did best. While he had trouble sending an email and had very little knowledge of computers, he counted on Chuck Ross and Russ Halcome for such technical expertise. And he had Jack Burnette and other investigators working on other trial preparations. Burnette had assigned Investigator Bob Slezak to work with Scott Peebles in arranging to bring witnesses from Augusta, while Russ Halcome and Investigator Mike Pearson were braiding any loose ends of missing evidence together into one seamless cord of physical exhibits.

The usually upbeat Porter called in his teams for a strategy meeting. He outlined the Jennifer Corbin prosecution as he and Ross saw it, and asked for suggestions. After a few minutes of silence, Danny Porter looked up to see his men either shaking their heads, unable to come up with a different approach, or worse, nodding and agreeing with him. And that was the last thing he wanted. Porter's ego didn't require burnishing. He wanted answers, and he smacked the table with the flat of his hand.

"Quit saying yes," he shouted in his deep voice. "I'm not here for you to agree with me!"

"One of the few times I've ever seen him angry," one investigator remarked. "He didn't necessarily want to have all the answers. He wanted us to point out any weak spots. He sure didn't want us to sit there and nod. He wanted our input—not 'yes men.' So we all started pitching our own theories. And it worked better."

Chuck Ross, who had studied the photographs of Jenn Corbin's bed, noted that a pillow on the door side of the bed had a deep indentation in the middle of it. "It looks to me," Ross said, "as if the shooter knelt here on the pillow, as he shot her."

Porter agreed. The sheet on that side of the bed was slightly untucked, as it would have been after someone knelt on the bed. From the timing of Jenn's calls to Anita Hearn, they knew for sure that Jenn had been alive long after midnight. Marcus Head's report said that Anita estimated their last call was between 1:20 and 1:30 A.M. Bart had placed the cell phone call that emanated from the closest tower to his house at 1:58 A.M.

Anita Hearn had said that during one of Jenn's phone calls late that night, she had admitted for the first time that she feared Bart might murder her. She had been uncharacteristically pessimistic when she said she hoped to meet Anita some day. "Maybe we will," Jenn said, "if your plane doesn't crash on the way here—or if my husband doesn't kill me first."

"I think he walked in the house," Chuck Ross said, "straight back to the master bedroom, knelt on the bed, reached out and pushed her down, shot her, walked out of the house, and drove away."

Perhaps. Or he might have stayed long enough to

shout at Jenn before he shot her. Their boys hadn't heard anything, but they'd been sleeping soundly upstairs.

No. More likely, Bart Corbin had determined beforehand what he was going to do, carefully planning how he would kill Jenn and to have an alibi already in place for that night.

The prosecution team had the cell phone connections, and they felt they were close to getting a point-to-point tracking on the gun that killed her. Out of all the vital elements in their case, this one was still elusive. They needed to know where that gun had come from, and they needed to link it absolutely, categorically, irrevocably, to Dr. Barton Corbin.

They still weren't able to do that. But the prosecution, nevertheless, got a boost on March 24, 2006, when Judge Michael Clark announced that he was going to allow the similar transaction information into the upcoming trial for Jenn Corbin's murder. Jenn's jury would hear about Dolly's death.

He also said he hoped to avoid postponing the newest trial date, April 17. Finally, it looked as if the trial would be a "go" after all.

Chapter Thirty-Three

Fall 2005–Summer 2006

THE RICHMOND COUNTY district attorney's team knew where the gun that killed Dolly came from. Her father had given it to her. But the Gwinnett County prosecutors didn't have the full history of the .38-caliber revolver that killed Jenn. They didn't know the origin of the gun found in her bed. Her killer had placed it in a position which he mistakenly believed would indicate she had held that weapon. There had been no fingerprints on this gun; either they were wiped off or the killer wore latex gloves.

Where had that old gun come from? None of the people that the detectives had interviewed remembered seeing a .38-caliber revolver in Bart Corbin's possession, nor had any of his more recent acquaintances ever heard him talk about guns. He had once owned a shotgun, and that was missing from his closet. After he ran over Jenn's foot, she had told the police dispatcher that she was concerned about the missing weapon. Bart's permit to have a gun had expired, and he'd never bothered to renew it. A shotgun had also been stolen from the Barber home. But there seemed to be no connection between either missing shotgun and Jenn's murder.

The .38 was a mystery gun, but it didn't have to stay that way, even though efforts to trace it had been so far tantalizingly unsuccessful. But time was running out, and they were a few months away from trial.

In a sense, guns are like people. They don't come with a birth certificate, but a gun has a record of when and where it was manufactured, the date it left the factory, and its "life" through the years. Whenever a gun changes hands, it is a legal requirement that those exchanges be noted in police records. Of course, that doesn't always happen. Criminals file serial numbers off guns because they don't want their weapons traced, and many guns are transferred privately and secretly; some are simply stolen. Law enforcement personnel attempt to note the peregrinations of every weapon they come across, although that isn't always possible.

If Danny Porter and Chuck Ross could somehow link that old .38 revolver to Bart Corbin, it would strengthen their case tremendously.

When Jack Burnette, Eddie Ballew, Kevin Vincent, and Russ Halcome served a search warrant on the Corbins' residence on Bogan Gates Drive in Buford, they had looked for any record that might show where the .38 had come from—and found nothing.

But they had winnowed down the possibilities to one likely source. Jenn's family had mentioned a man named Richard Wilson, Bart's good friend for many years. Wilson lived in Troy, Alabama. Neither Richard nor his wife, Janice, had come to Jenn's memorial service, and that seemed strange, since everyone said that Jenn had gone out of her way to entertain them, and welcome them to the Corbins' Fourth of July celebrations every year.

Russ Halcome had first placed Bart at the scene of Jenn's murder by tracking his cell phone, all perfectly legal, despite the defense lawyers' motions to the contrary. Next, Halcome mapped the cell phone towers and the sectors where Corbin had used his phone on November 29, 2004. Once again, Halcome charted a path. This one showed that Bart—or his phone—had been on a long, apparently secret, round-trip to Birmingham and Troy, Alabama.

The DA's investigators and Marcus Head already knew that Bart Corbin had been in Birmingham on Monday, November 29, because Jenn had found a parking stub for that date in his clothing, and mentioned it to at least two people. That trip to Birmingham from the Atlanta area was 148 miles. Now, they wondered if Bart had also driven down to see his old friend Richard on the same day. It wouldn't have taken him that long to drive another 140 miles south to Troy. If he drove the hypotenuse of this "triangle," on his return, the direct route from Troy back to his clinic in Hamilton Mill was approximately 193 miles.

No one had seen Bart on that Monday, so he could have taken a side trip to Troy and been home in the evening, having covered something under 500 miles in one long day.

But why would Bart have gone to Troy? Was Richard Wilson such a close friend that Bart had driven all that distance to gain some comfort or wisdom from him? Or was there a dark reason for his trip? The detectives suspected that Wilson might have provided Bart with the .38 that he used to shoot his wife five days later.

Within a week of Jenn Corbin's murder, Kevin Vincent and Gwinnett County Police Detective Eddie Restrepo left to drive to Troy, Alabama. Leaving Lawrenceville at 6 A.M., Vincent and Restrepo arrived at Wilson's home at 9:15. His home served as his business, Troy Small Motors, which was basically small engine repair, and some selling and trading of items like lawnmowers, tools, and anything with a motor that is of use around a home or farm. The shop had a brick façade, two bays to hold larger vehicles, and was plastered with signs reading "Stihl," "Dixon," and "Dixie." There were some all-terrain vehicles parked outside.

Janice Wilson said her husband wasn't home, but should be shortly. Wilson drove into his yard ten minutes later and invited them to come into his kitchen to talk.

"Do you know why we're here?" the Gwinnett County investigators asked.

"I have a pretty good idea."

Wilson explained immediately that no matter what he told them, he was sure to upset "one side of the family or the other." He was grateful to Gene Corbin, who had put him to work right out of college, and he didn't want to offend him. He had known Bart's father for about fifteen years, but he said he'd only known Bart since about 1992. Janice Wilson chimed in to say they usually took a yearly trip up to Lake Lanier for the Fourth of July, although they hadn't been able to make the trip this year.

"The last time I saw Bart and Jenn, and their kids," Richard recalled, "was this year—in August—when Janice threw a surprise birthday party for me here in Alabama."

The Wilsons said Jenn Corbin had become very ill during that visit. The Corbin family had to leave early on

Sunday morning after Jenn threw up all night. Richard said the last time he had spoken with Bart before Jenn's death was sometime around Thanksgiving. Bart had told him then that he was getting a divorce because Jenn was having an affair with someone on the Internet.

"He said she had a second cell phone that she didn't tell him about, and she only used it to call her 'lover.' "

Wilson was sure that the next time he spoke to Bart was on December 5 when Bart called and told him that he couldn't talk on his cell phone—but he would call him back. Bart did call back about 8:30 P.M. and asked him if he had heard what happened. Richard Wilson told him he hadn't heard anything, and it was then that Bart had told him that Jenn was dead, and the police were "all over him" for it.

Their conversation had been very awkward. "What do you say," Richard asked, "when you hear that?"

Janice and Richard said they had gone directly to the Internet and looked up newspaper websites in Atlanta. After reading the coverage of Jenn's death, they had come to the conclusion that the media had already convicted Bart. Janice pointed out that they also felt that Dalton could not have said all that he said about his father's guilt—not unless someone had coached him. "Absolutely no way!"

The Wilsons obviously didn't care for Heather Tierney and said they were concerned that she had the children, but, when pressed, they could give no reason for their feelings about her.

"Do you know of any guns that Bart owned?" Kevin Vincent asked.

"All I know about was a Ruger Red Label shotgun, and that was it."

"You never gave any member of the Corbin family a gun?"

"No."

"We do know that the gun that was used to kill Jenn Corbin was purchased someplace in Alabama—as far as we can track it."

Wilson said he knew nothing about that. And he denied having a visit from Bart on November 29.

The Georgia detectives asked Richard Wilson if he would accept a subpoena to appear before the grand jury in Gwinnett County. He shook his head, saying he knew they could not make him come to Georgia because he didn't live in that state. "I won't be there," he said flatly. "I'm not going to appear before any grand jury."

He was right. At that point, they could not force him. They would have to have evidence connecting Wilson to the death gun before they could extradite him. While it was against federal law to give or sell a gun to someone in another state who then used it in a crime, they could not prove yet that Wilson was "a party to a crime."

They were a long way from being finished with Richard Wilson, although they could not have realized the long and tortuous road they would have to travel.

On the way out of town Vincent and Restrepo stopped by the Troy Police Department and talked to Sergeant Calista Everage. She asked her radio operator to run a history of any police contacts at the Wilsons' address. One entry reported that Janice Wilson had purchased a .38 revolver in 1994—a Charter Arms .38 special.

This wasn't the gun they were looking for, and it wouldn't have meant much to them, except that Janice had just told them she didn't own any guns and had very little knowledge of firearms.

Other than some minor complaints the Wilsons had reported about thefts at Troy Small Motors, Sergeant Everage couldn't add anything more.

During 2005, Kevin Vincent called Richard Wilson sporadically, and found him no more forthcoming than he'd been in person. Wilson still denied knowing anything about any .38 revolver.

In October 2005, Jack Burnette, preparing for the upcoming trials, had assigned his newest investigator, Mike Pearson, to help track the .38 revolver. Pearson, a former military policeman, had been an investigator with the Georgia Bureau of Investigation for ten years before he'd joined the Gwinnett County DA's office only a month earlier. It looked then as if there would be a trial in January—and in Augusta. If the judge there agreed to similar transactions, they wanted to be ready with information about where the .38 had come from.

Mike Pearson lived up in "the mountains" outside of Atlanta. They would have been called foothills in Colorado or the Northwest, but it was beautiful country and Pearson didn't mind the long commute to Lawrenceville. He was a easygoing man whose humorous façade often disguised the tenacity with which he followed the trail of a suspect or a vital piece of evidence.

Kevin Vincent and Mike Pearson drove back to Troy that October 2005. Even though Bart remained behind bars, Richard Wilson had consistently refused to talk about the gun that killed Jennifer, always claiming he knew nothing about it. They wanted to confront him again in person.

They found Wilson was just as cordial as he had been on Vincent's first visit, but he didn't want to leave his property. They talked to him on the sidewalk outside. Maybe he was afraid they were going to grab him and "abduct" him to Georgia.

Wilson explained once more that he didn't want to "take sides," and Pearson said, "If you know something, you should tell us."

It seemed a wasted trip. But Vincent and Pearson stopped by the Troy Police Department again and distributed pictures of the murder gun, and also took some by local pawn shops.

Twice in the next few months, Mike Pearson phoned Richard Wilson. "I just wanted him to know that we were still interested in talking with him. They were only five-minute conversations, and he was still stonewalling us. We knew the gun was 'born' at a Smith & Wesson factory, went to a distributor in Birmingham, and then to a pawn-shop in 1957," Pearson recalled. "But that's where its trail ended. We needed to know where it had been over the prior forty-eight years."

When Pearson got Wilson on the phone, he continued to deny even talking to Bart Corbin about a gun, and "hemmed and hawed" when he was asked a specific question. It wasn't, Pearson felt, that Wilson was telling an outright lie; some code of ethics was preventing that, but he was dancing around the edges of questions. "I don't want to be involved," he said firmly. "Not then—and not now."

"You're not being fair to Jennifer," Pearson said, pressing him. "You owe the truth to the kids."

Pearson realized that the mention of Jenn Corbin struck a nerve with Wilson, but he still would not budge. Wilson's memory grew hazier.

"Mr. Porter wants you to know you're gonna come to Georgia—and you're going to sit on the stand—"

Wilson took a deep breath, and sounded offended. "You're threatening me," he complained.

"No," Pearson said. "It's the truth."

But that was all Pearson was going to get. He was making headway, but not nearly enough.

After yet another trip to Troy, Mike Pearson stopped in Montgomery and Birmingham on the way back to Atlanta. He was determined not to go home without finding something—anything—about the deadly .38. He had the pictures of that gun whose lineage so far eluded him. He knew the serial number by heart: 397676. He stopped in pawnshops, knowing that the chance he would find a receipt matching that serial number was infinitesimal.

In Birmingham, one of the pawnshop owners opened up his attic to Pearson. It was the storage place for decades of prior records—possibly thirty or forty years' worth. The attic was hot and dusty as Pearson pored through box after box of gun sale receipts. The law said that gun records had to be saved for thirty years; he hoped that these might go back even further.

From 8:30 A.M. to noon, he crouched in the pawnshop's attic, searching for what—for him—would be buried treasure. He might need to go back fifty years to find what he needed. And he was perfectly willing to do that.

But, as he opened the last box of files, Pearson's heart sank. They only went back to 1971: thirty-four years.

"If you had only been here last year," the pawnshop owner said sympathetically. "We purged everything before 1971 then."

Disheartened, Pearson drove back to Gwinnett County. There had to be another way or someplace else to look for the trail of the Smith & Wesson .38, 397676, and how it might have ended up with Richard Wilson.

Mike Pearson had little doubt that Wilson had given the murder weapon to Bart Corbin on November 29, 2004. But no jury would be convinced of that just on Pearson's say-so. Danny Porter and Chuck Ross thought the way Pearson did. The gun was the missing link. They were prepared to go ahead without it, counting on circumstantial evidence, the cell phone tracing that Russ Halcome had done, and the maps he had' made of where Bart was.

Bart Corbin's attitude after Jenn's death would work for the prosecution; he hadn't behaved like a grieving widower who was concerned for his children. He had told lies. They felt he was the kind of defendant who would insist upon testifying in his own defense, even though his attorneys would probably throw their bodies in front of his to keep him off the stand. And that would be to the prosecution's advantage.

The Gwinnett County District Attorney's Office and the Gwinnett County Police Department was prepared to go to trial, and confident that they would get a conviction.

But they still wanted the gun. Just in case.

Richard Wilson did not want to come to Georgia, and he particularly did not want to become involved in the search for Jenn Corbin's killer. He seemed confident that as long as he stayed in Alabama, there wasn't any way the Georgia detectives could get to him.

They had to find a way to convince him otherwise.

The January 2006 trial date, and the April 2006 trial date had come and gone, with more trial delays. Bruce Harvey and David Wolfe, stunned when Judge Clark agreed to the "similar transaction" testimony, had asked the Georgia Supreme Court to rule on whether that was legal. Clark agreed to that—as long as the higher court would put the question on a fast track. They had waited long enough for trial.

Once more, the defense team lost, but they seemed only moderately concerned. They had other issues to bring up.

It looked, however, as if there would finally be a trial in September 2006. It was now the second summer since Jenn Corbin's death. She had been gone for twenty-two months.

Mike Pearson wondered if Wilson believed he didn't have to worry much about the district attorney's men because they were from Georgia. He seemed convinced that he could not be forced across the state line to testify. Maybe if Mike could bring in somebody impressive from Alabama, Wilson would sit up and pay attention.

"I had a friend in Alabama who had certainly made an impression on me," Pearson said. "His name was J.D. Shelton and he had an Alabama badge because he worked for the Attorney General's Office there. J.D. was a big, burly guy who worked out. He fit the angle I had in mind exactly. I ran my problem by him, and asked him if he would take a ride with me down to Troy. He said 'Sure,' and the next morning we headed for Troy."

Once more, Mike Pearson, now accompanied by J.D. Shelton, walked into Wilson's shop. Mike made the introductions and he thought he saw a little more concern in Wilson's eyes. Early in their conversation, J.D. asked Wilson if he and Bart had ever smoked marijuana together.

Wilson stood up indignantly, and said, "I am a Shriner and a Mason. We don't do that."

Pearson filed that information away in a corner of his mind. Maybe it would turn out to be useful.

Pearson had written out a list of all the cell phone calls Bart had made to Wilson's home, office, and cell phone, and drew lines on it, showing the connections between the two men—especially on November 29 and 30, 2004.

"I showed it to Richard Wilson, and I said, 'You are involved—I want you to acknowledge that Bart Corbin called you on November 29, 2004.' "

Wilson said no again.

"That's no longer an acceptable response from you," Pearson said, holding out the page of phone connections. "Here's where he calls you. Here. And here, and, late at night, here."

Pearson wasn't expecting any sudden confession about the gun, but he hoped to have Wilson simply acknowledge that Bart had been there at his house, or that they could at least talk about the phone calls. But Pearson felt Wilson slipping away, finding him vague and reluctant to give up any specifics. They were beginning to go nowhere again.

Pearson pointed out that Wilson had clearly talked to Bart long after his August birthday party, and before Bart called him to tell him that Jenn was dead.

Backed into a corner, Wilson finally conceded that was true. But when he'd talked to Bart, it wasn't about a gun.

"He said he had problems."

"What problems?"

Wilson wouldn't answer, and Pearson moved closer. "Look, this isn't a poker game. I'm showing you everything I have. Was he here that day?"

Wilson half nodded.

"Why was he here?"

"Well, probably he needed to get his weed eater fixed."

That was patently ridiculous, and Pearson and Shelton stared back at him, unconvinced.

"That's a $10 job," Pearson said. "I don't buy that. Who needs a weed eater bad enough in the winter to drive all the way from Atlanta to Troy?"

Wilson only shrugged.

Pearson and Shelton headed out of Troy, without having gained the information they had come for. Once more Pearson drove back to Gwinnett County disappointed, but far from ready to give up.

*   *   *

DANNY PORTER'S STAFF huddled to discuss a different approach that might work with Wilson. Pearson mentioned that Richard Wilson was interested in squirrel-hunting dogs. And so was Jack Burnette, although Jack seldom hunted; he just liked the dogs. Burnette was a Mason, and so was Wilson, and very proud of it.

"It was Jack's turn at bat," Mike Pearson said. "And he was game."

Investigators from Porter's office had practically worn a rut in the road between Gwinnett County and Troy, Alabama. Now Mike and Jack headed down that road again. Pearson hoped that the sly fox of the DA's office could establish some rapport with Wilson because they had "so much in common."

Burnette and Wilson exchanged the secret handshake, and Wilson was perfectly willing to talk about squirrel-hunting dogs and the Masonic Lodge, but, other than that, Burnette "hit a brick wall."

If anything, Richard Wilson was even more cagey, still secure in his belief that he could not be forced to appear in court in Georgia.

CHAPTER THIRTY-FOUR

SUMMER 2006

THE DETECTIVES, investigators, district attorneys' staffs, and even Judge Michael Clark were looking forward to seeing Bart Corbin stand trial for murder. Partly it was because this promised to be a precedent-setting case, and for those who loved the law, a fascinating one. And, realistically, it would be a chance to observe—and hopefully listen to—a defendant who had resisted all efforts to question him. From the very beginning, Corbin had maintained an arrogant attitude, figuratively thumbing his nose at those who sought the truth in the death of his wife. The curious public was also anxious to see what a trial would bring. Gwinnett County had a reputation for catching some of the more bizarre cases in America, but the tangled story of Dolly Hearn, Jenn Barber Corbin, and Dr. Bart Corbin surpassed them all.

The families of the dead women viewed the upcoming trials with dread. They had gotten a glimpse of the defense case in pretrial hearings, and they were horrified. Bart's attorneys had demonstrated their mesmerizing skill, and Jenn's family knew they would work to paint a picture of her that wasn't at all like her.

It would be hard enough to sit through testimony and look at photographs of crime scenes, location of wounds, and autopsies. It would be agony to hear their beloved daughters' names besmirched, and to hear the defense case that was undoubtedly choreographed to suggest that both Jenn and Dolly had been unstable enough to commit suicide. Narda Barber lost sleep worrying about how the defense team would use the hundreds of emails exchanged between Jenn and Anita Hearn. She hoped that both jurors and court-watchers would understand that, except for the last fifteen days of her life, Jenn had believed that she was writing to a good, honest, man who loved her—a man who was going to take care of her and her sons. "Christopher" had helped her get through the last year of an impossibly painful marriage.

"Jenn was intelligent and kind," Heather said. "But she was totally naïve. Sometimes, as much as I love her, I still get mad at her for being so dumb! I tried to warn her—we all did, but she kept believing. She could have lived another sixty years if she just hadn't been so trusting of someone she didn't know—and if she had only realized how dangerous Bart was."

Narda hated the thought of sitting in the courtroom in Lawrenceville, but it would be harder on her to stay away. Max would be there with her, along with Rajel, Heather, and other family and friends. She didn't know if she would be testifying or not. Narda didn't want to cry on the stand, or get confused by questions from Bruce Harvey or David Wolfe.

In the summer of 2006, as the first trial lay just ahead, Danny Porter and Chuck Ross met with the potential prosecution witnesses to see how they might come across on the witness stand. Narda's emotions were probably too close to the surface, but they thought Heather and Doug Tierney could maintain their equilibrium. It was going to be rough, but victim/witness advocates in Gwinnett County were helping Jenn's family cope.

During one witness orientation day, there was an unfortunate meeting in one of the DA's conference rooms. Narda's interview lasted longer than they expected, and she had to walk by Dara Prentice—who she firmly believed was Bart's longtime lover. Dara apparently didn't realize that Narda could not forgive her for having an affair with her daughter's husband, and she greeted Narda brightly. But Narda sailed on by, her face set in stone.

Barbara and Carlton Hearn would also be attending this first trial in Lawrenceville, along with Dolly's brothers, Gil and Carlton Jr.

That summer was very long for all of them. They had geared up for trials three times before, only to have the dates pass without the prosecution going forward.

*   *   *

AS PREPARATION for the trials continued, Porter and Ross reviewed their potential witness list. There were eighty-four names there, and they had fifteen pieces of evidence set. Porter would probably handle the opening statement and the closing arguments, along with questioning the families and friends of the two victims. Ross would question the witnesses expert in forensic technology: the Internet explorations, the information caught on the hard drives, and the way Bart Corbin's cell phone calls had left damning trails behind him. Ross would also lead Russ Halcome through his explanations about a myriad of charts and displays in a way that jurors could understand.

The gun? They still had no evidence that would allow them to connect it to Bart Corbin.

Chapter Thirty-Five

AUGUST–SEPTEMBER 2006

DANNY PORTER AND CHUCK ROSS were prepared to dig in as the September trial approached. Once it began, they would have tunnel vision, thinking only of what went on in the courtroom.

The Corbin family gathered round Bart. They believed in him totally, and were determined to stand by him. Brad's wife, Edwina Tims, had become the family spokesperson, although she and Bart's twin hadn't been married very long when Jenn died. Perhaps inevitably, the once-friendly relationship between Jenn's and Bart's families seemed irretrievably broken.

As August became September, it was still warm and humid in the suburbs of Atlanta, but the sun set earlier. Heather bought school clothes for her youngsters—Dalton, Dillon, Max, and Sylvia. Max and Narda took a short vacation, but they were afraid to go very far, in case there were no further postponements. Once the trial started, they expected to be in Judge Michael Clark's courtroom until almost Thanksgiving.

Orientation for prospective jurors was set to begin on September 8. Danny Porter had asked that there be a huge pool of jurors available. Beginning with 650 possibles, they would need to find fourteen people who, supposedly, had formed no opinions about the guilt or innocence of Dr. Barton Corbin. Winnowing that number down to find twelve jurors and two alternates could take two or three weeks. Only then would the actual trial begin.

Narda and Max Barber were taking it one day at a time. They decided to attend jury selection and to keep going if they found they could bear to hear the testimony. So did many of Bart's family members. Edwina Tims planned to be in the courtroom every day, sitting in a back row of the courtroom. Word was that Dr. and Mrs. Carlton Hearn would be attending this first trial. They wanted to see Bart Corbin face a jury of his peers. They had endured sixteen years when it seemed that everyone but her family had forgotten Dolly and how she died.

There was pain on every side; a family watching someone they love on trial for murder suffers anguish, too. Connie Corbin had done her best to raise her three boys without the presence of their father, and she had been so proud of Bart, her son, the dentist.

* * *

IT WAS LABOR DAY, 2006, and jury selection for Bart Corbin's trial in Gwinnett County was only days away. David Wolfe and Bruce Harvey were still lobbying for a change of venue, which is a standard defense motion in almost every murder trial with any pretrial publicity. They announced that the voir-dire process (where attorneys question potential jurors directly) would probably reveal how many people in Gwinnett County had already formed opinions about Bart Corbin's guilt, as a result of what the lawyers considered massive publicity that would make it impossible for their client to get a fair trial.

While Judge Clark had ruled earlier against moving the trial, he agreed to consider hearing their renewed arguments if it should begin to appear that picking an unprejudiced jury in Gwinnett County was unlikely.

Although they were continually making motions, Harvey and Wolfe were actually only patching up every possible crevice in their case. In truth, they felt confident. No one had heard the gunshot when Jenn Corbin was killed, and her exact time of death—measurable by several factors such as the temperature in her house that night— might possibly, in the defense team's opinion, have been as late as six in the morning. They would use that to lessen the impact of Bart's cell phone call at 1:58 A.M. hitting on the tower so close to Bogan Gates Drive.

They could say the cross-hatched gun butt pattern wouldn't hold fingerprints.

They also believed they could tear apart the similarities between Jenn's and Dolly's cases. They might have been whistling in the dark, but in front of reporters they scoffed at the idea, insisting that the two cases weren't all that much alike.

And, of course, they would take Jenn's sad little online romance and shape it to blend into their theory that she probably had been suicidal. They would portray Jenn as a distraught woman, who believed that Bart could successfully prove in a custody hearing that she was a bad mother and a wanton woman. Wouldn't suicidal thoughts be expected in a woman who had lost a "lover" who never existed, and was soon to lose her home and her children?

In the hands of brilliant defense attorneys, a case that was heavily circumstantial and with physical evidence that might confuse a lay jury was certainly no slam-dunk for the prosecution.

*   *   *

THERE WOULD BE TWO PHASES in jury selection. The Court would hear first from people who felt it would be a great hardship on them to serve—those with small children to care for, or health issues, or those whose jobs assured the public good. Those who did not speak English would certainly be excused. Gwinnett remained a small-town county in many ways. There were bound to be some who actually knew the principals or the attorneys, or felt they might be called as witnesses.

Forty people from the first pool asked to be excused. By September 12, only five people who had been questioned were deemed neutral enough to go on the second list. There were forty-two more possibles in the second pool. Both the prosecution and defense teams would have nine peremptory challenges to excuse jurors without cause. And they would undoubtedly lose a few more for cause.

Nevertheless, Danny Porter said he expected to begin opening statements on September 25.

It was true that the charges against Dr. Barton Corbin had garnered widespread publicity, but perhaps it wasn't so pervasive that it would be difficult to select a jury.

Heather Tierney's website in memory of her sister now had almost 400,000 "hits." Some of those, however, were multiple drop-ins by the same readers, and posts had come in from all over the world. Court TV, Greta Van Susteren, Nancy Grace, *Inside Edition,* and *People* magazine were all interested in covering the trial. *Dateline NBC* and *48 Hours* were preparing documentaries of the Corbins' story.

As the trial date neared, Bart Corbin was anxious to present his side of the story, convinced that any jury they picked would believe him if he testified. Always before, he had referred questions to his attorneys and he remained a somewhat mysterious figure, his image caught briefly on television or newspaper cameras as he was led in and out of various court proceedings or back to jail. To those who didn't know him, he was an enigma. But those who did know him were sure his arrogance would not allow him to plea-bargain to lesser charges. Surely he would demand to get on the witness stand and explain his innocence.

The consensus among most Georgians seemed to be that the lanky dentist was guilty, but survivors of the two dead women still worried about the possibility of an acquittal. Narda Barber kept going back to the what-ifs of a trial. The tenth anniversary of Jenn and Bart's wedding had passed on September 1, but no one seemed to remember it or the joy and hopes Jenn had then. Her mother had been stunned to learn that Bart had been able to walk away from Dolly's death and go on with his life, brushing Dolly's memory off his shoulders as he would a shred of cobweb.

Would the same thing happen with Jenn's death?

This wasn't a television drama; this was real life. And the likelihood of some decisive evidence being discovered at the last minute was slim.

*   *   *

CHUCK ROSS AND INVESTIGATOR BOB SLEZAK were absent from the courtroom activity on September 6. They had a date in Superior Court in Troy, Alabama. Ross had drafted a material witness order that he planned to present to a judge in that city. Court in Troy started at nine, and Ross and Slezak rolled out of Gwinnett County at 5 A.M., even before the sun began to lighten the sky.

Richard Wilson didn't know what a "material witness" was, and he had consistently refused to leave his hometown. But now, he would have to. Ross's testimony convinced the Alabama judge to issue the material witness order, a ruling that was an unpleasant surprise for Bart Corbin's good friend.

What Porter and Ross would ask Wilson once they had him on the witness stand was still up in the air. Mike Pearson had never given up on tracking the revolver that had killed Jenn Corbin. He was just stubborn enough to keep trying. But he'd run out of options.

Pearson was about to get an idea from the investigator who shared his office, one of the many cubicles opening off the long hallways of the Gwinnett County District Attorney's Office.

Jeff Lamphier might have been the only investigator in Danny Porter's office who didn't have a smidgen of a Southern accent. Lamphier was from New York State, and he was a natural. He didn't have a college degree. He believed—and rightly so—that for him the best training came on the job. Lamphier signed on first with the DeKalb County, Georgia, DA's office. After eighteen months, he moved to Gwinnett County. There they quickly began to call him "The Smartest Man in the World."

Mike Pearson described himself as a "blabber," who was always talking, while Lamphier spoke only when he had something important to say.

"Jeff was over there typing," Pearson remembered. "And we're sitting back to back. I'm saying, 'I know that guy in Alabama knows something, but I can't prove the .38 came from there. Everything points to Alabama.' "

As Pearson vented his frustration about his unsuccessful search to link Bart Corbin to the death gun, Lamphier whirled around from his computer, and asked quietly, "Have you tried this?"

"Tried what?"

"An off-line search."

"No."

"Has anyone else?"

Mike Pearson had done any number of traces—through the ATF (Bureau of Alcohol, Tobacco, Firearms, and Explosives), NCIC (National Crime Information Center), the GCIC (Georgia Crime Information Center), with no luck.

Now, Lamphier reminded him, "You have the gun, you have the serial number, and an off-line search goes back ten years. Try it."

He handed Pearson the name of a young woman at the Georgia Bureau of Investigation, and said, "I hope it helps."

They were so close to trial. They needed this badly.

Most legitimate gun buyers check with police departments to see if secondhand weapons have ever been stolen or used in a crime. The Georgia Bureau of Investigation and the Georgia Crime Information Center can get access to those inquiries about guns by auditing the NCIC records over the preceding ten years.

"If any police department or police agency in the United States has ever checked a gun, it will show up on an off-line search," Pearson explained. "It will show the day, the time, the place, and the officer who asked for the information—usually by radioing the dispatch operator to see what's on record for a particular gun."

Mike Pearson gave the woman at the GBI the information on the make, model, and serial number of the .38 that killed Jenn Corbin.

"By lunchtime, she called me back. She said that she had been able to go back ten years, and she hoped it helped. She had found six entries off-line on this gun."

The first four weren't useful. They were the inquiries that the Gwinnett County DA's office itself had submitted.

But there were two more.

Pearson ran his finger down the page. There was a query in 1996 radioed in to the Montgomery, Alabama, Sheriff's Office at 2 A.M. That was ten years back, but at least it placed the mystery gun in Alabama.

"But the next one was from the Troy, Alabama Police Department—September 2002. Bingo! I thought I'd fall out of my chair!" Pearson recalled. "I couldn't even talk at first because I was so excited. I finally yelled at Jack, "This gun's been run in Troy!'"

Pearson and Jack Burnette made a phone call to the Troy Police Department and learned that the officer who asked for information on the .38 in 2002 had been a captain in their department, since retired. Mike Pearson called him and asked for details about the gun. The retired officer did his best to remember the circumstances on that morning in September, four years earlier. But the memory evaded him; he'd run so many guns off-line. It could have been during a traffic stop, but it might just as well have been for somebody who simply hailed him over.

Pearson asked about the 911 tapes in the Troy Police Department, knowing it was a long shot. It would take a massive search to find a tape four years back, and there was always the chance that its contents had been erased and taped over with more recent calls.

Jack Burnette and Mike Pearson tried the other—more remote—possibility: contacting the Montgomery County Sheriff's Office about the 1996 inquiry in their jurisdiction. The request to have the .38 checked out had been a full decade earlier. At 2 A.M., it had to be a traffic stop.

They were a year too late. Montgomery had had gone computerized in 1997—not 1996. The operator told Pearson he would have to go through files stored in the attic.

For Mike Pearson, it was a replay of an old, bad dream. He wasn't surprised when no records were found in Montgomery. That was the way his luck had been running in this case.

*   *   *

AFTER THE MATERIAL WITNESS ORDER naming Richard Wilson was issued, he had no choice but to appear in court in Troy. And the news appeared in the local newspaper that he had been ordered to testify in Bart Corbin's trial.

After reading that, the chief of police in Troy, Anthony Everage, called his detectives in and asked them, "Are we helping these guys in Georgia as much as we can?"

Everage was a tall, good-looking man, and, incidentally, another squirrel hunter. "But we'd tried that avenue already," Pearson said with a grin, "and it didn't work."

But now, Anthony Everage believed more could be done by his department, and decided to step in to help nudge Richard Wilson toward a witness chair in Gwinnett County, Georgia. He called Jack Burnette, and said, "I know Wilson. I've known him for ten years. I'll help if I can."

Everage's most important offer came next. He said that his department's 911 system had gone digital—and that he would have it searched for a call-in from the now-retired captain.

And, finally, something solid popped up in the Troy Police Department's 911 system. Almost as if he still couldn't believe their luck, Mike Pearson said, "The chief pulled out a twenty-second conversation where the Troy captain was asking for information on a gun with the same serial number that we'd all memorized: 397676. Best of all, they had it on tape!"

It was a twenty-second blip on a long-ago tape that could very well change the whole outcome of the Corbin trials.

Everage called Burnette and let him know what he had found. He said, "I've got the tape. Do you mind if I go talk to Wilson?"

After so long and so much disappointment, it seemed almost miraculous that things were suddenly moving so fast. Burnette looked at Pearson and asked, "What can it hurt if the chief goes to see Wilson?"

The two Gwinnett County investigators waited tensely to hear back from Anthony Everage. When the phone rang, they both jumped.

The Troy chief of police filled them in on what had happened, quoting the conversation he'd had with Richard Wilson.

Everage said he'd driven up to Wilson's small motor repair shop, and Wilson had been perfectly willing to walk out to sit in his police car, something he had always refused to do with the Georgia investigators. But he knew Everage, and he felt comfortable with him.

"He said to me," Everage told Burnette, " 'I have a feeling you're not here about lawnmowers.'

" 'You're right,' " I said. " 'I'm here to talk about you doing the right thing.' "

At that point, Everage said he'd popped the tape of the 911 call made four years earlier into his dashboard, and Wilson listened intently to the crackling voices, as the captain asked for information on the gun.

"Who do you think he was running that gun for?" Everage had asked.

"Probably me." Richard Wilson's shoulders had slumped at that point.

"Richard," Everage had said firmly, "you're gonna go to court, and those people over there in Georgia are really good. You're gonna end up telling a lie on the stand, and you won't be coming back to Alabama, and I'm gonna have to find someone else to fix my lawnmower."

After almost two years of protecting Bart Corbin, Richard Wilson had run out of ways to avoid the truth. He told the Troy Chief that he had, indeed, given Bart the gun. And, yes, he had done it on November 29, four days before Jenn was shot.

"How do you want me to handle it?" Everage asked Burnette. "Do you want to come on down and ask him more details? No matter what he says, I just heard it, so I guess I'm on your witness list now."

Chapter Thirty-Six

September 2006

It was Tuesday morning, September 12, and in Lawrenceville, Georgia, jury selection had moved into a kind of rhythm. They were beginning to make progress. Narda Barber was sitting in the back row beside Jennifer Rupured, Jenn's fellow teacher at Sugar Hill Methodist, when she became aware of someone walking toward the prosecution table as Danny Porter and Chuck Ross interviewed prospective jurors. Porter turned slightly and saw Jack Burnette approaching. These two old friends had worked so many cases together that they knew how each other's minds worked. There was no way that Burnette would interrupt a court session if he didn't have something really important to impart.

Burnette handed Porter a folded slip of paper, and the DA glanced at it. Narda and Jennifer saw his shoulders straighten. It wasn't a broad gesture, but it indicated a bit of surprise.

"The note from Burnette read, 'Come out of the courtroom, NOW! Wilson copped to the gun!" There were five lines slashed under the "NOW."

It took a lot of acting skill for Porter to maintain a casual attitude, but he managed it as he asked Judge Clark's permission to step out of the courtroom for a moment. Burnette and Mike Pearson were practically bouncing off the ceiling with their amazing news. They told Porter and Ross that Richard Wilson had finally admitted to giving the old .38 to Bart Corbin. Someone had to get down to Troy and talk to him further, and arrange to bring him up to Georgia as a prosecution witness.

Back in the courtroom, Porter asked Judge Clark for a sidebar session and the four attorneys—prosecution and defense—moved up to the bench where they held a whispered conversation.

Court-watchers fidgeted, straining to hear what was being said. Everyone tried to guess what was in the note that might have made Porter ask to approach the bench, but neither the judge's nor the attorneys' faces betrayed what they were thinking.

The sidebar seemed normal enough; there had been others. And Narda didn't sense that anything had changed. Judge Clark remarked that it was almost time for lunch, and dismissed the jury pool and gallery a few minutes early. Narda and Jennifer Rupured headed downstairs to the cafeteria for lunch.

But there had been rumblings in the courtroom, and those who knew the prosecutors and defense attorneys felt an almost palpable electricity, despite the effort they and Judge Clark made to appear blasé.

When Narda rode up the escalator after lunch, she encountered Danny Porter in the hallway. They locked eyes, and she questioned him silently. Now, she was sure that something had happened. The DA and his staff had been unfailingly responsive and considerate of her family—of all victims' families. But she sensed that at the moment Danny Porter didn't want to talk to her.

"I can't tell you," Porter finally said, reading her mind. "I just can't tell you anything."

"Is it good or is it bad?" Narda asked quietly.

"It's good," he said. And with that he walked away, leaving her with a slight surge of optimism. She wondered if he had come up with some piece of evidence or a witness for the prosecution. He seemed both uncommonly cheerful and tense.

Surprisingly, the Tuesday afternoon session began routinely, as if nothing had changed. The attorneys questioned more potential jurors. But not for long. Judge Clark announced crisply that he had a sudden scheduling conflict, and that he needed to accommodate that. He dismissed the jury pool until Thursday morning.

A little bemused, Narda headed home. She had come to know Danny Porter well enough over the past twenty-two months to suspect that something was up, something of earthshaking proportions for the trial of her son-in-law. When Porter called her on Wednesday, there was no question about it. There was obviously some kind of detour along the path toward trial.

Porter didn't spell anything out; in fact, he told Narda once more that he couldn't give her any details. But then he asked her, if there should be a request by the defense for a plea bargain, would she still want the trial to go ahead?

Why on earth would the defense ask for a plea

bargain? Narda knew Bart, his bottomless need for control and his damnable pride. He had maintained all along that he had nothing to do with Jenn's death, and he still carried himself with a certain haughtiness, his body language showing how positive he was that, once more, he was going to walk away a free man.

Would she want the trial to go ahead? *No!* The very thought of sitting in the Gwinnett County courtroom for weeks and listening to her beloved Jenn being described falsely as a faithless wife, a bad mother, and a sexually promiscuous woman—all illustrated by the giant blowups of Jenn's and Anita's emails—nauseated Narda. She agonized that those who hadn't known Jenn in life might believe the smarmy picture Bart's attorneys were sure to paint.

If Bart could be imprisoned forever without a trial, she would have a sense of peace. And Jenn would be vindicated. That was what she wanted to say, but she couldn't speak for everyone. She would have to talk to Barbara and Carlton Hearn and to Max and the rest of her family. She wondered what could have happened to make Bart even consider pleading guilty. But she hoped that what Danny Porter was asking her meant that there was a chance he would.

*   *   *

JUDGE MICHAEL CLARK didn't have a scheduling conflict. He was meticulous about arranging the hours of his days, and his assistant, Greg Lundy, helped see to that. The Corbin trial had top priority with Clark and he had cleared his decks to be sure it ran smoothly. But Clark and all the attorneys had agreed to this ploy to keep the media at bay until they could follow up on the contents of the note that Jack Burnette had handed to Danny Porter.

Porter, Chuck Ross, Russ Halcome, Mike Pearson, and Jack Burnette would be heading out for one more trip—hopefully the last—to Troy, Alabama. Bruce Harvey and David Wolfe would travel south, too. Richard Wilson had already arranged for an attorney to represent him. They would all meet at 6 P.M. on Wednesday evening, September 13. At last, the prosecution's reluctant witness had promised to tell them the truth. If Wilson followed through, Bart Corbin might very well think twice about proceeding with trial.

Burnette and Pearson would conduct the interview—they probably knew Wilson better than any of the DA's staff.

Wilson was a large man with powerful arms, growing somewhat thick around the belly as he approached middle age. He sat nervously in his chair in the interview room as he faced the prosecutors' team from Georgia. Yes, he said, he had given Bart the .38 revolver. Bart had called him and said that Jenn "was fooling around on him," and that he was frightened that he might be in danger. "He needed a gun to protect himself," Wilson said. "He asked me if I had one, and I did, so he came on down here to get it."

Bart had once claimed that he feared for his life after Dolly Hearn was killed. After all, Dr. Carlton Hearn had warned him not to hurt Dolly. In November 2004, had he been referring to Max Barber? Was he really afraid of Max, a tall, gentle man? Or was he saying that Jenn's "Internet lover" would come after him? Or was it all only an excuse to put a gun in his hands once more? The investigators voted for the latter reason.

When the gun in question was handed to Richard Wilson, he studied it and said, "That certainly looks like it."

Wilson explained that he got the revolver originally by bartering. He'd traded it for something—maybe a lawnmower. He didn't remember any longer. And it didn't matter.

"At last," Danny Porter said, "we had the murder weapon in Bart Corbin's hand."

Wilson was extremely loyal to Bart Corbin, following some unwritten rule that you don't snitch on an old friend, but finally he could no longer withhold the truth.

His attorney arranged an agreement that would keep Wilson from being charged with hindering prosecution, and he agreed to testify against his old friend.

Mike Pearson couldn't resist one last question. "Richard," he said. "I gotta know. You could help me out if you'll tell me. What could I have done differently—to get you to tell me the truth?"

"Not a thing," Wilson said. "You're a nice guy. I just didn't want to get involved. I still don't."

At last, he had no choice. He *was* involved, and he had been from the very beginning. He seemed somewhat relieved that he no longer had to feel guilty about turning his back on Jenn Corbin, who had always been so nice to him.

It was very late on that Wednesday night when the caravan from Lawrenceville arrived back in Gwinnett County. As exhausted as they were, Danny Porter and his staff were happy. There was no way the defense could recover from what was obviously a death blow to their case.

Bruce Harvey couldn't disagree. He and David Wolfe had been prepared for all eventualities—except this one.

They had witnesses in the wings prepared to refute whatever Porter and Ross threw at them.

"We go from 'We're gonna kick your ass—let's rock and roll,' " Harvey said, "to 'How can we save this guy's life?' "

And Bart Corbin's life was now in jeopardy. Danny Porter had no compunction about seeking the death penalty. Porter had sent five killers to death row, and he had, thus far, attended two of the executions. "If I send them there, I have the obligation to see it through to the end," he remarked.

If any crimes had warranted a death sentence, Bart Corbin's had. He had crept up on two young women he purported to love—and destroyed their brains with two single shots. And he had planned his murders carefully, even to the point of annihilating their reputations. All to protect himself and his massive ego in the belief that he deserved to have anything he wanted.

*   *   *

ON THURSDAY MORNING, Narda and Max Barber, Heather and Doug Tierney, and Rajel Barber sat in Danny Porter's office. He warned them that they could not say anything to anyone because negotiations were going on between his office and the defense lawyers, and they were extremely delicate. But he indicated that there was about to be a massive denouement in the case. Bart Corbin was on the edge of changing his plea to guilty, and nothing must interfere with that. They couldn't tell their best friends, or their relatives. No one. The Barbers still didn't have all the details, but they trusted Porter absolutely.

Dolly's family was being told, too, that something huge was about to happen. And both families agreed that they could accept a plea bargain—as long as Bart Corbin admitted his guilt in public.

Nothing in Judge Michael Clark's courtroom had changed. During the Thursday morning session, three prospective jurors were chosen. Everyone went to lunch as usual. Another juror was questioned after lunch. As normal as the proceedings were, it seemed as though a certain current ran along the press bench, the families' section, and the spectators. It sizzled silently in the air.

And then Judge Clark announced that they would adjourn—to resume at 9:30 Friday morning. Jenn's family could wait no longer, and they were back in Porter's office that afternoon. He was grinning.

"He told us it was a 'slam dunk,' " Narda recalled. "That a plea bargain had been reached and everyone would know about it Friday morning."

There would be no trial.

The Barbers and Tierneys were a little surprised to learn that their estranged son-in-law wasn't going to receive a mandatory sentence of life in prison without parole. There was no Georgia statute that would assure that. He would avoid the death penalty, and he would serve a very long time in prison, but someday, he would probably get out.

As Heather and Doug Tierney drove to the justice center on September 15, Heather gasped. Three white doves flew low over their car, and then lifted their wings and soared skyward.

When court resumed that morning, no one in the Corbin family was there. The night before, Bart had summoned them to the jail so that he could tell them something they needed to know. After hearing what he had to say, they elected to stay away from Michael Clark's courtroom.

But the gallery was packed. Jenn's family and Dolly's family were there, along with most of the investigators from both Gwinnett and Richmond counties. DA Danny Craig and his chief deputy DA, Parks White, were there at the prosecution table. Sergeant Scott Peebles and De-Wayne Piper sat just behind them.

When Dr. Bart Corbin walked in between Bruce Harvey and David Wolfe, it was as if everyone in the courtroom held their breath. He was dressed in a dark suit, light blue shirt, and a blue tie with huge white circles on it. Any weight he had gained was gone now; he was rail-thin and his dark eyes burned holes in his pale face.

He rose to face Danny Porter, who stared back at him.

Porter described the morning of December 4, 2004, although there was probably no one in the courtroom who didn't know every detail of Jenn Corbin's murder. He spoke of a seven-year-old boy who wakened to find his mother dead, bleeding from a shot in the head.

"Did you, in fact, commit the offense of malice murder, which is outlined in the indictment?" Porter asked.

The room hushed, with everyone wondering if at last Bart Corbin would speak of what he had done and why. But his thoughts were still unreadable. His forehead tightened and three parallel, wavy lines appeared just below his left eyebrow and then snaked across the bridge of his nose. If the spectators behind the rail expected any emotion, this was all they were going to get.

He answered, "Yes." Simply "Yes." Somehow it didn't seem fair that he wasn't required to say more.

Only Danny Porter and Judge Clark had a front view of Corbin's face. "There was no reaction," Porter recalled. "It was like looking into the eyes of a shark."

Danny Craig rose to face Corbin. "Do you further admit that you committed the murder of Dolly Hearn on June 6, 1990?"

"Yes."

Bart Corbin sat down, but there were two other men who had asked to speak. Max Barber was usually a quiet man, a man who had lived for forty years in a house with a talkative wife and three talkative daughters. He had not planned to speak on this morning, but now he knew that he had to. He and Bart had been close, and he had loved his son-in-law, and enjoyed the times they'd gone fishing, talked about cars, and bonded on their side-by-side houseboats. In some ways, Bart had been the son Max never had.

As he came to the front of the courtroom, Bart looked frightened, diminished, as if the very air was seeping out of him.

At first, Max looked down at him and told him that he had done the right thing in confessing, and Bart seemed to relax a little. But then Max's voice took on a powerful, steely edge.

"God may forgive you," Max said. "I never will. I speak for my family when I say I just virtually hope that you burn in hell."

Bart Corbin crumpled.

Carlton Hearn Jr. was next. It had usually been his brother, Gil, who spoke for the family, but this time it was his turn.

"Bart Corbin stole from me," Carlton said. "He stole from my whole family. He stole from the world. He deserves no place in society. He's just a shell of a man. He's hollow."

The courtroom was perfectly silent.

When Judge Clark offered Bart the chance to speak to the Barber and Hearn families, he declined.

Although none of Bart's family was there, his younger brother, Bobby, spoke to reporters later, saying that his family had trusted Bart, had done everything they could to support him over the past two years.

"We chose to back the guy we believed in," Bobby said. "And we chose to back a liar. Had I known he did it, they would have got him. It's that simple. He took a mother from her kids. He took somebody's daughter."

There was nobody left for Bart Corbin to call up in the middle of the night.

AFTERWORD

JUSTICE ROLLS ON swiftly in the state of Georgia. Shortly after he pleaded guilty on that Friday afternoon in mid-September 2006, Bart Corbin was sentenced to two terms of life in prison. According to the terms of his plea bargain, the sentences will run concurrently, rather than one after the other, with credit given for the nineteen and a half months he spent in jail as he awaited trial. Concurrent sentences never seem quite fair—two murders for the price of one—but it had to be that way.

Under Georgia parole guidelines, he will be eligible to apply for parole consideration in fourteen years, but it's hardly likely he will get out so soon. As Danny Porter said, "I don't think Barton Corbin will ever see the [outside] world again. . . . He won't have a realistic chance of parole for twenty-eight years."

If he should be paroled at that time, he will be in his seventies.

Corbin was soon moved out of the Gwinnett County jail. Georgia Department of Corrections records show that the prisoner, whose ID number is 0001226826, entered the system four days after he pleaded guilty and was sentenced. On September 19, Corbin became one of 53,089 prison inmates in Georgia. After orientation, he was sent to the Forest Hays Jr. State Prison in Trion, a correctional facility in the northwestern part of Georgia that is designed for close security. Relatively new, it is a rather bleak penitentiary, dominated by a looming guard tower that resembles an air traffic control vantage point at an airport.

Hay State Prison's defined mission is "to house inmates with behavioral problems that cannot be addressed at other prisons." It is also constructed to keep those who need maximum supervision inside the walls.

In the general population, there are four-hundred beds—some of them bunk beds in dormitories, others in single cells. The "Seg Unit" and the Isolation Unit share one-hundred seventy beds. Outside the perimeter fence, there is a boot camp for inmates who are expected to return to civilian life one day. These trustees take care of the grounds and other exterior chores.

The prison where Corbin now lives is very bright, lighted constantly so that there are no shadowy corners, but it is stark. The floors at Hays State Prison are waxed to a mirror-like polish, probably with the aid of one of the Georgia Department of Corrections' prison industries. Inmates manufacture chemicals for household use (a cottage industry similar to Bart's father's business at Gecor). Some corrections facilities in Georgia make beautiful furniture, or prisoners' clothing and shoes, or have print shops. Inmates who qualify at Hays work in the prison's mattress factory. There is no job designed for an imprisoned dentist.

Back when Corbin was in the Gwinnett County jail awaiting trial, a prisoner who had been charged with stealing an airplane had a dental emergency, and he was moved to the cell next to Corbin's. The dentist didn't find that amusing; the local media did. Whether Bart Corbin will ever be trusted enough to be assigned to the prison's medical or dental clinics is questionable.

For now, Corbin is almost indistinguishable from other men in prison. He, who prided himself on his wavy dark hair and had only hundred-dollar haircuts, now has a shaved head. In his prison mugshot, his head is bald, either by prison policy or because he likes it that way. He looks healthier than he did at his sentencing, and his weight is listed at 218 pounds, his height at six feet three. Inside the walls, an inmate's physical strength or the illusion of power is a form of self-protection, particularly for a man who sneaked up on helpless women with a revolver.

Like most murderers who once dominated the news, Bart Corbin has already slipped into relative obscurity. His mother makes the trip to Trion to visit him; his brothers do not.

But he is alive, while Dolly Hearn and Jennifer Barber Corbin are dead. And yet, memories of the women's brief lives continue to blossom in the families who will always love them. The Hearns and the Barbers have refused to let their losses destroy the bonds that have carried them through a long ordeal of emotional pain, frustration, and disappointment to final justice.

After the verdict, Dolly's brother Gil wrote about her in a poignant statement to the press: "Our beloved Dolly was taken from us over sixteen years ago when she was a senior in dental school, one year shy of becoming Dr. Dolly Hearn. Since then we have been living two nightmares.

"We now live without Dolly's contagious smile, her positive outlook on life, and the joy that she brought to every room she entered. The pain of her loss is awakened each time we tell our children and grandchildren that Aunt Dolly was more than just a photo. We have thoughts of the dental practice that never was, and we think of all of the lives that remain untouched by her inspiring acts of kindness, her free-flowing words of encouragement, and the spontaneous manifestations of her unique sense of humor. This is the nightmare that we will never escape.

"In our second nightmare, we've lived knowing that Dolly was the victim of a pointless, cowardly act of murder, believing that every path for justice was seemingly exhausted. We've felt helpless, hopeless, and robbed of any remedy to set the record straight and to see justice served. We have always known the truth. Today we rejoice that this truth has been publicly revealed and that Dolly's name is now officially cleared. This nightmare is over."

Gil Hearn praised the detectives and prosecutors who brought a sense of peace, at last, to his family and "the happiest ending" the cases could have. Dr. Carlton and Barbara Hearn had lived for years with some bitterness because they felt that the first investigation into their daughter's death had been incomplete. In their hearts, they knew Bart had killed Dolly, but their lawyer, his investigator Sarah Mims, and their own efforts to find the truth hadn't convinced the 1990 team of Richmond County detectives.

Now, Barbara Hearn was finally able to say, "They redeemed themselves in our eyes this time. They really and truly did not investigate that case like they should have, and I don't think they made any bones about it. But when they learned . . . that Jennifer and Dolly had died in a similar manner, they opened this case again and they went after it with a vengeance."

Early on, the Hearns established a Memorial Scholarship Award—the "Dolly Award"—for dental students at the Medical College of Georgia. It isn't given to students with great scholastic ability or those recommended by faculty. Each Spring, approximately fifty members of the current junior class pick classmates who embody characteristics that reflect who Dolly was. The criteria was "P.E.P. for "Professionalism, Empathy, Perseverance."

And that was Dolly Hearn. Dozens of students have already benefited from the generosity of those who loved her. But, perhaps the greatest balm to her survivors came true on January 12, 2007. In May, 1990, a week before she died, Dolly was thrilled to announce that she would be "Dr. Dolly" in only a year. Members of her graduating class tried their best in 1991 to see that she received her dental degree posthumously along with them, but it didn't happen. They could only put her photo in their class composite picture, and present her parents with the hood she would have worn.

After Bart Corbin confessed to her murder, her once-fellow dental students—now in their forties—persuaded faculty members to join them in lobbying for Dolly's dental degree.

In June, Dolly Hearn will finally receive her degree in dentistry when the Class of 2007 graduates. "The degree really helps confirm that she did have the utmost respect of her mentors and her peers," MCG Dean Connie Drisko said. "And I think it speaks highly of her character and the wonderful memories people have of her."

"We have always called her 'Dr. Dolly," Barbara Hearn said, "And now she will be. We're very happy."

Dalton and Dillon Corbin, now nine and seven, live, of course, with Heather and Doug Tierney in a large house filled with cousins, sunshine, paintings, music, and dogs and cats. They often call Heather "Aunt Mommy," and she and Doug are always there for their four children. When they take a rare, short vacation, Narda and Max or their Aunt Rajel take care of Dalton, Dillon, Max, and Sylvia. Somehow, Heather manages to juggle the needs of a preschooler, three elementary students, and a husband, and she coaches Dillon's basketball team as well. Doug is unfailingly patient, and didn't hesitate for a moment about taking responsibility for raising two more children.

Heather still breaks into tears when she speaks of Jenn, and she probably always will. There will be numerous challenges for Jenn's sons as they grow older, and the Tierneys will see that they have the counseling they need. Heather understands why Bart's mother and sister-in-law, Suzanne, sometimes come to watch Dalton and Dillon at their ball games, and she hopes that the boys' relatives on their father's side can be a part of their lives.

The Corbins have asked for huge time chunks of visitation, more than they had when Jenn was alive and she and Bart were together. For now, that isn't workable, but Jenn's relatives don't want her boys to be totally cut off from half of their heritage. Dalton and Dillon love their cousins—Bobby's children—and Jenn always made sure that they celebrated Connie's birthday, and other important dates in Bart's family.

Dalton is extremely bright, and still carries within him a sense that he failed to protect his mother, along with a continuing fear of his father. As Bart approached two trials, Heather attempted, with the advice of a counselor, to answer Dalton's questions. "I told him that his father was going to trial for Dolly Hearn's murder, and that he might also be on trial for killing his Mommy."

Dalton asked her how long Bart would be in prison, and she told him that it might be a very long time. Even though she knew how frightened Dalton was, she wasn't prepared for his next question.

"Don't they have an electric chair anymore?" Dalton asked.

Dillon is a far less intense child, younger when his mother was shot, and his memories are blurry and a little confabulated. Neither of the boys has asked to visit their father.

The Tierneys' house is seldom silent, full of shouts, laughter, and typical sibling arguments among the younger family members, along with barks and meows from Fuey, Sophie, and Zippedy Doo Dog: "Zippo," the dog who came with Dalton and Dillon. Someone is always hungry—dogs, cats, and humans.

Heather has a number of cartons that had once been in Jenn's house in Buford. She finally came to a place where she was able to open a box from Jenn's pantry. It held her sister's spices, Lipton soup packets, rice, and a jar of peanut butter. When Heather opened the peanut butter, she saw three little swipes had been taken from the jar, and felt one of the thousand pangs that catch her unawares.

"All I could think of was that Jenn didn't know this was her last jar of peanut butter."

Heather put a label on it that said, "Do not use. Do not throw out." Someday, she will have to deal with it, but not at that moment.

The Jennifer Barber-Corbin Memorial Playground at

Sugar Hill Methodist Church was dedicated On November 13, 2005. Both Narda and Heather have their own memorial gardens in their yards, where they grow Jenn's favorite flowers.

Within a week of Bart's guilty pleas, Narda opened her mail and was stunned to find a bill from the funeral director Bart had retained in 2004. This was the mortuary where she had been told she had no say over whether her daughter would be buried or cremated. All the arrangements had been Bart's prerogative. Narda and Max, understandably, protested. Narda had begged the director not to go ahead with the cremation, but she could not stop it; Bart had made that decision.

This bill for thousands of dollars could not possibly be their responsibility, but it seemed that the funeral parlor now believed that Bart wouldn't—or couldn't—pay, and they had turned to the Barbers.

It was yet another blow for Jenn's family. They contacted an Atlanta television reporter who had always treated them fairly and asked to go on the air to tell about this indignity.

The bill was withdrawn.

Just before Thanksgiving 2006, Brad Corbin left a letter for the Barbers and Tierneys at their church. Jenn's family wanted to get through Christmas before they read it and waited until January 3, 2007, to pick it up. It was part apology, part condolence, but it was full of Brad's continued insistence that he hadn't believed that his "twin" was guilty. Rather than using their given names, Brad referred to Bobby as his "younger brother" and Bart as his "twin."

He assured Jenn's family that he had never met Dolly Hearn, and had never known how she died. His letter was strangely flat; it was more a plea for them to understand how rough Bart's crime had been on him, and his family. He wanted to mend fences.

Brad stressed that the Corbin family had absolutely trusted Bart, although they had never asked him outright for the truth. They had all been shocked, Brad said, when they met with Bart at 9:30 P.M. on September 14, 2006. Only then had he confessed the murders and told them that the murder gun had been traced to him.

In his letter, Brad Corbin referred to Jenn as "his sister," and said he missed her. Certainly, the Corbin family has suffered losses, too, although they apparently used denial to deal with them as long as they could. Whether there will ever be any healing of the rifts that remain after Jenn's death and Bart's imprisonment, no one knows.

For months after his arrest, Dara Prentice faithfully picked up Bart Corbin's mail from his clinic address and either took it to him in jail or forwarded it to him. She remained ambivalent about his guilt or innocence, and, even after his guilty plea to both murders, she had a great deal of trouble believing it. She is still married, believing that her husband was unaware of any personal involvement she had with Bart. Ironically, Dara isn't so different from Jenn—at least when it came to what matters the most to her—and that is that her two children won't be hurt. Her goal is to see them through to adulthood, and to be as good a mother as she can be.

The last time Dara saw Bart was in March 2005. Although he wrote several letters to her from jail and prison, she hasn't written back. Her regret, guilt, and stress over the final denouement of her affair with him may have been the cause of many illnesses she has suffered since Jenn's death.

A reader asked me recently if I remember the homicide

victims that I've written about in the past, or if I move on to future books and reach a point where I no longer think about them or their families. I do remember every victim I've "met," even though I never knew them in life. After spending a year or two researching each book, meeting their families, talking to detectives and prosecutors and judges, I write the victims' stories, including some of the most personal parts of their lives. It would be impossible for me to forget any of them.

I may have been as close to Jenn Barber Corbin and Dolly Hearn as I have been to any victim. That is partly because I have daughters who are close to their ages, and also because the investigations into their deaths were so thoroughly documented by law enforcement agencies. But I suspect the real reason is because their families have kept them within the circle of love, even though they are gone.

When I visited Narda and Max Barber's split-level home in Lawrenceville, Narda led me downstairs to their guestroom. That evening, I had just come from Danny Porter's office. Bart Corbin had already pleaded guilty and been sentenced, so journalists were allowed to read certain investigative files, and that afternoon I had looked at the crime scene photos. Although I don't include body pictures in my books, it's necessary for me to see them so I can be accurate when I describe a crime scene. And so I had studied the pictures in the Corbin files. It was obvious that neither Jenn nor Dolly had any warning that they were about to die.

I will never become inured to or blasé about homicidal tragedy, no matter how many books I write, and I was somewhat shaken by the crime scene investigators' photographs.

As we walked into the guest room at the Barbers'

home, I instantly recognized the bed with its four posts with pineapple-like carvings. I had just seen pictures of it—the bed where Jenn had died. Her mother and I sat on the side of that bed as we talked. And then I became aware of a huge photo of Jenn on the wall; it was a lovely self-portrait, taken when she was years younger, and her long blonde hair spread out like a shining halo.

Beneath the portrait, a candle glowed atop a handsome, transparent container, and I realized that it held Jenn's ashes, finally released to her family after two years. I felt the infinite sadness in the room—a place not in the least haunted, but somehow encompassing the monstrous loss of a precious life.

We drank Jenn's favorite—mojitos—in her memory before dinner, and the soup served was one of the recipes she—the gourmet cook in their family—was known for: a thick and hearty squash soup. Although I would never meet Jenn, I now felt closer to her than ever.

Less than a week later, I was in Washington, Georgia, welcomed into the historic white house where Dolly Hearn had grown up. An almost life-sized portrait of her dominated the entry hall. The same photo is displayed at the Medical College of Georgia in Augusta. Dolly's bedroom is little changed since the last time she left it, but it isn't a memorial; the memory of Dolly is alive, a part of her family's lives. Her nieces wear the small dresses with smocked bodices that she once wore. The old tree that Dolly posed in almost twenty years ago grows just outside the private entrance to her room.

Almost miraculously, Dolly's cat Tabitha lived to be twenty-one years old. She was a comforting cat, albeit a little deaf and crotchety with arthritis, usually sleeping in a chair next to the fireplace in the parlor where Barbara

Hearn and I talked. The old cat allowed me to pet her, and I couldn't help thinking how amazing it was that she not only survived Bart's kidnapping in 1989, but was more than a hundred years old in "cat years." Tabitha died on March 6, 2007, leaving an empty place in the Hearn family home in Washington. When I heard that Tabitha had left this earth, I immediately thought how happy Dolly must have been to see her again.

We walked in the yard where Dolly and her brothers played under a pecan tree. That tree is no longer safe, but Dolly's nieces and nephews play the same games on another side of the huge yard.

We looked at her father's garden, and her mother's magnolia tree, won at a garden club years ago, and now twenty feet tall. It was October. The Confederate Rose bush had just burst into bloom, and Barbara picked a rose for me. I pressed it between the pages of my notebook, and I kept it on my desk as I wrote this book at home. I'm not sure why—probably for the same reason that I carried home a baggie full of seeds from Jenn's garden. They will soon be flowering in Seattle.

At the end of the afternoon, I followed Barbara Hearn's car as she led me to the cemetery. We stood at the foot of Dolly's grave. After Bart Corbin's guilty pleas, both friends and strangers sent dozens of roses to the Hearns, and to this cemetery. Bart's staff placed a red rose in every room of his clinic.

The *Atlanta Journal-Constitution*'s headlines about Bart Corbin's plea on September 15 had filled almost half of the front page. Barbara had that front page laminated and she had placed it on a wire stand at the head of Dolly's grave. The headlines shouted "Guilty! Guilty!" twice—once for Jenn and once for Dolly. We saw that the display still stood there a month later, undisturbed by anyone who had driven or walked through the quiet graveyard. There were still a few faded red roses on Dolly's grave, and one ceramic red rose that would never fade.

I have written scores of stories about young women who died much too prematurely, and I always have the thought of "If only . . ." If only their lives had played out differently. Both Dolly Hearn and Jenn Corbin were women who wanted other people to be happy, who worried that they might have hurt someone's feelings, and when things began to spin out of control, they continued to believe that they could find a way to leave a violent, jealous, maniacally possessive man without a bitter ending.

And that became impossible. Knowing who they were, I'm sure they would be at peace to know that their tragedies may well warn other women for whom it is not yet too late.

Bart Corbin's guilty pleas were both a triumph and a disappointment for the men and women who had worked overtime for two years to build a case against him and to prepare for trial. They had done that, but even so, the investigators and the prosecutors were left with an empty feeling. So was Judge Michael C. Clark. Clark had done his best not to have "Corbin tried on the Internet," and to keep a lid on too much information leaking out before trial. For twenty months, everyone involved—literally scores of people on the prosecution side—had done their best to protect their case against Corbin. Every conceivable loophole had been sealed up, and they had all chosen their words carefully. They had planned the State's cases—one in Lawrenceville in Gwinnett County, and the other in Augusta in Richmond County—with the utmost precision. Their witnesses were on deck, and the charts, tapes, forensic tests, cell phone records, all the audiovisual aids, were ready.

And suddenly, it was all over. Many of them felt like athletes who had trained, practiced, and visualized how they would compete in the Olympics or in a championship game—and then had the game called off for good. Even though they were professionals, and they knew that some trials never go to a jury, they had all been geared up to perform at their peak, and they were curious, too, about how the Corbin cases would play out in court.

But, above all, justice itself was the most important issue. And Dolly and Jenn had been avenged. Next to that, Porter and Craig wanted to save the dead women's families from any more pain, and they had managed to do that, too. They were relieved for the Barbers, the Tierneys, and the Hearns, and both Danny Porter and Danny Craig and their staffs thought first of what would be best for the victims' survivors.

Bart Corbin's defense team had been ready to compete, and were very confident. But they had been shot down by things their client had failed to tell them, so their disappointment with the outcome was especially sharp.

It was finally over.

Several months after the sudden end to Corbin's trial, Anita Hearn, the mystery woman who some believed had been the catalyst who—knowingly or unknowingly—set a disaster in motion finally came forward to speak on national television. Anita's hair was jet-black, long and straight, and her heavily made-up eyes appeared to be black, too. Her mien was almost gypsy-like. She was a small woman who looked to be somewhere between thirty-five and forty-five, and she spoke in a flat, husky voice with virtually no affect, often laughing or smiling inappropriately.

Seeing her, it was impossible to view her as the masculine, tender persona that "Christopher Hearn" had been to Jenn.

"At first, we were just pretending," she said, as she attempted to explain away her false seduction of Jenn on the Internet. "We were playing. Things were getting intense. I said [wrote], 'My name isn't Chris—My name is Anita.' Jenn logged off."

But, later, Jenn had come back on, trying to understand what had happened. Anita insisted that she had grown to love Jenn, and made no apologies for her own actions. She said she was sure that Jenn would not have killed herself, and, speaking as if she were an expert about a woman she had never really known at all, Anita said, "She was stressed out—but not suicidal. I don't think that's a path Jennifer would have taken."

And, of course, Jenn had not committed suicide. On the night she died, she was looking forward to a happier life, one that was free of Bart's influence. Perhaps the part of Jenn's story that many people find the most puzzling is that she forgave Anita Hearn for her cruel subterfuge, and even continued to correspond with her.

I believe that Jenn Barber Corbin was brainwashed, and that, had she ever met Anita Hearn in person, she would have quickly moved on.

But images deeply embedded in the human brain are not easily erased. And what Jenn was feeling was a phenomenon peculiar to the age of the Internet. A year after Jenn was murdered, television documentaries and talk shows began to feature segments about women who had fallen in love with men they met online.

All of them were intelligent and successful women, albeit lonely, and they had thought it safer and more discreet to exchange emails with perfect strangers when they would never have considered going alone to a bar or a singles dance.

They were prime prey for con artists. They were not the "Nigerian scammers" that Heather once warned Jenn about, but men who wrote increasingly seductive emails that promised everything from romantic meetings to marriage. Many of these men sent photographs purported to be of themselves. But they seldom were.

In the fall of 2006, three attractive women appeared on a well-known talk show, and were shocked to find that, although each of them had been writing to a different man, their correspondents had all included the same photograph—that of a handsome, well-dressed businessman. The real man existed, but he had no part in this scam. Nor did he know how the con-men had obtained his picture.

These duped women admitted that they had sent money, plane tickets, and personal information to their potential lovers. Yet none of them had ever met their correspondents in person. And still, these perfectly sane and bright women had agreed to a meeting. Instead, they all waited in vain at airports as passengers deplaned, watching for the man in the pictures, who had promised to bring roses.

Of course, the men weren't on those flights, but later they all came up with seemingly plausible reasons about why they had missed the magical moment of first meeting. Several even had the nerve to ask for more money to take care of last-minute complications. One man explained that he had become suddenly ill and been rushed to a hospital. And the woman who waited for *him* actually sent him more money to pay his hospital bill!

The most astounding revelation on the talk show was not that the women had been duped; it was that they all said they were still in love with the men they had trusted. Even faced with solid evidence that they had been fooled, they stubbornly refused to accept that the romance they hoped for didn't exist. Two of them said they intended to stay in their Internet relationships. Their disillusionment was so great that they had to cling to what they hoped for. They still believed in a future meeting with their "fiancés." Jenn Corbin died only two weeks after she learned that there was no Christopher; she hadn't had time to process the truth about Anita Hearn. For her, Christopher lived on—at least in her mind, caught somewhere in the tunnels of EverQuest. Jenn, sadly, never got the chance to emerge from the deception, and go on with her life.

Some of the mysteries that were connected, however tangentially, to Bart Corbin remain in shadow. Harriet Gray's murder in September 1995 has never been solved. Like Jenn, Harriet Gray left a journal behind—although its contents remains secret because her case is still open. One jarring note, however, is the whispered information that the entries in those journals are not in Harriet's hand-writing.

There is little question that Bart Corbin and Harriet Gray worked in the same dental clinic; but there is some debate about whether they ever worked there at the same time. Her relatives believe that they knew one another other.

As this is written, Mary Denise Lands has been miss-ing for almost three years. It is unlikely that Bart Corbin had anything to do with the disappearance of this fourth woman he knew who apparently met with violence. There is no new information on where she might be. Cold case detectives from the Michigan State Police are still investi-gating her disappearance.

—Ann Rule

JENN CORBIN'S SQUASH SOUP

3 large cans chicken broth (12 cups)
1 butternut squash (3 or 4 pounds)
2 tablespoons olive oil
1 package of kielbasa sausage (1 pound)
2 cans of corn or 2 cups fresh corn
1 box of wild rice (approx. 1 cup)
1 medium carton of half-and-half or heavy cream
    (1½ cups)
2 large sweet onions (chopped)
Fresh ground pepper
Salt to taste
1 tablespoon chopped fresh parsley

Preheat oven to 400 degrees F. Poke holes in squash and bake for at least one hour until it is soft. While squash is baking, in a saucepan, bring four cups of stock and ½ cup of onions to a simmer. Stir in the rice and cook until rice is tender, stirring occasionally with a fork. Put in bowl to cool. In a large saucepan or pot, heat olive oil, and brown cut-up sausage, remaining chopped onions, and corn. Sauté for 3 minutes. Cut baked squash in half and remove seeds. Scoop out squash and puree in blender, adding a little chicken broth. Add to the sausage-corn mixture, and then add remaining chicken stock.

Season with salt and pepper. Bring pot to a boil, then turn down to simmer for 20 minutes. Skim off any excess fat. Stir in the rice and cook for 10 minutes. Remove from heat. Stir in heavy cream and top with parsley.

Note: Add leftover chicken, turkey, vegetables, if you like.

About the Author

ANN RULE came to her writing career with a solid background in law enforcement and the criminal justice system. Both her grandfather and her uncle were Michigan sheriffs, and she was once a Seattle police officer herself. She has five children and five grandchildren, two dogs, and five cats. Ann has been a full-time true-crime author since 1969, publishing 28 books, and 1,400 articles in such publications as *Cosmopolitan, Ladies' Home Journal, Good Housekeeping, Readers' Digest, Chicago Tribune,* and *True Detective.* She serves as executive producer of the miniseries of her books. She is a certified instructor for police training seminars in the thirteen Western states, lecturing on serial murder, women who kill, and high-profile offenders. She has presented papers four times for the National Academy of Forensic Science, and has lectured at the FBI Academy and to the National Association of District Attorneys. She has testified twice before the Senate judicial subcommittees on victims' rights and serial murder. She worked on the U.S. Justice Department Task Force to set up VI-CAP, the Violent Criminals Apprehension Program. Ann supports crime victims/survivors' groups, domestic violence support organizations, pet rescue organizations, and organizations like Childhaven and Child Help that try to save abused children and work with their families on better parenting. Ann, who is almost always working on a new book, now lives near Seattle, Washington, on the shores of Puget Sound. Information on Ann's books, and discussion groups on her guestbook, can be found on her website at www.annrules.com. Write to her at AnnieR37@AOL.com.